D0854049

PRIVATIZATION AND THE WELFARE STATE

Privatization and the Welfare State

Implications for Consumers and the Workforce

Edited by
PHILIP MORGAN

Dartmouth

Aldershot • Brookfield USA • Singapore • Sydney

Published by
Dartmouth Publishing Company Limited
Gower House
Croft Road
Aldershot
Hants GU11 3HR
England

Dartmouth Publishing Company
Old Post Road
Brookfield
Vermont 05036
USA

British Library Cataloguing in Publication Data
Privatization and the Welfare State:
Implications for Consumers and the Workforce
I. Morgan, Philip I.
361.941

Library of Congress Cataloging-in-Publication Data
Privatization and the welfare state : implications for consumers
and the workforce / edited by Philip Morgan.
p. cm.
Includes bibliographical references.
ISBN 1-85521-404-0
1. Privatization–Great Britain–Case studies. 2. Municipal services–Great Britain. 3. Public utilities–Great Britain. 4. Industrial relations–Great Britain. 5. Great Britain–Economic policy–1945- 6. Great Britain–Social policy–1979- 7. Welfare state. I. Morgan, Philip I.
HD4145.P723 1995
338.941–dc20 95-7436
CIP

ISBN 1 85521 404 0

Printed and bound in Great Britain by
Ipswich Book Co. Ltd., Ipswich, Suffolk

Contents

Contributors

Nigel Allington	Cardiff Business School, UWCC
Peter Anthony	Swansea Institute of Higher Education
Thomas Clarke	Leeds Metropolitan University
Charles Ford	University of Strathclyde
Colin Harris	Brighton University
Tony Hazell	Health Care Development Advisory Ltd.
Colin Mair	University of Strathclyde
Miguel Martinez Lucio	Cardiff Business School, UWCC
Peter Morgan	Cardiff Business School, UWCC
Philip Morgan	Cardiff business School, UWCC
Charles Okeahalam	University of Manchester
Nicholas O'Shaughnessy	University of Cambridge
Chris Potter	School of Medicine, UWCC
Madsen Pirie	Adam Smith Institute
Marsden Preece	Cardiff Business School, UWCC
Michael Reed	University of Lancaster
George Thomason	Cardiff Business School, UWCC
Robert Smith	Centre for Housing & Urban Planning, UWCC
Peter Saunders	University of Sussex
Richard Walker	Centre for Housing & Urban Planning, UWCC
Roy Wilkie	University of Strathclyde
Peter Williams	Cente for Housing & Urban Planning, UWCC
Dolph Zubick	Health Care Development Advisory Ltd.

Preface

> ....the ideas of economists and political philosophers, both when they are right and when they are wrong, are more powerful than is commonly understood. Indeed, the world is ruled by little else. Practical men, who believe themselves to be quite exempt from any intellectual influences, are usually the slaves of some defunct economist. Madmen, in authority, who hear voices in the air, are distilling their frenzy from some academic scribbler of a few years back. ... it is ideas, not vested interests, which are dangerous for good or evil.

John Maynard Keynes, *General Theory of Employment, Interest and Money: Collected Writings*, vol. vii (1936) McMillan Publishing Co. 1973 pp. 383-4.

Introduction

This book was conceived in an attempt to examine some of the questions raised by privatization. A number of authors currently engaged in researching various aspects of privatization agreed to contribute to this volume by presenting their evidence. This evidence is either in the form of case studies, empirical or secondary research.

Since privatization is multi-facetted, it was considered necessary to view it from a multi-disciplinary perspective by drawing on the expertise of economists, political scientists, public service consultants and human resource management specialists. All contributors are well qualified to comment on the effects of privatization from the vantagepoint of their specific disciplines and experience. The resulting chapters are representative of the changes that have taken place since privatization policies were introduced in Britain.

Although privatization is a largely global phenomenon, much of the impetus has come from Britain. (It is reputed to be Britain's biggest service industry export and many consultants are in the process of spreading the word abroad.) In the UK the public sector now accounts for over 30 per cent of the British GDP which includes public corporations, local authorities and government departments (Naisbitt and Aburdene, 1989). For this reason, attention is focused on the British model alone, since it was felt that much can be gained from a study of this system.

The book endeavours to offer a balanced view of the successes and failures of privatization (in so far as these can be judged, bearing in mind timescales and the absense of baseline data). Each chapter discusses a different aspect of privatization and enables the reader to gain some insight into what differences (if any) exist between the Conservative Government's expressed aims in adopting a policy of privatization versus what is actually happening. In the process, it is hoped this present volume will be a useful addition to the burgeoning literature and continuing debate on issues surrounding privatization.

Summary of chapters

The following is a summary of the various chapters in this volume.

Chapter 1 attempts to put privatization in historical perspective by briefly reviewing the capitalist and socialist systems, from their beginnings to the present day. A comparison is made between Adam Smith's 'self-interest' ethic and Calvinism and the neo-human relations ethic of the 'me-generation' of the 1960s and 1970s. The latter emphasized self-actualization and personal growth. It is contended that this latter ethic was largely misunderstood and became transmuted into the 'selfishness' of the 1980s and 1990s during the Thatcher years.

The chapter also traces the changing value system of the population from the liberalism of the 1960s to the conservatism of the 1990s and shows how these values underpinned and supported the political and economic theories of their respective times. Thus, during the 1960s in a period of economic growth, social welfare programmes were supported, but as the economy took a downturn, support declined and more conservative views became *vogue*. However, it is contended that capitalism and privatization with their emphasis on competitiveness undermine community spirit and create alienation for its members.

Research findings are also presented which appear to contradict the expressed aims of the Conservative Government's privatization programme. Also discussed are the costs of providing welfare programmes and how many of these have been curtailed, or partially privatized, by the Conservative Government in an attempt to reduce the PSBR. Finally, 'communitarianism' which emphasizes individual, family and collective responsibility for solving societal problems, is proposed as an alternative to the twin dilemmas posed by privatization and socialism.

In Chapter 2, Madsen Pirie presents the Conservative Government's case for privatization. He notes that privatization resulted from the Conservative Government's desire to correct the perceived failings of state industries and utilities which '... were loss-making, inefficient, over-manned, under-captialized, out-of-date, unresponsive (to consumers) and politically troublesome'. A policy of privatization was also adopted, Pirie contends, in an attempt to control costs which were too often thwarted by Civil Servants. Although nearly all of the privatization measures taken were initially unpopular with the electorate the Government was able to swing popular opinion around once they were perceived as being 'successful'. Pirie contends that the Government's privatization programme has been a resounding success.

In Chapter 3, Hazell and Zubick discuss the role and availability of capital markets to facilitate privatization. They argue that the mere sale of public assets clearly will not do anything on its own to achieve greater efficiency, higher quality or increased consumer sensitivity. They contend that full and free access to capital markets is a lynchpin of the whole process if ultimate cost-efficiency of the financial management function is to be achieved. However, as they note, there are serious barriers to achieving this. These barriers centre around the available skill base existing within the various privatizing agencies themselves.

The authors go on to identify and evaluate constraints and opportunities and positive models from which to secure realistic trading positions for all concerned.

In Chapter 4, Anthony and Reed argue that the simplicities of the market economy ignore the realities within which managers operate in organizations. They contend that in the private sector, competition between managers can lead to disaster. In the public sector, the flexibilities required to meet market turbulence are incompatible with the continuing provision of important services to defend which managers will fend off market forces. In both private and public sectors, managers seem to exercise control over their environments rather than being controlled by them. The market model does not reflect the real world, private or public, in which managers operate. In the public sector in particular, reality demands the balancing of efficiency and care and the ability to deal with complexities beyond the simple dictates of market demand.

In Chapter 5, Allington assesses the economics and politics of the Conservative Government's privatization programme in an attempt to determine whether the parable and the reality of privatization have any connection. Whether the programme was successful or not, in terms of their own criteria, the symbolic significance of the programme as a demonstration of the benefits to be attained from greater economic freedom and democracy are shown to be important.

The problems associated with the former nationalized industries in addition to the intellectual background to privatization are examined. Certain theoretical developments in the economics of politics and bureaucracy and in public choice theory are then highlighted. Following privatization, the whole regulatory framework becomes crucial to its success, but for various reasons discussed here, the optimum competitive environment was not created in Britain.

He suggests that the newly independent East European states and those Western states currently planning or enacting privatization programmes might gain useful insights from a consideration of the British experience. To this end, the final parts of the chapter consider a number of alternative methods for the disposal of state assets which might strengthen competition, but also widen the base of capitalism, raise efficiency and even reduce unemployment.

In Chapter 6, Allington and O'Shaughnessy contend that over the last fiteen years there has been what amounts to a sustained political attack on Britain's universities. Originally inspired by the obvious untenability of the then existing arrangements, the attack proceeded to develop a momentum of its own. As a consequence the authors believe that it is debatable whether anything like the traditional idea of a university can survive in Britain. The attack is articulated through bureaucratic intrusiveness, regular reductions in financial support and even verbal denigration. Central to the attack is the exploitation of an extreme inequality in the power relationship existing between the government and the universities.

Thus, universities are subject to annual (per capita) reductions in funding under that persuasive rhetorical conceit of 'efficiency gains'. Moreover, the authors believe that the universities have been subjected to crude accountancy criteria that are insensible to the ends and meanings of the academy. The chapter outlines both the case for formal independence for some universities, and the various mechanisms by which this can be achieved. The central idea is of the repayment of grants and tuition fees via additional taxation for university graduates: the key mode of market exchange would be higher education voucher, which in conjunction with the ability to raise loans in the city, would make independent universities sustainable for the first time since the nineteenth century. The authors conclude that faced with such a massive governmental attack, independence for some institutions is no longer an ideological absurdity, it becomes a practical necessity.

In Chapter 7, Morgan and Preece look at the way in which existing educational and training structures have been shaped by perceived past societal needs, the way in which the education structure has been adapting to changing societal structures and the possible changes implied by the increasing emphasis on privatization as an aspect of societal imperatives. After reviewing some of the main factors which have shaped the existing educational structure and process, the move towards an emphasis on privatization is placed in context and various government and educational establishment initiatives to respond to this process are also reviewed.

After assaying the changing societal expectations of the education process implicit in privatization and the practical career needs of students expected to cope with this changing worklife scenario, examples of relevant educational initiatives are explored and evaluated in terms of their putative contribution to a positive improvement in the outcome of educational practice.

In Chapter 8, Martinez Lucio discusses the obstacles that have existed regarding the commercialization and privatization of the Post Office and the way in which the Conservative Government has attempted to deal with these obstacles. The obstacles include the organization's public service ethic, the popularity of the service and the high levels of quality achieved well before the Conservative Government took office in 1979. As he indicates, the irony is that, unlike other public services, the Post Office has not been an 'unsuccessful' organization and hence it has been difficult for the Government to mobilize public opinion in favour of privatizing it. The various ways the Government has attempted to transform the autonomy and peculiar nature of the Post Office in an attempt to change it are discussed. These strategies include the use of commercial language, the development of performance measures and increasing decentralization.

In Chapter 9, Wilkie, Mair and Ford, after discussing various 'privatization' issues related to the police service, including civilianization, from a value-free perspective, argue that these measures are redefining policing, police work and performance without explicit debate or consultation. They argue that the core-ancillary distinctions underpinning privatization of the police force are extremely questionable and they doubt whether they would survive explicit policy discussion. Nevertheless, they suggest that the implications of privatizing the police force are so enormous that they need to be addressed by a Royal Commission. Such a commission would be tasked with reviewing and redefining the role and function of policing and setting future policy. The commission would, they feel, help to prevent much of the 'creeping privatization' that had such a deliterious effect on the service in the recent past.

Privatization of the police is examined within a definitional framework that emphasizes two related themes: (i) That privatization typically involves the transformation and dilution of state involvement in an area of activity, not the complete elimination of it; and (ii) That privatization often involves an implicit distinction between core and ancillary aspects of state involvement. Within this framework the authors show that a substantial erosion of the public policing function has occurred since 1979, and that a significant growth in private sector involvement in policing occurred as a consequence. This shift has been largely presented as efficiency improvement or cost control, but the authors argue that cumulatively it is transforming the nature of the police service. They conclude that an explicit preview of the nature and role of the public police service is now necessary, preferably in the form of a Royal Commission.

In Chapter 10, Clarke discusses how the creation of hundreds of quasi-autonomous agencies to carry out the executive functions of government in the early 1990s in the UK represented a transformation in the machinery of government by stealth. Proclaimed as an alternative to privatization, allowing the executive agencies to prove they could be highly efficient with more autonomy within the public sector, at times it has seemed the Agencies were simply one step towards the privatization of most of the civil service. The introduction of extensive market testing has confirmed the view the government sees the Agencies as part of a process of transition towards the market.

This raises fundamental constitutional questions. Because the Agencies were ostensibly to remain within the public sector, no legislation was required for their creation. Agencies are supposed to be distinct from quangos (non departmental bodies) as they remain departmental bodies, ultimately responsible to the Minister concerned. This intrusion of the business form into the management of government threatens the traditional public service values of impartiality, universality and accountability. The performance improvements attained by a number of the Agencies, if proper constitutional arrangements are not worked out, could be at the price of the impartiality and integrity of the civil service.

In Chapter 11, Okeahalam discusses some of the implications for franchise operators and consumers as a result of the possible privatization of British Rail (BR) passenger services. He concentrates on three issues: i) the debate on the efficiency effects of the introduction of the private sector; ii) the importance of competition to reduce the likelihood of privatized monopoly, and iii) the likely impact on consumer welfare and service quality. He discusses the financial, competitive and administrative implications of implementing a railway privatization programme.

He maintains that the Government must ensure that the bidding process is fully transparent and that clear guidelines are set to enable potential franchise operators to make rational investment decisions. He also maintains that the Government regulatory body - Railtrack - has a duty to the consumer to ensure that all franchises face true competition so as to protect the welfare of consumers.

In Chapter 12, Potter investigates the question of the extent to which the internal market reforms of the NHS constitute privatization. In the process of answering this question, he examines the problems of providing an undefined range of services with limited resources and reviews the various meanings of privatization. He notes that the reforms have changed how the range of services delivered are defined, emphasizing clients' needs rather than professional preferences. But he concludes that as the service remains substantially free at the point of use the reforms do not amount to privatization. However, he allows that the foundations may have been laid for privatization in the future.

In Chapter 13, Harris, using a case study of two water companies, examines how privatization has affected the attitudes and working lives of employees in those companies. It is argued that privatization has achieved some of the objectives that its proponents set; namely it has increased managerial autonomy and possibly reduced the willingness of workers to follow a strike call from their union. But there is no evidence to show that one of the key objectives of privatization - to overcome the 'them and us' division between workforce and management in British industry - has actually been accomplished. Indeed, there is strong evidence to show that the reverse has taken place - that privatization has actually caused a polarization of attitudes between higher and lower grades.

In Chapter 14, Thomason explores the progress made in pursuing the Conservative Government's cost-saving and efficiency-enhancing strategies relating to the delivery of public services in the UK. He argues that outright privatization has had some success in creating a 'new realism' among former public sector workers, but that the strategies of market-testing and internal market creation appear less likely to foster a strong commercial orientation among the professional employees involved.

In Chapter 15, Saunders focuses on the effects of privatization on consumers. He begins by refuting Ernst's basic claim that privatising the four basic utilities - gas, water, electricity and tele-communications - has harmed consumers of these services. Saunders maintains that in the case of water privatization the evidence on prices, quality of service and accountability, that consumers have probably gained more than they have lost. Saunders reviews the evidence and draws upon a recent 'before-and-after' study of the privatization of the water industry to demonstrate that, even in this most contentious of privatizations, consumers have not been disadvantaged by the move from government to private ownership.

Finally, in Chapter 16, Smith, Walker and Williams examine alternative approaches to housing provision and allocation in the UK, setting social housing in the context of different political attitudes and considers the ways in which market oriented approaches to housing have been advocated during the 1980s and 1990s, with the emphasis on the privatization of housing. The changing position of the consumer in the social housing sector is analysed, with a growth in tenants's rights and participation acknowledged alongside an examination of the exit rates from social housing. The authors conclude that, despite reforms and positive shifts in the relationships between social landlords and tenants, the increasing marginalization of social housing has often undermined the changes introduced designed to benefit the consumer.

Since privatization has never before been adopted on quite this scale it is impossible to provide anything more than an interim report at present. I shall now permit the various authors to speak for themselves.

Philip Morgan
Cardiff, 1994

References

Nesbitt, J. and Aburdene, P. (1990), *Megatrends 2000*, London: Sidgwick and Jackson.

Acknowledgements

I should like to thank numerous people for their help in preparing this book, in addition to the authors. I should especially like to thank Nigel Allington for his helpful comments and Louise Jones for the careful preparation of the final drafts and typesetting, and Nancy Morgan for preparing the Index. I should also like to thank Anne Govier and Kate Stephenson for their help and library research.

Section I

Rationale & Implications of Privatization

1 The privatization and the Welfare State: A case of back to the future?

Philip Morgan

Introduction

Privatization is arguably one of the most profound and far-reaching legacies of the three Conservative governments of the 1980s. It has not only changed the public sector, it has changed the face of British industry and introduced new ways in which former public service organizations must relate to their workforce and to their customers. It has also redrawn the social contract between the government and the individual regarding the degree of responsibility that is to be assumed by the welfare state. Privatization policies have aimed to 'roll back the frontiers of the welfare state' so that, rather than the state taking care of people from the 'cradle to the grave', people are now expected to assume a much greater responsibility for their own welfare (Klein, 1988). On the face of it, all of these initiatives may sound like good ideas. However, while the intent of privatization has been to ensure that many hitherto public sector organizations are run along more efficient and business like lines, the human costs are only now being counted. These have included increased unemployment and alienation for some and loss of community for many more, as privatization measures take effect.

The general purpose of this first chapter is to provide a context for the chapters that follow. It commences with a brief historical overview of the beginnings of capitalism and the development of the Welfare State especially in the US and, to a lesser extent, in the UK and traces the changing value system of the majority of the population from the liberalism of the 1960s to the conservatism of the 1980s. It is this conservatism that helped the Tories in the UK and the Republicans in the US (until 1992) to retain their hold on political power. Also presented are some research findings which appear to contradict the positive claims made for privatization by the Conservative Government. The Chapter concludes with a discussion of 'communitarianism' as an alternative to the twin dilemmas posed by privatization and the Welfare State.

Generally speaking, privatization is a term used to cover a variety of policies aimed at re-establishing the primacy of 'market forces' as the best means of distributing jobs, wages, goods and services and that through competition public industries and services can be made more efficient, by eliminating waste and providing greater 'value for money' (Pulkingham, 1989). It also involves the sale of public sector assets and the transfer of ownership and a large element of control from the public to the private sector and the total or partial dismantling of the nationalization process begun in 1945 (Klein, 1988). Pulkingham (1989) argues that as such, privatization is, among other things, both an employment and wage policy, the intention of which 'is to govern, not simply the general type of service provision but also, the method of wage determination itself' and that it is the culmination of post-war policies in the public sector concerning wage determination. (This is borne out by the collective bargaining strategies trades unions have supported for decades.)

The Conservative Government, in their 1992 *Manifesto*, maintained that privatization promotes greater efficiency (by reducing wastage), increases job opportunities and provides incentives, benefits consumers (in the form of lower prices through competition) and benefits the public by widening share ownership (*The Conservative Manifesto*, 1992). However, there is considerable controversy as to whether privatization actually accomplishes these results. Buckland (1987) suggests that privatization actually increased prices to the consumer and placed an added burden on the taxpayer. (For example, if shares are sold too cheaply there is a loss of revenue for the taxpayer. Also, if the former nationalized industry made a profit, this is now lost, so either taxes must rise or expenditure must be cut.) Additionally, privatization has made large segments of the workforce redundant: Haskel and Szymanski (1991) after examining the effects of privatization on jobs conclude that: 'Privatization has led to large scale labour shedding as companies have become more profit-oriented.'

Privatization has also changed the way in which much of the work has traditionally been conducted, such as for example, contracting out for specific services. Block (1986) contends that asset sales, and contracting out, have also done much to weaken the power of the unions. Moreover, while it may have reduced costs in some instances, Thompson and Whitfield, (1990) note that this is often at the expense of service quality. Many organizations now complain that many contracted out services, such as cleaning and catering have proved unsatisfactory.

Additionally, while share ownership may have been widened initially, over time it is the institutional investor who has become the largest shareholder; something which has been repeated throughout Europe. (For a more detailed discussion, see Allington, Chapter 4.) While these are only a few examples, there nevertheless does appear to be a considerable gap between the Government's avowed intent in adopting a privatization programme and what has actually occurred.

Since privatization appears to raise more questions than answers, it would seem appropriate to examine its general philosophy, together with its results, in more detail. This requires a brief review of how capitalism developed in America and Britain at the turn of the century and how it was later modified in the 1980s.[1] During this period also, societal values changed considerably which further served to underpin, reinforce and support the various political and economic theories of that time.

The roots of privatization

The roots of private enterprise, as opposed to public enterprise, can generally be traced back to the eighteenth century economic theories of Adam Smith.[2] Smith's belief in a free-market economy based on the pursuit of 'self-interest' guided by the 'invisible hand' of competition to promote the common good, complemented the dominant Calvinistic religion and philosophy of the time. This stressed that the road to salvation lay in hard work, self-sacrifice, self-denial and the accumulation of wealth (Weber, 1947; Tawney, 1938). Industrialists were free to display their diligence and, hence, godliness by accumulating wealth.

Governments of the time believed that permitting businesses complete unregulated freedom to pursue economic goals would eliminate economic scarcity and, eventually, poverty. However, when market forces were allowed a free hand *a la* Friedman, unhindered by any regulatory machinery in the US at the turn of the century, it simply enabled the so-called 'robber barons' to prosper at the expense of the poor. It also permitted certain employee abuses to flourish: 'sweat shop' practices, child labour, unsafe working conditions, starvation wages to be paid and pollution to go unchecked. (Of course, Smith would have seen these as an example of market failure demanding government intervention through some regulatory framework.)[3]

It was only after the Great Depression of the 1930s, following the stockmarket crash in 1929, that a Democratic Government in the United States saw the necessity of intervening in an attempt to remedy many of the problems caused by laissez-faire capitalism, including the political instability that resulted. Roosevelt's New Deal owed a considerable debt to the economic theories of Maynard Keynes (1936) that were propagated in the US by Alvin Hansen of Harvard University. Keynes provided the revolutionary theory that the Government should assume responsibility for the level of employment, either through manipulating fiscal policy or public expenditure, or both. (Social welfare came later in Britain, post-Beverage.) This interventionist approach, most typically associated with the welfare state was built on the principle of service provision, outside the market, on the basis of need and regardless of ability to pay.[4] (It is interesting to note that it was largely due to the failure of the free market economy at that time to ensure even minimum living standards for all workers that the welfare state was begun.) Therefore, following on from the New Deal in the 1930s, and culminating in the 1960s with Kennedy's New Frontier and Human Rights Bill to Johnson's Great Society and the War on Poverty, government interventionist programmes became the norm. As these programmes grew, so the social welfare budget quadrupled, rising from $3.9 billion in 1929 to $52 billion in 1960 (Merriam, 1967).

It was during the 1960s and the early 1970s that a sea change in fundamentally shared cultural values occurred, first in America and later, in Britain. The belief that hard work, self-denial and moral rectitude were their own rewards, was replaced with the rise of the human potential movement of the neo-human relationists (Argyris, Maslow, McGregor, etc.). This group's message became somewhat distorted in the minds of certain sectors of the population, so that the pursuit of 'self' and the realization of one's full 'potential' came to be perceived as the real purpose of life. It was no accident that this 'narcissistic' cult of individualism arose at the same time that the economy was booming and most citizens had attained a high level of material wealth. This decade is often ridiculed as the 'me-decade' when, 'Americans believed that they could have it all - wealth without work, sexual freedom without marital problems, self-absorption without loss of community' (Bode, 1981). This is the type of argument that Smith would have used to suggest that the pursuit of self-interest benefits the community.

Viewed in this light, we seem to have come full circle back to the eighteenth century economic theories of Adam Smith. Smith's theories seem particularly apt today in relation to the Conservative Government's privatization policies since these policies aimed to 'get government off people's backs' by allowing them greater freedom to pursue their own 'self-interest' and by making them assume a greater responsibility for their own welfare. Needless to say, this had great appeal to a population brought up on the exhortations of the human potential movement, which preached individual growth through 'self-actualization'. Little wonder that the new 1980s 'me-generation' (i.e. those born in the 1960s) were most anxious to jump on Thatcher's 'market-forces' bandwagon, since it appeared to offer the best means of securing their own particular 'place in the sun'. Thus, throughout the later 1980s in both Britain and America, 'self-interest' was pursued with renewed vigour as 'paper entrepreneuralism' was encouraged through speculation on the stock market and people were urged to take on enormous debt (sometimes 3 or 4 times their annual salary) in order to own their homes. Following on from this, inflation and lack of investment severely eroded the British industrial base during that period.

There is, however, one important difference between the present-day free-market philosophy and the Calvinist doctrine of laissez-faire capitalism. That is, that while Calvinism preached self-denial and delayed gratification, the 'me-generation' of the 1960s and 1970s emphasized self-gratification and having it all now. As Yankelovich (1981) observed, selfishness often masquerades as 'self-actualization' and 'nothing has subverted self-fulfillment more thoroughly than self-indulgence.'

Consumerism and alienation

An additional effect of the rise of capitalism in the nineteenth century was that it destroyed man's sense of community since it tended to 'put man against man'. De Tocqueville (1840) in discussing American society under capitalism during that period, describes it as: 'Multitudes of men incessantly endeavouring to procure the petty and the paltry pleasure with which they glut their lives. Each lives apart (and) is a stranger to the other's fate ... he does not know anybody else, he exists only in himself and for himself alone...' This was the beginning of the alienation process later described by Marx as being endemic to the capitalist system. Since then the process has escalated under privatization.

Mrs Thatcher said, 'there was no such thing as society, only individuals,' and envisaged a kind of social Darwinism taking place in Britain where only the fittest survived. The net result of the privatization measures taken was that 'citizens' were turned into 'consumers'. (*The Citizen's Charter* might more properly be called the *Consumer's Charter*, since the emphasis is not on citizenship but on consumerism. Citizenship implies belonging to a community with rights *and* responsibilities, not simply 'rights'.) When everyone becomes a consumer 'getting and spending' in the market place, involved solely in a pure cash nexus with their neighbours, the glue that binds society together becomes infinitely weaker. This may result in alienation for many members of society. This is alienation not simply in the Marxian sense but in a social sense (or anomie as Durkheim (1952) described it), where man becomes not only alienated from the product of his labour, but alienated from his neighbours as well. Yankelovich (1981) noted that what he called the 'Maslovian escalator' was responsible for much of the loneliness and isolation he found among American society.

Tawney (1938) noted, over half a century ago, that society was no longer organic but rather had become a mass society in which all relationships were contractual. This process has been accelerated today with the advent of compulsory competitive tendering (CCT). While competition may be effective in some instances in keeping prices low, it also has the negative effect of perpetuating a kind of artificial conflict predicated on selifishness. The result is that co-operation (and community) are sacrificed to the gods of consumerism. Consumer-man, therefore, cannot feel himself to be a whole person or a member of a community as he is pushed and pulled in different directions by 'market forces'. Soon, he too simply becomes another mere depersonalized commodity to be bought and sold in the marketplace like any other thing. Also, when individual self-worth and self-esteem are determined by a bank balance rather than who the person is - society is the loser.

'Traditionalists' and 'Strong Formers'

In addition to the increasing commercialization and alienation in society, there has been a definite political swing to the right in the past decade or so in most Western democracies. This is obviously reflective of the attitudes of the electorate and it is informative, therefore, to review how societal values have changed since the 1970s, enabling a Conservative Government to remain in power for over fifteen years.

Yankelovich (1981) in a ten-year study of the changing values of American Society has identified two distinct groups of people; one he named the 'traditionalists' and the other the 'strong formers'. (Although this study was conducted in America it reflects the changes that occurred in Britain during the same decade.) He found that the 'traditionalists' represented 20 per cent of the population who still adhered to the values of hard work, family loyalty and self-sacrifice. They comprised the poorer, older, more conservative and more rural population in the US.

He found that the strong formers comprised only 17 per cent of the population and had self-fulfillment as their main objective in life. However, this group was important, he believed, because they represented the vanguard of a new social ethic. This group was younger, better educated, less religious, different from the mainstream in their reactions and tended to agree with statements like, 'I spend a great deal of time thinking about myself,' and 'satisfaction comes from shaping oneself rather than from home and family life.'

Yankelovich also found that the vast majority (63 per cent) still believed in some of the more traditional values but they also held more liberal views that would have been considered heretical only a decade before, but have now become fairly commonplace. They were tolerant of abortion, premarital sex, remaining single and not having children and were dubious about the importance of work, feeling that it did not have to be the centre of their lives.

However, just as this psychocultural revolution was gaining ground, led by this vanguard group, it ran into serious economic problems in the shape of rising oil prices, and inflation, increasing costs of government entitlement programmes, and a decline in the competitiveness of US industry. All of these had significant public policy consequences attached to them. Bode (1981) noted that:

> Ever since Roosevelt's New Deal the credo was to help the poor so long as it did not actually hurt the rich. As long as the economy was booming, 'the rising tide that lifts all ships' was the dominant metaphor. But as soon as economic scarcity occurs and people feel vulnerable they begin to resent helping others (Yankelovich, 1981). They become 'bored with the problems of race and unemployment that (they had) begun to address in earlier decades.'

Nevertheless, Yankelovich contended that a new 'ethic of commitment' was dawning, particularly among the strong formers, where self-denial and self-fulfillment would be synthesized into a 'search for community'. However, he seemed a little uncertain in his optimism and instead, suggested that a period of chaos might lie ahead: 'Our current mood is one of all-encompassing disorientation; a muddled confusion has now become the hallmark of the search for self-fulfillment. If we can overcome it, a good journey to the end of the century and beyond is still possible. But if the confusion persists, a bad trip is inevitable' (Yankelovich, 1981).

With the benefit of hindsight it can be seen that Yankelovich tended to ignore the political realities of the time, especially the Reagan administration's dismantling of fiscal and social policy in the wake of the anti-liberal backlash. He also largely ignored the 20 per cent tradition-minded population of mainly Reagan supporters who were appalled by the permissiveness they had witnessed under previous democratic administrations. In fact, it was this increasingly vocal group which set the moral tone for both sides of the Atlantic in the 1980s and well into the 1990s.

The aims of privatization

Given the conservative mood of the UK in the early 1980s, the newly elected Tory Government was able to draw on much support for their revolutionary privatization programme, largely because it seemed to offer a way of reducing the PSBR. However, two questions remain: (i) Why did the Conservative Government decide to adopt a comprehensive programme of privatization?; and (ii) Has it been effective in achieving their aims?

Vickers and Yarrow (1988) in their influential book, list seven possible reasons for privatizing, two of which will be discussed here, i.e. improving efficiency and gaining political advantage.[5]

Haskel and Szymanski (1991) note that it is difficult to assess the overall effectiveness of privatization, since much of the attention has been focused on the efficiency issue in terms of reducing costs (although prices have risen due to lack of effective competition). They write that it seems to have been accepted as a truism that private enterprise is more efficient than public enterprise. However, this proposition has never really been rigorously tested.

The avowed aims of the Conservative Government's 1979 election manifesto was to: master inflation, through monetary discipline; reduce the size of the Government's borrowing, reduce waste and bureaucracy, cut income tax, and reward hard work, responsibility and success. (Interestingly, the term 'privatization' was not used originally in the 1979 *Manifesto*.)

As Marsh (1991) notes, in his comprehensive review of the literature on privatization under Thatcher, the initial emphasis of privatization was to buttress a policy of controlling the money supply (which failed), by reducing public expenditure. Privatization gave rise to income tax cuts somewhat later (which were usually introduced immediately before an election as a means of winning votes for the Government.) Marsh also found that privatization was pursued even when there was no demonstrable benefit to consumers. And, Young (1986) notes that privatization was often pursued for political rather than economic reasons, on the assumption that it was easier to sell public assets and more popular than cutting public expenditure.

Bishop and Kay (1988) argue that privatization was: 'a policy which was adopted almost by accident but has become politically central; a policy which has no clear-cut objectives, but has become almost an end in itself.' In contrast to most theorists, Young (1986) argues that there was a coherent policy and that 'it was applied as a philosophy on a sustained and continuing basis.' As evidence for this he cites the way privatization policies were pursued even when they incurred public expenditure or did not promote competition.

Marsh concludes that privatization had a number of aims, some of which were contradictory. For example, he notes that increased efficiency conflicted with the need to ensure quick and successful asset sales; competition was compromised because of the need to ensure the co-operation of management. Haskel and Szymanski (1990) contend that privatization was characterized by a change in objectives in public sector organizations that was possible only if the organization was privatized. They maintain that it is competition rather than privatization itself that is important, since privatization *per se* changes very little from an efficiency perspective, unless it is accomplished by liberalization of the market. Without liberalization, privatization would not reduce wages or unemployment. (See Chapter 4).

Where liberalization was not feasible, the Government set up a number of regulatory bodies to invervene on behalf of consumers (e.g., OFTEL, OFWAT, OFGAS, etc.). These 'watchdog' bodies were established to oversee pricing in industries where competition is limited, e.g., British Telecom, gas and electricity. Here, market forces were not allowed to operate unhindered because of substantial monopoly conditions, since it was believed that this was against the public good (Haskel and Szymanski, 1991). However, the general perception among the public is that these bodies have not protected consumers to any great extent and that they 'lack teeth' to enforce their recommendations.[6] (It has even been suggested by the media that there has been collusion between the regulators and certain utility companies themselves (see Chapter 4).

Thus, rather than a coherent strategy, these apparent inconsistencies strongly suggest that, in terms of Vickers and Yarrow's identified aims, gaining political advantage would appear to be high on the list. In this respect, privatization is in danger of assuming many of the trappings of an ideology, since it is being pushed as a panacea for all that ails the British economy, regardless of whether it is suitable to a particular type of institution. When political and economic decisions are based on ideology rather than on the needs of a particular situation or system, they can indeed be 'dangerous'. And, while a policy of privatization may be entirely appropriate when applied to running a commercial organization where the profit motive is all important, it may be entirely inappropriate when applied to an agency like the National Health Service where making a profit would conflict with society's needs.

The end of the Welfare State?

But perhaps an equally important reason for privatizing was to staunch the flow of deficit spending on 'welfare programmes'. Therefore, starting in the 1980s, both the Reagan and Thatcher Administrations, in consultation with economists such as Friedman and Enthoven,[7] concluded that the 'free market' was capable of allocating goods and services more effectively than the state could. In an attempt to lower domestic programme costs these administrations advocated greater competition among service providers and more cost-sharing among consumers. The assumption, according to market theory, was that competition lowers costs by making services more efficient and by improving quality. Cost-sharing, this same theory holds, saves dollars by increasing consumer costs relative to those of the government and by encouraging consumers to use services more selectively.

Faced with large scale deficit spending, welfare and social programmes were severely curtailed, especially in the 1980s by the Reagan Administration. This Administration quickly started to dismantle many of the social programmes of previous democratic administrations in the firm belief that much that was done was the result of muddleheaded liberalism causing good money to be thrown after bad.

The net result was, according to Abromovitz (1986), that

> since 1981, the Reagan Administration proposed and enacted numerous privatization measures. Taken together, these measures have (1) undermined liberal social welfare principles, (2) sent consumers from public agencies into the private service market, and (3) validated the idea of replacing standard entitlement programs with private market alternatives. The result of this strategy, in addition to enlarging the role of private enterprise in a scaled-down welfare state, have been larger profits for private providers; lower wages, fewer jobs and weaker unions in the public sector; and less service for those most in need.

'Reaganomics' rested on a firm belief in the 'trickle down' effect. That is, by turning almost all public service industries over to the private sector they would be run more efficiently and that this would provide more jobs for people who would then start to disappear off the welfare rolls. Needless to say, this did not immediately take place. Instead, unemployment steadily increased and the number of people made homeless escalated.

Not only that, but according to Eshag (1994) writing in *The Times*, 'during Reagan's presidency (1981-88) the Federal budget deficit and public-sector borrowing more than doubled; the public debt almost trebled; and the money supply rose by more than 90 per cent, to permit a fall in interest rates.' Nevertheless, he concedes 'the rate of inflation was almost halved and gross private investment rose by 30 per cent in real terms, compared with 12 per cent in the preceding eight years' (*The Times*, Friday October 28 1994).

Larry Elliott, Economics Correspondent for the *The Guardian* (27 November, 1993) notes that government spending on welfare programmes was noncontroversial throughout the 1950s and 1960s. Elliott, quoting from Mullard's book, *The Politics of Public Expenditure*, writes that:

> government capital expenditure as a proportion of GDP was running at well over 4 per cent in the late 1960s, while social security spending was just over 7 per cent of GDP. The latest figures reflect how mass unemployment and the concomitant growth of poverty have changed the balance of spending. Social security benefits now account for more than 12 per cent of GDP, while overall capital spending - admittedly somewhat deflated by privatization - has shrunk to 1.4 per cent. (*The Guardian,* 27 November, 1993).

Elliott observed that 'the welfare state accounts for two-thirds of present state spending, with the money concentrated on the "five giants" identified by Beveridge - disease, ignorance, idleness, want and squalor'. For example, in 1993 the Government spent £34.6 billion on the NHS (just under 6 per cent of GDP); education received £32.3 billion or 0.17 per cent compared with 0.5 per cent in the 1960s; for unemployment and poverty the total social security budget was £85.6 billion - pensions alone account for £35 billion (income support and housing benefit have doubled since the boom of the late 1980s); public housing has recently been cut. During 1992/3 the Government spent just slightly over £6 billion on housing. Elliott concludes that 'overall, the welfare state accounts for more than 26 per cent of GDP, double the levels of the 1960s. By international standards Britain is not generous, ranking 17th out of 21 industrialized countries in 1989, down from 13th in 1981.'

A third way

While capitalism made growth and economic prosperity possible for some, it abandons those who cannot compete in the marketplace. (Also, with many hitherto welfare programmes either being abandoned or privatized this cushion has all but been effectively eliminated.) Socialism has been successful in creating the welfare state but it has also produced third and fourth generations of dependent families. As a result of these and other abuses, governments are finding that public money cannot support the welfare system at present levels. Both the left and right are, therefore, seeking alternatives to the ever increasing demands of the welfare state and the unbridled workings of the free market economy, as neither capitalism nor socialism appears to offer any way out of the current dilemma.

Both economists and sociologists have joined the search for a better way. For example, Etzioni (1989) echoed Yankelovich's findings that there was a 'need for community' among the majority of the population when he put forward his idea of 'communitarianism'. The basis of the communitarian ideology is the community, and its themes are family, work and mutual responsibility. It also owes something to Schumacher's (1974) idea that 'small is beautiful'.[8] Etzioni similarily maintains that big government should be replaced by small, informal government and the family should become the basic unit of society. Everything should be decentralized so that communities, not big government, can become more effective (Phillips, 1993).

In determining where ownership of a problem exists, the principle of 'subsidiarity' is invoked. This maintains that the responsibility for any problem or situation belongs first to those nearest to the problem and then only if a solution cannot be found by the individual does responsibility devolve to the family. If the family cannot cope, then the local community should become involved. Only after these possibilities have been tried and the problem proves too intractable should the state intervene. This type of thinking justifies levying fines on all who do not comply and imposing 'workfare' instead of welfare on the unemployed. Etzioni is well aware that these proposals are controversial and require a radical restructuring of society's attitudes and values. Nevertheless he confidently predicts that communitarianism offers a way out for politicians.

Communitarianism is not without its critics, however. Stone (1994), points out that communities can be more repressive and bureaucratic than big governments e.g. the Salem Witch Trials (*The Sunday Times*, October 1994). And feminists like Betty Friedan believe that if communitarianism is adopted it may wipe out the gains made by the women's movement in the past decades, since it appears to require women to return to the home and to adopt the more traditional roles of homemakers. Etzioni believes that these criticisms are unjustified and are due to a misunderstanding of communitarianism. He maintains that the concept of subsidiarity should take care of many of the problems the changeover would create.

While there appears to be considerable merit to communitarianism, especially in making individuals and communities more responsible for solving their own problems, Etzioni does not answer the basic question of how this fundamental change in societal values is to take place, nor where the money is to be found. Nevertheless, in the absence of any other alternative, and if only as an antidote to the consumerist *zeitgeist*, perhaps what *is* needed is a new ethic of co-operation akin to that proposed by communitarianism. Such an ethic would have the effect of forcing us to become more interdependent and societally conscious and might end some of the self-seeking and alienation-inducing behaviour encountered today. As of this writing, however, the traditionalists in the form of free-marketeers appear to be in the majority and the revolution that Etzioni seeks, seems a long way off.

Summary

While privatization may have produced some benefits in the form of increased efficiency and accountability where resources are finite, the Conservative Government's claims for privatization (increased job opportunities and incentives, greater benefits to consumers through lower prices due to competition and increased public ownership of shares) remain largely unsubstantiated. Instead, it is argued that privatization has been used as a means of maintaining the Conservative Government's hold on power under the guise of increased benefits to consumers and the workforce. Also, now the Government has virtually reached a limit for cutting the PSBR it must either raise taxes or privatize more assets. (Between 1979-92 the Government raised £42 billion through privatization.) The Conservatives have also retained their hold on power by virtue of the social backlash that occurred among the majority of the public against the liberalism of the 1960s. Subsequently, Adam Smith's concept of a free market economy found new favour with the 'enterprise culture' of the 1980s which gave new meaning to the term, 'self-interest'.

A way forward is suggested by Etzioni and others through 'communitarianism' which stresses individual, family and community responsibilities. This system appears to offer an alternative to the polar extremes of increased socialism or increased privatization. However, the way ahead seems fraught with difficulties since this system appears to require a radical restructuring of society's values.

The challenge ahead for our political leaders is, therefore, to balance the gains made by 'market- forces' with concern for the welfare of the individual. In other words, this means becoming both efficient *and* humane at the same time.

References

Abromovitz, M. (1986), 'The privatization of the welfare state: a review,' *Social Work*, July/August, 1986.

Bender, F. L. (1972), *Karl Marx: the essential writings*, London: Harper Torchbooks.

Bishop, M. and Kay, J. (1989), *Does privatization work? Lessons from the UK*, Centre for Business Strategy, London: London Business School.

Bode, K. (1981), 'The Identity crisis of the me generation,' *Washington Post*, July 5.

Block, F. (1986), 'Political choice and the multiple "logics" of capital,' *Theory and Society*, 15, pp. 175-192.

Buckland, R. (1987), 'The costs and returns of the privatization of nationalised industries,' *Public Administration*, vol. 65, no. 3, pp. 241-57.

De Tocqueville, A. (1840), *Democracy in America*, 2 volumes, London: Longman, Green, Longman and Roberts,1862.

Durkheim, E. (1964), *The division of labor in society*, New York: The Free Press (copyright by the Macmillan Company, 1933).

Durkheim, E. (1952), *Suicide: a study in sociology*, London: Routledge & Kegan Paul, first published in 1897.

Elliott, L. (1993), 'As the balance of spending tilts away from long-term investment, room for manoeuvre is constrained,' *The Guardian*, 27 November.

Enthoven, A. C. (1985), *Reflections on the management of the NHS: an American looks at incentives to efficiency in health services management in the UK*, London: Nuffield Provincial Hospitals Trust.

Eshag, E. (1994), 'How labour could avoid trap set by the Treasury,' *The Sunday Times*, October, 28.

Etzioni, A. (1989), 'Towards an I & we paradigm,' *Contemporary Sociology*, 18, March.

Friedman, M. and Friedman, R. (1980), *Free to choose: a personal statement*, London: Secker & Warburg.

Haskel, J. and Szymanski, S. (1991), 'Privatization, jobs and wages,' *Employment Insititute Economic Report*, vol. 6. no. 7, December, 1991.

Kay, J. and Thompson, D. J. (1986), 'Privatisation: a policy in search of a rationale,' *Economic Journal*, vol. 96, pp. 18-32.

Keynes, J. M. (1936), *General Theory of Employment, Interest and Money: Collected Writings*, vol. vii Macmillan Publishing Co. 1973, pp. 383-4.

Klein, R. (1988), 'Privatization and the Welfare State', in *Lloyds Bank Annual Review: Privatization and Ownership*, Vol. 1, London: Pinter Publisher, (Edited by Christopher Johnson).

Marsh, D. (1991), 'Privatization under Mrs Thatcher: a review of the literature', *Public Administration*, Vol. 69, Winter 1991, pp. 459-480.

Merriam, I.C. (1967), "Social Welfare Expenditures, 1927-1969", *Social Security Bulletin*, 30, December.

Mullard, M. (1987), *The politics of public expenditure*, London: Croom Helm.

Naisbitt, J. and Aburdene, P. (1990), *Megatrends 2000*, London: Sidgwick and Jackson.

Phillips, D. L. (1993), *Looking backwards: a critical appraisal of communitarian thought*, Princeton, NJ: Princeton University Press.

Pulkingham, J. (1989), 'From public provision to privatization: the crisis in welfare reassessed', *Sociology*, Vol. 23, No. 3, August 1989.

Schumacher, E. E. (1974), *Small is beautiful: a study of economics as people mattered*, London: Abacus edition by Sphere Books, Ltd.

Smith, A. (1976), *An inquiry into the nature and causes of the wealth of nations*, edited by R. H. Campbell and A. S. Skinner, (Glasgow edition) Oxford: Clarendon Press.

Stone, N. (1994), 'A mad scramble for the centre: there can never be a middle way,' *The Sunday Times News Review*, 9 October.

Tawney, R. H. (1938), *Religion and the rise of capitalism: an historical study*, with a prefatory note by Charles Gore, Harmondsworth: Penguin.

The Conservative Manifesto, (1992), *The best future for Britain*, published by Conservative Central Office, 32, Smith Square, Westminster, London, SW1P 3HH.

Thompson, D. and Whitfield, A. (1990), 'Express coaching: Privatization, incumbent advantage and the competitive process', *MIMEO.*

Vickers, J. and Yarrow, G. (1988), *Privatization: an economic analysis*, MIT Press; Cambridge, Mass.

Weber, M. (1947), *The theory of social and economic organizations*, edited by Talcott Parsons, trans. by A. M. Henderson and T. Parsons, New York: Free Press.

Yankelovich, D. (1981), *New Rules: searching for self-fulfillment in a world turned upside down*, NY: Random House.

Young, S. (1986), 'The nature of privatization in Britain, 1979-85', *West European Politics*, No. 9, pp. 235-52.

Footnotes

1 Since Mrs Thatcher worked closely with the Reagan Administration during this period of considerable reform what happened in America is closely mirrored by what occurred in Britain. It is necessary, therefore, to review how America influenced Britain during that period.

2 When Mrs Thatcher became Prime Minister in 1979, Sir Keith Joseph, the Minister for Industry, sent copies of Adam Smith's book to all senior civil servants, advising them that if they wanted to understand the new Conservative Government's policies, they should read it. It is not reported how many did, however.

3 Smith *did* approve of some degree of government intervention, if this became necessary. For example, he argued that the price mechanism was pre-eminent and that it was the duty of governments to ensure that there was competitive pricing. When this did not occur some form of government regulation was required. However, Smith believed that this should be used only as a last resort.

4 Smith argued that competition should be guaranteed by government regulation, if necessary. But he believed that the price mechanism thus regulated would work to allocate efficiently factors of production, goods and services. Keynes, on the other hand, argued that the price mechanism does not work. Rather he argued that capital stock adjusts in a recession (i.e., it contracts) and prices adjust much later and inadequately (i.e., they rise rather than fall to maximize the firm's revenue). Thus, Keynes argued that aggregate demand and, in particular, investment need to be expanded to raise employment.

5 The seven possible reasons for privatizing listed by Vickers and Yarrow included: (i) improving efficiency; (ii) reducing public sector borrowing requirements; (iii) reducing government involvement in enterprise decision making; (iv) easing problems of public sector pay determination; (v) widening share ownership; (vi) encouraging employee

share ownership,and (vii) gaining political advantage. The first and seventh of these are discussed in this Chapter; the remaining five are dealt with in other chapters in the book.

6 It is in the privatization of water, where competition is non-existent, that consumers appear to have suffered most. OFWATT agreed that the average water bill for consumers in England and Wales has gone up by an average of 68 per cent in 1993/94. (Northumberland Water has increased its charges by over 500 per cent!) Coupled with this is the fact that the directors of the water companies and other recently privatized utility companies have awarded themselves annual salary increases of 180 per cent or more and have accepted subsequent yearly increases of 20 per cent ever since. (Although a number of 'watchdog' committees were asked to contribute to this book, all declined for various reasons.)

7 Enthoven, an American, who knew little about the British NHS was nevertheless quite undaunted when asked to review it from the point of view of an outsider. He thus provided the genesis for many of the subsequent reforms carried out on the NHS, including *The Griffith Report*, (1983) and *Working for Patients,* (1989).

8 Schumacher (1974) in *Small is Beautiful* contended that the pursuit of progress which promotes giant corporations and increased specialization has actually resulted in economic inefficiency, pollution and inhuman working conditions. Schumacher proposed a system of Intermediate Technology based on smaller working units, communal ownership and regional workplaces utilising local labour and resources emphasizing people not things.

2 Reasons for privatization

Madsen Pirie

Why privatize?

One reason why privatization has become so significant a force in modern economies is that it achieves many objectives simultaneously. Put another way, there are many reasons why governments might undertake a campaign of privatization, but the chances are high that there will be additional unintended benefits if they do so. The initial motive which prompted the British Conservative government first elected in 1979 was probably a desire to correct the perceived failings of state industries and utilities. That these were an economic burden is evidenced by their poor performance. Most of them made losses and had to be supported by annual subsidy from taxpayers.

The state industries tended to be inefficient and over-manned. They took more workers than private competitors overseas to produce each unit of output. Attempts by government and its appointed managers to control production costs proved relatively ineffective alongside the threat of bankruptcy and closure faced by their private counterparts. At its bluntest, they had little incentive to be cost effective since government would foot the bills and no-one would lose their jobs. State industries were notoriously under-capitalized. This is a straight consequence of Public Choice Theory. Faced with strident demands on its resources, government finds it easier to raid the capital account. Future voters do not affect its current electoral performance. They do not exert real pressure like today's pensioners and parents. In one state industry after another, cash-strapped governments had cut investment plans, leaving the industries insufficiently capitalized to be cost-effective. This is one reason why the state industries in Britain had an out-of-date air, and were often characterized by old fashioned equipment.

Lack of any consumer responsiveness was a major public criticism. Since they had access to taxpayer funds and rarely had to attract custom against competition, consumers were not a major factor. They could not take their money elsewhere because it had been taken in taxation and because a public monopoly often meant there was nowhere else. Thus customers were sometimes seen as an inconvenience. Producers, on the other hand, had real power and had to be taken account of. Workers could stage disruptive strikes or go-slows, leading to public pressure on governments. The state industries were thus producer-oriented instead of consumer-oriented.

Attempts to control costs could be thwarted by Civil Service managers putting on line the most valued part of the service, rather than attempting to achieve economies by internal saving and rationalization. The fact that they were nominally owned and directed by government made government responsible for their failings. Government was pilloried daily for the poor performance of the state industries. Always it was urged to do the same thing: pump even more money into them. It was because the publicly-owned industries were loss-making, inefficient, over-manned, under-capitalized, out-of-date, unresponsive and politically troublesome that the 1979 government decided to attempt privatization. It had not been elected on such a mandate. Its 1979 manifesto had referred to the Aerospace and freight industries as possible candidates for a return to the private sector. The supposition must be strong that it was the early success with its new policy which emboldened the government to attempt even more of it.

The Conservative Government's programme

If government's first aim was to stem the losses, it succeeded. The subsidies which the nationalized industries had required from the taxpayer were translated into contributions to the Treasury in the form of taxation on their profits. In the private sector taxpayers do not normally step in to support losses; these are borne instead by shareholders, employees, and sometimes by creditors.

Government had to restructure most of its state industries in advance of privatization. Often this meant writing off huge swathes of past debt. This money had nominally been 'invested' in state firms, but in reality it had been spent. The value was no longer there to be retrieved. Government was not interested in the argument that past taxpayers 'should get their money back'.

It took the view that it was more important to give the firm a chance to succeed. What government was doing in some cases was the equivalent of bankruptcy in the private sector. It was restructuring, paying creditors (mainly itself) a fraction of past loans, and setting a reorganized and unencumbered firm free to succeed. One measure of its success may be assessed from the fact that government received more at the end of the decade in corporation tax (35 per cent) on the profits of privatized industries than it took at the start of the decade when it owned the whole of them.

The desire to stem losses was one aim, but a desire to solve the political problem posed by state industries was another. It is commonly supposed that the prime aim of privatization must be to make industries profitable to make them competitive, or to make money from the sale. In fact the prime aim should be to make them private. All of the other targets are certainly worth achieving, but the very act of making an industry private involves political gain for the government which does it.

Depolitization of state industries

When a state industry goes private, it goes commercial. It is depoliticized to a great degree. Instead of expansion or closure plans bowing to the government's political needs of the day, they bow instead to commercial pressures. Instead of investment being determined by what government can afford, given its other pressing priorities, it is determined instead by what the market will offer. Privatization in Britain took the state industries out of the political domain. In doing so, it removed a considerable part of the flak which their failings directed towards government. It did not do so immediately. In fact it takes time before people regard the firm as wholly private. Its links with government take time to fade. But the experience in Britain suggests that as years go by after privatization, people are less and less likely to blame government for their behaviour. By 1994 few people were laying at government's door the troubles of British Aerospace, or blaming them for the loss of jobs at British Telecom.

This depoliticization is one of the most important gains brought by privatization. It leads people to see themselves (correctly) as consumers of services by these firms, rather than as participants in them through the democratic process. As such, people seek out and use consumer rights when they feel let down, rather than attempting to gain satisfaction through the political process.

Other objectives

After the desire to stem the losses and to get rid of the constant political problems posed by state industries, the other aims include the desire to make money from the sale, to introduce competition and choice, to create successful industries for the national economy, and to spread wider share ownership and employee share ownership. Not least among the aims is a desire on the part of government to achieve a perceived success and to be more popular and more electable in consequence of this. The aims of privatization are not always mutually compatible. Government must strike a balance, achieving some of each at the expense of others. It has certainly made money from its sales. By the late 1980s it was realizing £5.5 billion per year from its sales, a figure which it has since maintained.

The traditional three ways by which a government raises revenue all have their costs. Taxation is unpopular. Borrowing pre-empts the cash needed by the private sector to finance expansion. Inflation leads to a breakdown of trust and an inability to plan; it sets wages chasing prices chasing wages. The new method is only possible because Treasury rules count asset sales as 'negative expenditure'. Britain does not have an asset account; any nationalization has to be paid for out of current spending. The reasoning says that the reverse follows logically. If purchases come out of current spending, sale proceeds must go in to current spending. Lord Stockton, the former Harold Macmillan, famously characterized this as 'selling silver to pay the butler's wages.' His own background was surprisingly free of silver and butlers. His mistake was not to realize that it was the family junk being sold, and that it was being sold to the family. The state industries were national assets after they had been sold, rarely before.

The 'hidden' privatization was that of council houses, bringing in as much by the mid-80s as all of the other sales put together. Undoubtedly one factor which directs government even today towards further asset sales is the desire to gain revenue without taxing, borrowing or inflating.

Competition in the short and long term

The desire to introduce competition conflicts with the desire to get a good price. A competitive private firm will be worth less to potential buyers than a monopoly. Government's record, given this temptation, has not been bad. It has usually managed to introduce some element of competition, and always to extend it after time. It has used regulators as temporary expedients, to protect the consumer until competition could perform the task more effectively. Mercury was admitted only as a business competitor to British Telecom, but soon allowed by OFTEL to enter the domestic market and to provide rival telephone boxes. A further six entrants were admitted at the end of the seven year review. This seems to be developing as a pattern. Government gives shareholders seven years of the status quo at privatization, and then reserves the right to introduce more competition. Government has pragmatically decided to privatize when it can, by whatever method it can, and then put it right later if necessary. This is sound use of Public Choice Theory. State enterprises have powerful friends in Parliament. When they become not only private capitalists, but monopoly capitalists, they lose their political clout and are reasonably easy to change later.

It was undoubtedly a poor choice to privatize British Gas as a single unit, but government could probably not have done it otherwise. It knew that it could return after a few years to break up the company if necessary and introduce more competition. As long as the original buyers had the seven years they were promised, this could be regarded as a reasonably fair procedure. The share market tends to discount government-imposed changes as the case for them becomes more pressing. Government managed to introduce some degree of competition into Electricity by separating producers from distributors, and then by further moves to bring in new producers. The hardest to make competitive is probably water, but they could take a leaf out of the French book and use private tenders to give water boards competition. If water boards were required to put out perhaps 50 per cent of their work to outside tenders, but were themselves allowed to tender outside their own area, a reasonably competitive position might be created.

Some consequences

Privatization has undoubtedly led to the emergence of some strong national industries which are economic assets to the nation. British Telecom and British Gas have world-wide aspirations. British Airways is attempting to turn itself with partners into one of the few mega-carriers: it expects to dominate air travel. Some of the privatized industries have become British subsidiaries of foreign owners. Jaguar passed to Ford, Rover to BMW, both after very effective recoveries which re-established their reputations and restored value to the marque. The British government could never have secured political acceptance for privatization to foreign buyers, as the aborted negotiations with Ford for British Leyland divisions had shown. It was probably relieved that foreign owners were prepared to secure British jobs at no further cost or embarrassment to itself.

The aim of wider share ownership, both by the public at large and by employees in their own industries was achieved to a limited extent. Government offered shares to employees, getting to the point where 8 or 10 per cent of shares would be set aside for half price offers, or at least very attractive ones, to the work force. This helped to secure the acquiescence of union members, if not of union leaders, for the privatization. Typically, over 90 per cent of the work force would take up the offer (sometimes 98 per cent). Cut price shares for workers was less costly than it seems. Companies whose workers own shares in them are less likely to have disruptive disputes or strikes, will feature better morale, and are worth more in consequence. Thus the price of the rest of the shares goes up if some are sold to the work force.

In so far as it attempted to turn the general public into share-owners, the 1980s governments enjoyed more limited success. They famously turned around the ratio of trade unionists to share owners. In 1979 there had been four times as many trade unionists as share owners. Within a decade the latter exceeded the former. However, analysis of the new owners showed that most owned only one or two of the privatization issues. The habit of equity investment had not spread as deeply as the government had hoped. It was not for want of trying. The advertising blitz which accompanied the mass sales starting with BT certainly attracted popular interest and attention. More to the point, perhaps, attractive pricing led media pundits to predict immediate gains. The government aim appears to have been for a combination of good price and popular success, which in practice meant aiming for a first day premium of perhaps 10-15 per cent. Sometimes they were spectacularly wrong, and were accused of serious under-pricing to benefit 'their City friends'. It is truer perhaps that for industries which had never been valued before and had never kept proper accounts, no-one really had any accurate idea of what they were worth. The premiums were popular, and persuaded new buyers that privatization investment was a good thing. Government grew quite sophisticated at reducing the commission it had to pay. It did this by introducing competitive bidding, and succeeded in dramatically lowering the percentage it had to pay. Its argument was that many of these companies were blue chip, and did not involve the risk of more average firms. The under-writers earned their money when the BP issue coincided spectacularly with the 1987 crash, and they lost huge sums.

More sophisticated still were the mechanisms by which government could reward small share-holders, without pouring cash into the institutions which invested. It held two-tier sales, with part fixed by price and part by tender. 'Clawback' was introduced in the event of popular over-subscription, to take shares out of the tender sale and reassign them to the fixed price issue. In this way government sacrificed a little of its price in order to spread ownership and satisfy its citizenry. This, indeed, was one of its undeclared aims. It wanted privatization to be an electoral asset, a vote winner. To do that it needed to have a perceived success in which many ordinary citizens participated, and from which they benefited. This was undoubtedly achieved. Privatization was seen to have stemmed the losses, to have hived off the political problems endemic in state industries, to have helped keep taxes down, to have introduced elements of competition and choice, to have created industrial successes, and to have spread share ownership among employees and the general public.

This enabled it to achieve the undeclared aim of attracting votes and securing re-election. The unprecedented four-in-a-row election victories may have owed something to the privatization programme. With hindsight, the curious fact is that none of the privatizations was popular before it was put through. Many incurred huge majorities opposed. It was when government went ahead anyway and achieved its successes that opinion swung round.

The legacy

The final testament to the programme is that similar ones are under way in virtually every country in the world, and that an unexpected bonus for Britain has been the emergence of a growth industry in privatization expertise and advice. Since Britain did it first, its firms have an experience which is sought world-wide.

And the British opposition, which opposed every single piece of privatization, has one by one withdrawn its pledges to reverse them. It now accepts privatization as a policy which by its performance created a new reality. Privatization was pursued for disparate and sometimes incompatible aims. It solved the problems of the state industries, however, and it achieved enough of its aims to make it the most significant economic development of modern times.

3 Private finance: A driving force to enhance efficiency

Tony Hazell and Dolph Zubick

Introduction

Privatization was perceived at the outset as the representation of an ideology that public assets should be held in the hands of the public, either through direct, wider share ownership or through institutions such as pension funds. Along with this ideological aim came the desire to instil far greater levels of organizational efficiency through the imposition of private sector-type disciplines.

Towards the end of the 1980s, the privatization process started to falter for a range of reasons, not the least of which was the fact that it might be argued that the prime targets for this process had already been selected and actioned. The criteria by which this judgement could be made ranged from the inherent 'commerciality' of the entity to be privatized (the internal, cultural consideration) to the political and commercial attractiveness of the entity (the external consideration). Thus the remainder of the public sector was less attractive for these purposes. It was also less manageable for these same purposes.

At the same time, Government revenues were falling due, in part, to recession and due to the slow down of privatization proceeds and there was a clearly stated commitment to eliminating the budget deficit. There was also little scope left for the one-off gains which had earlier been achieved through the likes of rate-capping local government and re-phasing tax and excise payments. The combination of these principle factors (there are other, lesser ones) was to motivate the UK Government to explore ways in which it could limit, reduce and ultimately obviate the need for capital spend as far as possible. The brainchild it produced was the Private Finance Initiative or PFI.

It is also valid to point out that the above combination of 'need factors' is one which has exercised the minds of politicians of a broad range of views. Thus it is clear that the British Labour Party had in mind this same analysis when producing their policy document - Financing Infrastructure Investment. There are, naturally, differences between their views as to the roles to be played by the private sector in delivering any solution(s), but the central message remains the same: the private sector is needed to provide skills, finance and experience.

The above really confirms that the Government has, in the opinion of the authors of this chapter, identified that through the introduction of PFI made one of the principle inputs to infrastructural service delivery transparent thereby bringing the entire process into the open challenge of the marketplace. We shall bring this into focus - in particular in the cornerstone of the welfare state, the NHS - by subsequent reference to the transformation processes under way therein.

The NHS has been selected for the purposes of analysis in this chapter on the basis of its relative importance to the Government and society as a whole: the NHS costs approximately 6 per cent of GDP which is equivalent to 20 per cent of the Government's share of expenditure. The NHS expenditure exceeds government expenditure for either education or defence and is under continuous scrutiny for both its sufficiency (backlogs of service) and efficiency (year on year performance improvements). As this service is of universal interest in the UK, its transparency in measuring the effective use of resources is everyones business. Lessons learned in the NHS resource management process are by extrapolation of critical importance to the quality of wider government service provision throughout the UK.

The Genesis of PFI

Unveiled in the Chancellor of the Exchequer's Autumn, 1992 budget statement, PFI has been represented as a practical, highly robust and attractive means of enabling the private sector to invest and participate in the remainder of the UK public sector. As with all such initiatives, much has been said about it, some has been written about it but - in practice - little has been achieved truly under its banner.

The Channel Tunnel (the Chunnel) is presented as a direct result of the PFI which is an interesting assertion given the fact that the Chunnel predates the PFI by some ten years or more. However, it is equally true to say that much of the thought processes and resultant procedures which are now being embodied into PFI are borne of this experience. This is clearly a wise move given that the Chunnel is, in every sense, a ground-breaking development but that same body of experience must not be used to form a rigid template of procedures. Rather it should form the platform on which revised, continually evolving practices and guidelines are formed.

Analysis of the business case for the Chunnel reveals very early on that the Chunnel simply had to be financed out of private sector finance since the UK Government was in no position to directly manage its development. The task for all concerned was therefore to render the proposition as practically attractive as possible given that it was by then (the early 1980s) established truth that the UK's home market was clearly the EC and that, for this country's manufacturers to be in a position to exploit this home market without the economic disadvantages of relative remoteness and the associated high transport costs to the centre of the market, the Chunnel was an imperative.

It is certainly interesting to consider the role of the Government in relation to the Chunnel since it is a practical example of all the practical and political sensitivities which relate to such an important development. Perhaps the most important, singular issue is that of the role which the Government had to play in order to promote private investor confidence and, through this, to stimulate private investment itself in any large form. Whilst it has never been publicized to any discernible extent, it is clear that a project of the mammoth proportions of the Chunnel could never have been allowed to have been considered as just another private sector venture with all the propensity for mid-term failure which that might bring with it. Thus the Government of the day had to consider what role it might play to make it happen. This is discussed further in the next section.

One thing remains almost painfully clear to this day and that is that transport remains far and away the most visible area of private sector investment in the UK's government managed infrastructure. However, much is being achieved right now to widen the scope of the PFI and it is our belief that significant, wholesale changes are afoot to bring about radical changes to the view of how resource inputs need to be managed to produce effective infrastructural outputs. With the shift to efficiency of resource use rather than focus priority given to the issue of who owns the related assets, radical changes in the process of managing the means to deliver 'government' service provision is taking place.

Making it happen

In order for the private sector to be able to play the necessary role in relation to this and future ventures, it became necessary to consider the stance of the Government which had, of course, to stop short of actually either funding or guaranteeing the funding of the Chunnel itself. Herein lies the difficulty confronting the Government in relation to the PFI today: how to encourage its development and delivery of infrastructural support without actually turning the whole process into some simplistic debate over ownership of assets required to deliver the outputs demanded by the public.

The Government has made a number of very understandable moves in recent months in order to breathe life into the PFI. The first of these has been to appoint Sir Alastair Morton to head up a working party whose brief is simply to 'make the PFI happen'. This has spawned the Private Finance Panel (PFP), the membership of which is undoubtedly of the highest calibre of individuals drawn from private and public sector mixed backgrounds, all of whom have gained very real insights into either what is now being branded as PFI or have had real responsibility for running sections of the public sector which are now targeted as recipients of PFI attention.

Given the combination of the uniqueness of Sir Alastair's own working life over the past ten years and more and his own well catalogued personal qualities, he is an entirely understandable choice for this role.

The PFP has, itself, appointed its own executive support office in order to give the PFP itself some of the 'thinking and doing muscle' to assist it in the achievement of its aims. This executive office too is peopled by highly skilled, experienced individuals whose tasks are threefold in number, viz.:

- To identify blockages in the PFI process and to work with the relevant parties to identify ways round them where this is possible;
- To identify success stories from within the broad basis of PFI activity and to promulgate them as lessons and experiences from which the broader initiative can benefit;
- To sponsor individual projects where they are capable of developing broader applications within the context of the PFI.

Conversation with any of the senior players involved in any of the above leaves one very clearly with the message that they are all (both individually and as a combined team) being judged by the numbers, types and values of the transactions which actually get done: the criteria for success are thus clearly stated and recognized. Of critical importance is the drive towards transparency and clarity in effecting an open market of goal awareness and competitive responses through structures combining resources from wherever they may reside being drawn into combination to meet the tasks at hand - rather than spending the time engaging in debate over who should have the 'right' or 'responsibility' to pursue which goals with which assets. Essentially one has an open market of buyers and sellers from both the public and private sectors combining their skills and resources in the best way that experienced minds can orchestrate to meet the goals proclaimed and prioritized through the parliamentary process.

Thus the provision of the nation's infrastructure needs to be taken - as far as possible - outside of the day-to-day framework of parliamentary interference, combining the best required resources and co-operation of both the private and public sectors that can be encouraged to work together. The Private Finance Panel does therefore represent a first bold step in acknowledging this need and is thus to be welcomed provided it can continually demonstrate its value and its relevance to its parliamentary sponsors (of whichever political persuasion).

The combined impact of all of the above is undoubtedly to announce to the World at large that the UK Government is determined to see PFI work and that it will brook no possibility of failure.

Why such a high priority - the NHS example

In asking the above question, one has merely to return to the reasoning at the beginning of this chapter to establish a degree of measurement of the raw elements but this is to ignore other critically important components of the equation, such as the demand for PFI from the customer (public sector) side and what precisely does PFI really comprise?

For the purposes of developing this level of analysis and response to these questions, it is worth looking at the real example of the NHS, a critically important part of the fabric of the nation and one in which, it might reasonably be thought, PFI can play a major, influential role. At the same time, very little has been done and this point too needs addressing.

All the above is merely political consideration but it needs the reality of the demand from within the NHS to complete the picture. At the beginning of April, 1993, there was an annual actual and forecasted continuing requirement in the order of £2.0 billion for capital expenditure alone. This breaks down into

- approximately £1.0 billion on long term assets (primarily on new or significantly refurbished building programmes);

- £0.5 billion on new, major capital equipment items - scanners and the like; and
- the remainder on maintenance of a capital nature.

Assuming that PFI is to be largely directed to meeting all of these needs, it very soon becomes abundantly clear that the lack of progress demonstrated thus far will need to be jettisoned, to be replaced by solid achievement in which the issues of value for money, risk transfer and skills transfer are demonstrated to all concerned.

As if the above task were not daunting enough in its own right, there have been studies undertaken - most notably that undertaken by Professor Ceri Davies - which have identified an additional and growing backlog of capital refurbishment in the region of a further £2 billion. This only adds to the pressing case for a form of PFI in the NHS which will work well, not just for a few transactions but on a continuous basis over time.

The above figures, even then it may be argued, do not take into account the need for wholesale re-modelling of the NHS in the light of the changes which will arise from a market-driven structure (the Trusts, fund-holding GP's etc. with their supplier/purchaser disciplines). It is, for example estimated in one RHA alone that they will need to spend considerable resources in rationalizing their extant fourteen acute general hospitals into four to six new ones within the next few years.

Even these additional pressures do not take into account the ever increasing pace of technological change and statute driven changes such as Care in the Community.

Add to this, the Chancellor's avowed intention of obviating the PSBR in its entirety by the end of the millennium and the need for a successful and widespread PFI becomes apparent. Another way to describe the overall requirement is that one must recognize the enormity of the resource management problem of the NHS, and that our society requires the best resources be brought to bear to deliver necessary improvements - and this overall task implies a blending of government and private resources which are jointly managed.

Practical obstacles

What the Government appears not to have either understood or acknowledged yet is the extent to which the UK's public sector does not appreciate the nature and requirements of the private sector when it comes to considering lending or investing large sums into government sector activities. To this lack of understanding can be added a very real level of cynicism and fear in both sectors that this is merely just another gimmick or device at this relatively early stage in its development.

It is easy to see why these attitudes abound. In an environment where there is a good deal of fear about the reality of any job security. In other words, 'Why should I, as a senior civil servant put in a great deal of additional effort merely to produce a scenario in which I may ultimately end up losing my own job?' As a result, the overall level of morale and motivation within many areas of the remaining public sector stands at a critically low ebb and this is clearly not a good platform on which to build the resilient delivery processes which the public sector will require as it moves into the next millennium. Management forces must be directed to the achievement of explicit goals in an open environment of transparent needs and resource costs if real progress is to be made.

The Government clearly has a significant management task on its hands in terms of both motivating and educating those of its staff who are charged with delivering PFI. Additionally, the Government appears thus far to have failed to understand the interrelationship between the various players who are on its own payroll. Thus little has apparently been done to address the perceived conflicts which are very real issues for individual government departments. For example, in the case of financing a new NHS hospital, the Treasury will want to see the most cost effective solution for the Government as a whole, i.e. after taking into account any taxation issues. The NHS Management Executive will wish to bring in other re-structuring issues such as the transfer of private sector skills into subsequent service deliveries. The NHS Trust, who wish to borrow the money in the first place, will merely wish to have access to the cheapest available money source and have neither conditions imposed upon them.

All of this paints a picture where little has been done to define exactly what PFI really means and what is therefore going to be acceptable in proposing a case to the regulatory departments. This is clearly an understandable state of affairs in the early days of such a critically important and much needed programme but it cannot be allowed to last otherwise it will become a highly ridiculed embarrassment rather than the seizure of the innovative opportunity which it undoubtedly is.

A hidden agenda?

Add to the above the fact that the Chancellor of the Exchequer is now clearly stating that '.....the PFI is not merely about private sector finance'. In other words, the introduction of selected private sector skills and disciplines is an integral part of this Government's agenda in holding out the carrot of more widely available private sector finance.

We have mentioned 'skills transfer' in the previous section and it is vital that we explore what this may mean for those who wish to come into the PFI fold. Throughout the various published papers and other guidance made available, there is much made of value for money and risk transfer but little is spelt out in relation to skills transfer. This is the result of muddled goal definition and inadequate transparency in understanding of the value of using private sector 'input factors' to achieve a more efficient 'service output'.

In continuing dialogue with those at the centre of (NHS) matters, it has become clear that they are developing an agenda that has yet to see the clear light of day. Thus when a proposal is initially put forward to the NHSME, the initial feedback invariably makes reference to the need for a clear(er) demonstration of private skills transfer. Further digging into this sentiment reveals that the Government has a predilection for seeing an increasingly wider range of skills being transferred from the private sector to their own, extant 'businesses'. This does not reflect a problem of responsibility/control as much as it is a need to keep the costs of factor inputs relative to targeted outputs going down over time.

The skills thus sought are readily identified at the levels of, say, car parking management, hospital power plant management or even at the level of the forms of private sector project appraisal and project management before and during the construction of a new major hospital respectively. These are relatively simple and uncontentious deliverables which can be woven into a well thought through (NHS) business case, but they need to be thought through more clearly if such requirements are to make real business sense and - just as importantly - if they are to extend into the far more critical areas of clinical activity - i.e. the principles need to be applied to 'core' NHS activities and management processes.

It is thus possible to see a position arising where PFI can be used as a means of ensuring wholesale change not only in the ways in which NHS capital assets are appraised and financed but also in the actual ways in which future clinical services are provisioned. It has been repeatedly stated to us that the concept of the NHS remains sacrosanct, i.e. that treatment will always be available and that treatment will always be free at the point of delivery. What is at issue therefore is the manner in which these treatment processes are managed and what will it cost the taxpayer?

Before attempting to answer these issues, it is necessary to point out that, even in cases where private sector contractors have taken on the total management of, say, a mental health unit, the spectre of TUPE (the transfer of undertakings regulations) still remains and its cost implications have to be built into the vast majority of contracts where the private sector is bidding to provide such hitherto public services. Any private sector contractor who fails to do this will find him or herself in deep water from a variety of sources including his or her own shareholders (because of the failure to recognize and take into account what amounts to a contingent liability) as well as from those employees who transfer from the public to the private sectors in this brave new world.

The impact on the consumer

Bad management slows the process of new technology benefits reaching the consumer. This impact on the consumer is less easy to model in general terms but is rather more easily simulated by reference to individual elements of the public sector and we thus stay with the NHS model in order to explore this issue.

Before embarking upon this analysis, it is worth stating what in our view is likely to happen under the PFI over the foreseeable period. The base assumption must be that a breakthrough is achieved in introducing significant volumes finance to NHS Trusts which have capital (largely bricks and mortar) projects which have been able to demonstrate to the NHSME and to HM Treasury that they are of intrinsic worth through their carefully thought through structure of component parts of a business case. This same business case in turn will naturally need to address the issues of how the borrowing or 'joint venturing' NHS Trust intends to provide its services in an increasingly open and competitive market place.

It is essential to note here that it is emphatically **not** suggested that PFI will allow the building of hospitals, etc. of a lower standard, lesser demonstrated level of need, etc. than those currently financed through Treasury/NLF monies. Rather, it is likely that the credit committees of the financial institutions will want at least the same level of assurance as that currently sought under the existing regime. These same credit committees will expect to move the focus of their analyses more toward business risks and competition ends of the spectrum than is the case under the present regime.

At the same time, the potential lender(s) will expect to implant high level monitoring processes of a type with which the NHS is not yet familiar but which will roughly equate with the covenants regime found throughout the private sector. In order for this to work properly, these monitoring processes are likely to address themselves to the output of the NHS Trust's existing management accounting and activity monitoring systems but will also likely to contain additional requirements, some of which will be generic and others of which will be specific to the applicant Trust itself. Here too exists a significant transfer of private sector skills to the NHS whose finance staff have traditionally been cash-oriented. Addressing the issue of managing the financial structure and risk profile of their affairs will thus be stepped up a considerable amount.

At this stage in the development of PFI, it is probable that it will be those schemes which have been granted Approval in Principle (AIP) but will naturally not have been allocated Treasury funds which will form the natural target for initial PFI transactions. The average lead time between planning conception and ultimate commissioning of a major hospital can take anywhere between four and eight years. Even then, it is frequently the case that such schemes once started are phased over an even greater number of years. The evaluation of PFI as a component designed into new development programs will emerge as a result of 'forcing' PFI solutions into concepts designed around NHS/Treasury internal guidelines.

The net upshot of successful, widespread PFI funding as far as the patients are concerned is likely to be discernibly radical in many different ways, especially as PFI monies are likely to be made available in far greater supply than has been evidenced thus far. In the end, the speed of inevitable change in health service delivery structures, processes and the transparency with which all this will be observed, will be enhanced through PFI.

Under the existing arrangements and rules, schemes will still be subject to the same monitoring/screening processes and any funds released from the capital budgets will almost certainly be swallowed up by either the NHSME in reallocation processes or may, in time, be transferred to revenue budgets, doubtless subject to a plethora of centrally designed and imposed constraints and rules.

The impact of all this is that patients are likely to see much accelerated change at the service delivery end of the NHS as PFI becomes more successful in delivering the resources and structures needed to effect the radical change required. Other processes are also at work behind the scenes which will add still greater impact upon models of patient care, such as The Tomlinson Report, etc. and this is, in many ways, a blueprint for the future reorganization and rationalization of the NHS.

Specifically, what Tomlinson has done is to point out to NHS patients and employees that, in a market-force-driven activity such as the NHS, it is impossible to ignore the impacts of demographic changes. Further, when the accelerating rate of change of new surgical techniques (for example) is brought into the picture, it becomes impossible to ignore the need for wholesale restructuring of the NHS, especially in large conurbations.

Tomlinson goes further to point out that, in his opinion, it makes no economic sense whatsoever to entertain the gradual demise of the old, large district general hospitals found in many of our inner cities today. Many of these hospitals were designed and built in an era when none of today's non-invasive surgical techniques were envisaged. It is precisely this type of revolutionary innovation which has done much to make the old-style hospitals redundant. Recognition and careful planned management of this process will at least enable NHS managers to explain better the oft-times radical changes which PFI will bring with it.

PFI on its own will achieve little other than a mere shift of the supply of capital financing resources from the government to the private sector; as has already been explained above, this is clearly not the intention. However, when PFI becomes coupled with the above review and remodelling mechanisms it becomes clear that it is potentially an extremely powerful player in the NHS of tomorrow.

Tomlinson, for example, develops his argument in relation to London along the lines that the modern methods of treatment have changed so drastically that it is impossible to ignore their impact in modelling the NHS of the future. His further argument in relation to the gradualist shutting down of the old-style hospitals is also an economic one. Since the fixed costs associated with keeping any large hospital are so high, merely closing down one ward or one complete wing makes no business sense whatsoever. It is undeniably the case in the opinion of the authors that the whole process of developing a Plan for London and then delivering both its intent and ultimately its physical changes has been badly handled at the government level.

It is clear that the NHS of today - and certainly the NHS of tomorrow - will have to address its standing within the community whom it serves in much the same way as do the better managed corporations. It will have to develop a sharper, more effective and arguably better co-ordinated public relations activity as an integral part of its continuing business activity.

The net impact of all of the above as far as the consumer/patient is concerned is likely to be that of significant change in not only the ways in which NHS services are delivered but also in the actual locations of the health treatment units themselves. Thus it is probable that there will be a significant degree of rationalization of the existing hospital structure - viz. the fourteen to four/six analogy referred to above. It is almost inevitable that the freeing up of PSBR will also allow a greater rate of change in the whole area of primary health care. Thus while the numbers of megalithic hospitals reduces this will likely be balanced by a burgeoning growth in the numbers of health malls such as those already seen in the United States.

These health malls or health villages will accommodate general practitioners, dentists, pre-natal clinics, pharmacies and so on and will have a strong local community presence; in other words they will enable the clinicians to get closer to their customers in the truest sense of operating more effectively in a market force framework response to expressed and observed client needs and wants in a first hand way. Also incorporated within this innovation will be a patient day care hostel in which those receiving non-invasive surgery will be operated on and their recovery overseen by the resident clinical staff.

Clearly this model of health care treatment does not in any way obviate the need for the major hospitals but the overall means of treatment will probably dictate the increasing diminution of large, inflexible hospitals into smaller numbers with complementary specialist skill bases. At the same time, the roles of the ambulance services of the future will take on a degree of much heightened priority which is already being seen in this country. The role of the professional, well trained para-medic will thus come to the fore as the distances between each major hospital site become larger and the need to effect immediate remedial patient care becomes of paramount importance.

It is stressed that PFI alone will bring about none of the above since these glimpses into the future are way beyond the realms of influence of mere financiers. The decisions as to the ultimate shape of the NHS lie very clearly in the political arena, the banks and others being only providers of resource in much the same way as the equipment manufacturers, the facilities managers and so on. However, PFI will speed the process of this transformation by forcing a transparent open market process to bear on resource commitments required to get the job done.

The impact on the workforce

A further probable impact upon the NHS workforce does indeed loom somewhere in the background in terms of the need to develop and manage new skill sets which will doubtless come with PFI. The new skill areas circle around the wider management of increased ranges of facilities management contracts covering - in time - both non-clinical and ultimately the clinical service areas. Additionally, the models of PFI which we have seen being demonstrated thus far, will also bring in the need for far more sophisticated financial management skills. As we intimated above, the workings and resultant requirements of the banks' credit committees are as yet a black box to the vast majority of NHS Directors of Finance; much change will doubtless occur here over the next few years.

The question still remains as to the impact on the large numbers of skilled and dedicated personnel who work within the NHS of today. There is already a clear predilection for the implementation of a clear and yet simple regime of performance related reward structures albeit largely at the senior levels of management. It is probable that these same regimes will be extended to encompass greater and greater numbers of personnel as the whole of the NHS becomes more performance oriented.

It is also likely that there will be time-defined employment contracts which, already prevalent at the most senior levels, will similarly spread to all.

Most importantly, the decentralization of health care delivery to primary health care units capable of handling an increased spectrum of services will increase the skill requirements of those interacting with the public. This will have a dramatic impact on both patient and service staff satisfaction levels.

Taking all of the above together would represent a total impossibility for any management no matter how skilled or experienced unless the vision of the future is defined, planned for and then properly executed. This task needs addressing urgently and will need constant review and improvement. It seems that there is a very strong role for the leadership required to be taken on by the NHSME. Only time will tell if that body is sufficiently powerful and clear about its own destiny to be able to fulfil this critically demanding role.

The need for change

The need for change in itself is naturally not enough to produce change nor more importantly efficient constructive change.

As with all change processes, skills development will need to be identified on an objective basis and then it will need to be woven into a clear, organization-wide strategy which guides the allocation of resources towards its delivery.

There will also be further changes in the delivery process beyond those mentioned above, some of which will be more visible to the patients than others. A simple example of the more visible changes lies in the very design of the hospitals of the future. The lessons of the past reveal that mammoth, purpose-built structures cannot possess the flexibility of use that future uncertainties will demand. Thus the future hospital structure will be designed such that whole wings can be isolated from the central, common services area. In this way, should there be the need to sub-let large chunks of accommodation, this can be easily achieved without impacting adversely upon the continuing activities of the newly rationalized hospital. The NHS Trust of the future will need to have this flexibility of service delivery built into it so that it can always adapt to bring the best possible levels of service to their patients and at the same time balance their books.

Failure to achieve this balance - including the necessary return on Public Dividend Capital - will almost certainly result in the NHSME taking steps to replace the wayward Trust management. At the same time, the suppliers of PFI will be insistent upon the borrowing Trust taking measures to achieve this same balance. Managed flexibility are thus the watchwords of the NHS of the future.

Conclusion

PFI is thus a brave new world but, we would suggest that it is one which does not yet fully appreciate the nature and scope of change which it will bring. It is acutely obvious both at central Government level as well as at local service delivery levels that the impact is under estimated. PFI symbolizes the essential need to strengthen the management process to optimize the resource input/output equation, giving full access to private as well as public resources. The next few months and years will need to see a much greater clarity of thought being devoted toward understanding its impact and toward formulating flexible, cost effective responses towards it otherwise PFI may yet fail and be perceived as another golden opportunity for improvement which has passed by.

Equally clear is that there must be brought to bear an intelligent and robust degree of leadership of future developments of the NHS of the future within a strategic framework: this framework must be led and developed by the executive arm of the Government of the day - by the NHSE, by H.M. Treasury, by the Department of Health. At the same time, responsibility for flexible, high-quality service delivery must continue to develop at local NHS Trust levels.

The present position suggests that while the case for PFI is clearly understood and accepted across a very broad range of political community, its actual execution and the setting of a rule-based framework within which it will work are still in a very early stage of development. This position must change for the NHS to continue to deliver the quality and quantity of health care for which it is rightly renowned.

References

'A Review of Capital and Capital Charges in the NHS' (1991), jointly published by The King's Fund Institute and The National Association of Health Authorities and Trusts. ISBN: 0 946832 76 5.

'Competing for Quality' White Paper (1991), HMSO. Cmnd 1730.

'The Citizens' Charter: First Report 1992' White Paper. HMSO. Cmnd 2101.

'Unfreezing the Assets: NHS Estate Management in the 1990s (1991), published by The King's Fund Institute. ISBN: 1 870607 260.

National Health Service and Community Care Act (1990).

NHS Trusts Finance Manual - continually updated and added to.

Report of the Inquiry into London's Health Service, Medical Education and Research (1992), (the Tomlinson Report). HMSO.

S.I. National Health Service, England and Wales (1990), The National Health Service Trusts (Membership and Procedure) Regulations.

S.I. National Health Service, England and Wales (1992), The National Health Service Trusts (Originating Capital Debt) Order.

'The Citizens' Charter' White Paper (1991) HMSO. Cmnd 1599.

The Government's Expenditure Plans 1993-94 to 1995-96: Department of Health and Office of Population Censuses and Surveys - Departmental Report. HMSO. Cmnd 2212.

The Health of the Nation - Green Paper (1992), HMSO. Cmnd 1986.

'The Patients' Charter' White Paper (1991), Department of Health.

4 Public service and private profit: The managerial limits to enterprise

Peter Anthony and Mike Reed

Introduction

The enthusiasm for unlimited enterprise, happily associated with limited liability, rests on several claims, the most modish being that, as it is contrasted with command economies that are both totalitarian and collapsing, it is synonomous with success and with democracy. In these terms, the ultimate argument for enterprise is made to rest on the case for political democracy: even if economic success were not to be assured by competititon, the merits of political freedom would be so great that it would be worth some economic cost to maintain it. In this way the case for competition in the market is made to rest upon values beyond its premises and purpose: an argument couched in economic terms and aimed at material advantage comes to rest on different and overriding ends from which none of us can, with propriety, demur. Thus no explanation of the necessity of unenterprizing public service - we may note in passing the rhetorical achievement of securing 'unenterprizing' as a term of abuse - can convince if it is to be associated with dictatorship and the suppression of liberty. It must therefore be acknowledged at the outset that the maintenance of a public library service or prison system is not worth the price of a harsh dictatorship, although the one would seem to be incompatable with a totalitarian regime and the other its requisite condition. The qualified acknowledgement might be considered sufficient to raise some doubt about the reliability of the association between enterprise and democracy and between planning and totalitarianism. It seems to us unlikely that a national health service has to be driven by entrepreneurial zeal in order to maintain Parliament and we shall say no more about it.

Our concern is with an attempt to understand realities rather than dogmas. The case for market competition does not have to be made, it is a fact of social life which continues even when the most strenuous attempts are made to suppress it because it springs, as Adam Smith argued, from one of the most basic human characteristics; self-interest. He also pointed out that the less attractive aspect of this drive was selfishness and that, in many circumstances, it had to be controlled for both personal and the public good. It is hard to imagine let alone to observe a society which does not seek to control the pursuit of self-interest by law, by custom or by moral precept and to final apologists for such a notion of total freedom one has to turn to the extreme fringes of anarchism. Where the boundaries of such controls are to be drawn is a matter for political and ethical theory which should, no doubt, be informed by the technical advice of economists within their limited field but it cannot be a matter that can be left safely to be determined by them alone. Nor is it an aspect of reality that we can speak about with any competence, although we may have an opinion, like the next man or woman in the street. To voice opinions in public places and in authoritative tones is, however, to return to dogmatism.

The narrower area to be examined is managerial behaviour in organizations and the extent that it is and can be influenced by the forces of untramelled market competition. It is a timely question because, whether public services like health are to be described accurately or not as being subject to a process of 'privatization' , there is not much doubt that they are being encouraged in a process of commercialization in which market forces are to influence managerial values and actions. This change is to be brought about by subjecting the institution to the external forces of the market ('patient choice') and to internal competition ('competitive tendering') all for the sake, we are told, of the public good. That is as may be and once again we have to disclaim any right to express an informed opinion on the matter, except in so far as the changes concern the real or prescribed behaviour of the institutions' managers. It is our belief that in this particular context, the planned extension of private competition - if this is not a contradiction in terms - represents a serious misunderstanding of the nature of managerial relationships in both private and public institutions and, since it set out to overturn reality, that it will face disabling difficulties.

Let us take the most difficult case first, the institutions of private enterprise themselves.

Outside the Portobello Road, perhaps the purest example of free market competition, successful businesses become big businesses and are carried on by complex organizations which are managed, sometimes so successfully that they reach the status of oligopolies, form cartels and succeed in protecting themselves from the vagaries of the market from which they have grown. Competition, although they may never become free of it, is a threat against which they have provided themselves with a measure of protection. This may become a matter of regret for the theorists of market competition who tend either to ignore the instances of market suppression, ranging from Japanese national economic strategy and the importance of its department of trade in furthering it, to the smaller examples of oil companies, brewers and mercantilist constructs like Powergen, or alternatively, to acknowledge with regret the attendant difficulties of bureaucracy and sloth.

Within the bureaucracies of private enterprizes there is a paradoxical attempt to maintain the very competitive spirit from which they have managed to escape. There is much talk of the encouragement of risk taking by rewarding it as an end in itself, although elaborate machineries of control are established in an attempt to relate pay to performance. There is also much talk of the need for co-operation within the organization in order to overcome the effects of competition outside it. The co-existence of these two imperatives reminds us that, for many managers, competition is an abstract principle to which respectful reference is made on unpleasant occasions like the enforcement of redundancies; in their practical experience, competition between an organization's managers is a centrifugal tendency to disaster that has to be countered by measures to control it, unsuccessful to the extent that rivalries between marketing, production and accounts continue to show that they are all taking their eyes off the ball of the corporate goal. It is team work that gets the ball into the net: internal rivalry contributes to own goals. The football analogy is helpful because it reminds of both the usefulnss and the danger in the use of metaphors. Thus:

a) 'football is a competitive game representing all that is best in the striving for success';
b) 'football is a team game representing all that is best in the achievement of co-operation'.

Football is, of course, both and it is not an adequate account of the game to resolve this contradition by saying that it is competitive in terms of a team's relationship with its opponent while co-operative in the relationships between the team's members. It is a lot more complicated than that as any manager or fan will tell us. The competition with the opponent is controlled by rules which are sometimes ignored and sometimes interpreted by players' conventions - 'custom and practice' they are called in industrial relations. The co-operation between the members of the team depends upon personal skills which need to be demonstrated to the point where they can approach selfishness in order to assure continuing membership of the team. The reality of the game is a complex web of relationships, formal rules, conventions and understandings and to apply a single adjective in its description is, wilfully or innocently, to contribute to error or dogma. To use it as a metaphor for the much more complex business of management is to compound error or to entrench dogma.

Similarly, business enterprizes are engaged in competitive markets in which competition is limited by numerous forces. The most naive of market enthusiasts will recognize the necessity of legal regulation of market behaviour and of moral self-regulation as an alternative to the law, thereby recognizing the primary of values that cannot be adduced from the market itself and which are external to it. The market in this respect at least is acknowledged not to be alone, sufficient and pre-eminent as a determinant of its inhabitants' behaviour. In terms of the external relationships of business enterprizes, the theorists of the pure market have inflated a simple metaphor to the level of dogma, at best an idealistic expression of which the world should be like but lacking the capacity to account for reality.

As far as the internal relationship of business enterprizes and the behaviour of managers is concerned, there is a considerable body of evidence to suggest that the market model is not helpful as a source of explanation. Dalton (1959), Mintzberg (1973), Gouldner (1954), Stewart (1967), Burns (1961), Kotter (1982), all in separate accounts in different sectors of activity ranging over a period of some forty years, demonstrate the importance of networks of social co-operation, areas of negotiated order and of bonds of reciprocal obligation. This 'political perspective' is one of three analytical frameworks that have contributed to management theory (Reed, 1989) and stands in contrast to the technical perspective (and to the third, the Marxist, which need not detain us for the present) which sees management as engaged in the rational and systematic pursuit of clearly defined organizational goals, the co-ordinator of means towards ends. It would be fair to describe these two, frequently opposed, perspectives as together providing the only theoretical explanations available to managers of their activities and functions. Neither has much to say about the market as the prime mover of managerial action. That is not to say that the market is irrelevant and unimportant; it ultimately determines failure or survival, no doubt, but within its final imperatives managers behave as if they, not blind market forces, were in control of the complex relationships and systems that constitute large and effective organizations. In doing so they plan the achievement of predicted ends and they encourage the growth of communities based upon a considerable degree of mutual co-operation (it is the unnecessary weakness of each of the dominant perspectives that each derides the significance of the other) and both activities are intended to exercise a measure of control over a hostile environment. Whether they are engaged in rational planning or the much more frequent activity of building and maintaining networks of social co-operation, managers seem to be fending off rather than responding to the immediate influence of market competition. We might conclude that there is a significant measure of agreement between the available explanations of managerial behaviour about at least one thing; that managers try to behave like masters rather than like puppets of the market.

There is then some room for doubt about the immediacy of the market's influence on managerial behaviour even in its heartland - the private sector. The public sector was acknowledged to be different, concerned with the provision of services and held together by normative compliance in generally acknowledged values that this, too, is now claimed to be the proper arena for competition and market forces to determine needs and to allocate resources. While there has been no shortage of advice as to how and why education, health, the museum service, railway transport and penal detention should be opened to the spirit of enterprise (Du Gay, 1994), there are grounds for suspicion that there are political motives for off-loading escalating demands for scarce public resources into the neutrality of the market the blindness of whose forces saves the embarrassment of exercizing public and visibles choices. Even if the private sector does not conform to the model of competition, the model will serve to conceal unpopular decisions: it is not the minister but the market that closes hospitals. But the rational for introducing the disguise is that competition will improve services, that it will work.

It will certainly encounter difficulties special to the public service, not the least of which will be a problem in reconciling a sense of duty with the encouragement of an outlook that rewards effort and performance by a careful calculation of pay. The introduction of rewards related to performance encourages a spirit of negotiation as well as enterprise and a rational conclusion that commitment or effort that is not payed for is to be neither looked for nor provided; it is outside the new ethos that is being created so that a doctor or a teacher will be persuaded that a spirit of unrewarded co-operation on her or his part could result in demotion of discipline, evidence of unseemly conduct in the new regime. In the marketplace, haggling over the price is proper and consequently the delivery of a marginally acceptable return for the price is normal. One of the challenges to the autonomy of the clinicians in the Health Service is that the new spirit demands the replacement of what is best - professionally determined - by what is competitive and cost effective (Coombs, 1987). The opinion of the customers - they used to be called clients - is likely to be biased by self-interest on this matter. The challenge of the market to the established control of the managers of public service institutions is likely to be resisted for several reasons; professional and established self interest, a genuine concern with an ethical objective and with client interests, and suspicion about the competence, honesty and intentions of market-bred managers. These concerns find particular expression among managers of the Health Service.

A study of managerial roles and relationships in South Glamorgan District Health Authority (Reed and Anthony, 1990), reported the views of clinicians, nurse managers, administrators and managers. They revealed an extended network of collaborative relationships which went beyond the boundaries of the formal organization and hierarchical levels. In the pursuit of an overall concern with patient care, managers - broadly defined as those concerned with the control and co-ordination of others- sought their objectives by recruiting assistance wherever it was needed and from whoever could give it. In some instances the formal structure would be regarded as irrelevant or threatening, in others as a source of assistance that might be called upon to achieve the necessary ends. A considerable degree of consensus seemed to exist about what those ends were; disagreements about the means to achieve them tended to be referred to a long established ranking of professional status in which the clinicians, particularly the consultants, were pre-eminent. But others had their means of influence upon them, the result of practised social skills accumulated with close attention to experience and differences in personality. Managers spoke as though the formal structure of command was not simply irrelevant but that they had almost succeeded in inverting it, subordinating it to their own loosely constructed system of management. We concluded that what we had observed was something like a system of craft or task based management which was based upon professional competence but which extended well beyond the strictly professional groups.

The means by which managers managed in this Health Authority were not significantly different from the accounts given of general managers from Dalton (1959) to Kotter (1982). We have already suggested that this consistent explanation in terms of collaborative networks based upon negotiated order, while it stands opposed to explanations in terms of rational systems, shares with them an apparent immunity from direct influence by the market on managerial behaviour. There are specific features of public service managers that make that influence even more remote.

The extension of management to the autonomous direction of affairs by professional groups is always likely to create tension. MacIntyre (1981) characterizes the one as a 'practice' concerned with the pursuit of internal shared values bound together by tradition and concerns that are essentially moral. The other, an 'institution' engages in the exchange of external goods on a competitive basis and, extends its necessary influence over practices by diminishing their moral autonomy. To the extent that we have argued that managerial relationships, even in the world of unfettered competition, are essentially moral, this distinction must appear exaggerated (McMylor, 1994). Nowhere are managers engaged in an entirely ruthless struggle in a Hobbesian war of all against all - although Jackall's 'world of corporate managers' (1988) would seem to come very close to this condition. In any conceivable environment that depends upon the co-operative activity of its inhabitants, managers are likely to spend part of their energy in fending off the disturbance caused by impersonal market forces. Similarly, in organizations concerned with values rather than commodities, in practices, the professionals must manage if they are not to be managed and to see their essential autonomy reduced. Thus, in the NHS, doctors and nurses necessarily and continuously engage in management but they do not recognize what they do as 'managing', it 'seemed to be just plain doctoring' to them. A nurse manager confessed that she 'did not know too much about "managing" in the modern sense' but insisted that she 'managed all right'.

A state of affairs in which people who, while they are indisputably engaged in management, steadfastly deny that they have anything to do with it, requires some explanation. It is possible that they have their own perverse definition of the term so that, like Moliere's gentleman, they have been doing it all their lives without knowing it. To some extent that is the case; 'management' is something imposed on them by an alien order concerned with the pursuit of objectives that have nothing to do with their own real concerns with 'doctoring'. 'Management' is the paper work, the chores imposed by a distant bureaucracy, representing a hostile attempt to control their necessary autonomy, to subvert the co-operative system they have built to deliver the service of patient care. 'Management' is a dual strategy intended to secure their de facto recognition of a formal structure irrelevant to their purpose while wasting their time and distracting from their real work.

These may be the surface manifestations of a straightforward struggle for control which is taking place in hospitals, schools and universities, a struggle between practices and institutions. There may be a deeper confusion between entirely different conceptions about the real nature of the management. Management is an ancient activity, it did not have to be invented by Taylor and Ford for industrial manufacturing processes. Co-ordination on the scale required for the maintenance of Imperial Rome, the East India Company and the British Empire needed management but theorizing about management, the construction of an ideology of management, is a recent phenomena. It has advanced to the point at which it assumes institutional proportions in its own right, its founding ideology establishing an unchallengeable hegemony. An abstract conception of management pervades the market place and the production proceses that feed it and has advanced into those occupations 'hitherto honoured and looked up to with revered awe. It has converted the physician, the lawyer, the priest, the poet, the man of science into its paid wage labourers' (M. Cox and E. Nyles, *Communist Manifesto*, ed. by G.D.H. Cole, p. 123). The submission of health care, education, broadcasting and the arts to control by the market has been stealthy and it has been achieved by its outriders or functionaries. It was the apparent neutrality of management that made its presence within the gates acceptable, even welcome. Who, outside the majority measured by the market, could object to a more efficient health service, more relevant universities, more popular television, to performance related teachers and to libraries stripped of the costly storage of books that were rarely read? Management would assure more of what most of us wanted and would provide us with its expertise in the delivery. At the same time the introduction of management would surely be welcome to those occupations which, though they might be honoured and looked up to with awe, were often overworked and under-paid Their members would be offered salary progressions if they abandoned the mundane activities of teaching and nursing for the more important roles of the management of teaching and nursing. If reverence and awe had been maintained by any degree of professional mystification it would be removed by substituting for it the universal and accessable rationality of management.

Thus the nomenclature of management was put in place and was ready to substitute new meanings and a new culture in a process of transformation that was almost imperceptable. It was also ready to welcome the more direct assault on the autonomy of the practices. When a senior executive of a successful grocery chain was asked to report on the NHS (DHSS, 1983), there were two explanations available to counter incredulity; management is a science applicable to widely diverse businesses (itself a largely discredited notion even within the cannons of management theory by now) and, the market will better determine the allocation of resources than the complex processes of professional and administrative consultation so, who better to turn to for advice than to a shopkeeper from the market. Two foreign conceptions were introduced to the practice of health care as axiomatic truths; that there is a body of management theory available for instant application and that the market is a unique and capable determinant of human need

Neither was appropriate to the complex and collaborative structure that had evolved to focus the distinct and sometimes conflicting array of groups held together only by a moral concern with the delivery of a service commonly held to be important. It is quite possible to see organizations like the NHS as representing an alternative theory of management organization, based on task accomplishment and held together by craft-like affiliations (Reed and Anthony, 1993). Such a theory could be constructed on the actual practice, behaviour and working relationships of managers in service organizations and it could be extended beyond them to large areas of manufacturing as well. If it were to appear eccentric or idiosyncratic that is because it is made to seem so by the prevailing orthodoxy which, although established, in many respects does not reflect managerial reality.

An explanation of task based work shares some of the characteristics of craft work (see, for example, C. Wright Mills, 'White Collar', 1956) and some of professional work. These characteristics are unlikely to fit familiar distinctions between 'good' and 'bad' work, between self-actualizing and alienating work or between work that is high or low in disgressionary elements (Jacques, 1976). In other words, an explanation in terms of tasks and their management escapes the stultifying and scholastic problems in the discussion of alienation as well as the unrealities of orthodox management theory both in its hard and soft versions. It helps to explain, or at least it recognizes that a great deal of work and of its management is both alienating and self-actualizing at the same time. A task view of work recognizes that, while all work is done for economic ends, it inevitably acquires meaning within a social context and that it requires purposeful co-operation. It is complex in ways explained by Alasdair Clayre:

> In the first place, satisfaction with work - even with work that might seem extraordinarily unattractive to commentators from a distance - could be found existing side-by-side with dislike even in factory industry today; indeed it may well be that the peculiar nature of satisfaction with work can only be understood when both the enjoyment and the dislike are considered together ... Highly complex attitudes to work - dislike, and also satisfaction despite or even because of the intrinsic hardness of the tasks - can be found in different areas of industry and agriculture both before and after the industrial revolution (Clayre, 1974).

Let us consider the features of a task based view of work.

Necessity: A task needs to be done: over and above the fact that it has to be finished before you can go home, it is likely to be seen as important because its completion brings benefits to others - it will do them good or they depend upon it before they can begin their own work. Even when there is no product, as in maintenance work, the task can be seen to be necessary. The importance of the task can be perceived on a short time scale so it has nothing to do with the specious but troublesome distinction between value and utility.

Competence: The performance of the task requires accomplishments, skills and experience even in work defined as unskilled. No task is empty of the need for skill: if skill is not required by the job specification it is likely to be brought to it by the performer - see, for example, the account of Dolores, the waitress, given by Terkel (Terkel, 1975). Such free gifts are likely to be rejected by a management that is not task based.

Ownership: The task is possessed by the door because it needs to be done and because it needs skills and experience. It therefore confers some sense of responsibility for its completion which becomes dutiful; task completion is associated with a moral accompaniment.

Difficulty: Unpleasant, repetitive or dangerous elements in the task as part of what is owned; they can add to a sense of ownership because they contribute to the feeling that it has to be done and that others could not do it.

Relationship: The task may have to be completed before a higher order activity can take place, this is the case where work of preparation may be carried out by a learner or a worker of lower status. In these cases the preparatory work may be overseen by the worker of higher status to whose position the former may be an aspirant and who may be assisted in his or her ambition by the relationship of supervision.

The existence of tasks and the perception of their existence may be a matter of fact, of historical development and current arrangement, but they may be encouraged or destroyed by the managerial system that surrounds them. The network of collaborative relationships that make up the hospital service continue to exemplify several of these features (Strong and Robinson, 1990). Difficulty and unpleasantness is the ordinary experience of a variety of occupational groups of disparate status. The hospital porters, the catering and the domestic staff are linked into a pattern of relationships that are explained, necessitated and justified by what has to be done in aspects of patient care or by the need to prepare for the commencement of higher order tasks by nurses and doctors. The performance of tasks is monitored within task boundaries or across them by hierarchies of acknowledged competence that coincide, in some degree, with the realities of the perceived management system. Senior nurses supervise task activities by reference to standards that must be acquired by those aspiring to seniority and the tasks of nursing are measured by the judgement of clinicians, regarded as the arbiters of requisit standards. All is knit together by an infinite number of tasks that are, sometimes imperfectly, co-ordinated by a task based management system.

This is the system that has evolved at ward and hospital level. It is not the system of district and regional management which is perceived as remote, even hostile to task management. The interface between the two is always likely to be problematic. It is likely to occur in any large scale organization where the allocation of resources, the adaptation to the market, or the formulation of long term strategic plans is not only distant but essentially different from the short term production and delivery of the goods. Jackall's (1988) account of corporate managers and their Byzantine activities suggests that the disjuncture between strategic control and task management can assume catastrophic proportions which require separation into different worlds, necessarily out of touch with each other.

Strategic control, when it is not exercised on behalf of the personal interests of corporate managers - a state of affairs described by Jackall (1988) and familiar to us in recent British experiences (Pitelis and Clarke, 1993) - is concerned with relating the internal operations of the organization to the market, by adjusting them to its demands and by influencing them. If it requires the frequent and continual disturbance of the process of internal management, in any organization, the consequence is likely to be disturbance in what should be settled relationships of expectation and performance. Some such disturbance is inevitable and sometimes it is terminal; the organization ceases to exist and the market spawns other and no doubt more efficient suppliers. But there are areas of the public service where this sort of instant adjustment is not conceivable because the service delivered is not a matter of economic demand, it is deemed to be a public right which must be met without serious interruption. This is acknowledged in advanced societies by the recognition that the right to health care or to education is not limited, as it is in the market economy, to those who can afford to pay an economic price for the service. The concern about the closer intrusion of the market into the provision of health care and education is, in the first place, about whether provision is likely to become more closely linked to payment. It is worth noting that no one on the political spectrum says that this should be the case, the argument is about the probability of unintended consequences: the principal of open provision is not in contention, it is accepted by all parties.

The argument is that the closer influence of the market and of customer choice will assist the process of strategic control and make the provision of services more cost effective and hence more competitive. There is, as we have noticed, something specious (that is, superficially but erroneously attractive) about this contention because it is only a partial application of the market that is proposed The overall provision of funds is determined by social policy rather than market-priced demand, the internal competition between suppliers is limited to units rather than entrepreneurs and there is, fortunately, a massive professional control of standards of service and care. The result is something of an imitation of the market rather than reality.

But it is real enough to reinforce the rhetoric of market trading that accompanies it and to strengthen the culture of market management that will subordinate the network of task based management which has been legitimated by technical competence and an ethos of care. In an earlier study of hospital organization, Burns distinguished between the managerial system and the collaborative system and pointed out that, 'while there is an antithesis between the collaborative system and managerialism, it does not follow that the two are mutually exclusive' because managers and administrators often make use of the former (and, we would add, vice versa). He noted, however, that there was a real contradiction involved in the relationship between the two; 'managerialism is grounded in distrust in much the same way as the collaborative system is grounded in trust... Managerialism is a system imposed on top of the collaborative system.' (Burns, 1981, pp. 4-9). This subordination to a moral order, however loosely defined, beyond the formal boundaries and authority of the organization, legitimates its practices and submits them to a negotiated exchange with the wider social setting. In this sense, service delivering institutions like the NHS are different from, less isolated and discreet than business organizations. A retail business like Tesco interacts with its environment largely through the market of which it is a part: a hospital is part of a moral order.* The moral webb that encloses the hospital service has been demonstrated by a reluctance on the part of its inhabitants to engage in industrial action even when sorely pressed to do so. That degree of moral responsibility and the distinction it makes from market calculation of the value of its service is often encouraged by government. It

* (The distinction is broadly drawn: all businesses reflect moral relationships and all service organisations reflect market realities but, as Etzioni observed, they tend to conform either to the one or to the other).

is a distinction difficult to maintain when service is defined within the terms of a market economy.

The adventitious blindness of the market and the random grasp of its invisible hand are likely to be seen in schools, universities, hospitals and social agencies as threats that their guardians must fend off in order to defend the wider moral networks of which their organizations are a part. They are likely to be assisted in their efforts by the knowledge that we, their clients rather than their customers, approve of them because they seem to us to be made on our behalf. Within service organizations, co-operative relationships directed at the accomplishment of commonly agreed tasks seem to have been usual and their effectiveness has depended on the wider social and moral networks that have helped to form them. In service organization, the term 'negotiated order' extends to an order beyond the organization. None of this is to deny the existence of power struggles, resource struggles, sectional interests and professional closures and defences. But they are regulated, by and large, by a sophisticated network of relationships in which the tensions between different interests, occupational ideologies and rules can be brought into a workable, if precarious, 'modus vivendi' (Strauss et al., 1963; Strauss, 1978).

The market-led reorganization and the imposition of internal markets on the NHS in the 1980s and 1990s has imposed a non-negotiable order which challenges professionalism and the wider moral order in which it is located (Cox, 1991). The complexities of negotiated order set broad and contested limits to the untramelled exercise of pure professional power and control which produced difficulties, but they were never sufficient to threaten the elaborate form of work organization which recognized, often informally, the collaborative networks required to 'get the job done' to as high a standard as possible. The moral basis of that collaboration has apparently been threatened sufficiently to have introduced the Marxist language of alienation to the British Medical Association.

Unless management is conceived as the simple agent for the transmission of market forces into service organizations - in which case many of its widely advertised skills of co-ordination and control must surely become redundant - its practice must be concerned with the nurturing of organizational forms which facilitate the realization of 'goods' which it is the purpose of the organization to deliver. To do this it must work within rather than against the normative order upon which those forms depend. It is no small task. Managers, like their administrative predecessors, have to learn to engage with the uncertainties of complexity rather than the simplicities of market dictates. The engagement of management within service organizations entails the ability to cope with the unavoidable tensions and conflicts between institutional demands - such as external pressures for operational efficiency - and organizational imperatives - such as the maintenance of professional standards of patient care. And the resolution of these tensions has to be achieved while protecting the collaborative networks and the moral foundations which bind them within the organization and, externally, with its clients.

While the crude simplicities of market directed management can easily destroy the balances on which service organization are founded, the drive to superimpose it can seem attractive. Apart from the ideological attractions of a cure all general theory (laissez-faire), it has the great advantage of simplicity. It is much easier than real management, even if it kills the patient.

References

Anthony, P. (1986), *The Foundation of Management*, London, Tavistock.

Burns, T. and Stalker, G. (1961), *The Management of Innovation*, London, Tavistock.

Burns, T. (1981), 'Rediscovering Organization: Some Aspects of Collaboration and Managerialism in Hospital Organization,' *S.S.R.C.*, Unpublished Research Paper.

Clayre, A. (1974), *Work and Play*, London, Weidenfeld and Nicholson.

Coombs, R. (1987), 'Accounting for the Control of Doctors: Management Information Systems in Hospitals,' *Accounting, Organizations and Society*, 12 (4), pp. 389-404.

Cox, D. (1991), 'Health Service Management: a Sociological View', in J. Grabe, M. Bury and M. Calnar (eds), *The Sociology of the Health Service*, London, Routledge, pp. 89-114.

D.H.S.S. (1983), 'NHS Management Inquiry', *The Griffiths Report*, London, HMSO.

Dalton, M. (1959), *Men Who Manage*, New York, Wiley.

Du Gay, P. (1994), 'Colossal Immodisties and Hopeful Masters: Pluralism and Organizational Conduct,' *Organization*, 1(1), pp. 125-148.

Flynn, R. (1992), *Structures of Control in Health Management*, London, Routledge.

Gouldner, A. (1954), *Patterns of Industrial Bureaucracy*, New York, Collier MacMillan.

Jackall, R. (1988), *Moral Mazes: the World of Corporate Managers*, Oxford, Oxford University Press.

Jacques, E. (1976), *A General Theory of Bureaucracy*, London, Heinemann.

Kotter, J.P. (1982), *The General Managers*, New York, Free Press.

MacIntyre, A. (1981), *After Virtue: a Study in Moral Theory*, London, Duckworth.

McMylor, P. (1994), *Alasdair MacIntyre: Critic of Modernity*, London, Routledge.

Mills, C.W. (1956), *White Collar: The American Middle Class*, New York: Oxford University Press.

Mintzberg, H. (1973), *The Nature of Management,* New York, Harper and Row.

Pitelis, C. and Clarke, T. (1993), 'The Political Economy of Privatization', in T. Clarke and C. Pitelis (eds), op cit. pp. 1-30.

Pollitt, C. (1992), *Managerialism and the Public Services*, second edition, Oxford, Blackwell.

Reed, M. and Anthony, P.D. (1990), 'Managerial Roles and Relationships: the Impact of the Griffiths Report,' *International Journal of Health* 3(3), pp. 20-31.

Reed, M. and Anthony, P. (1993), 'Between an Ideological Rock and an Organizational Hard Place: NHS Management in the 1980's and 1990's,' in T. Clarke, and C. Pitelis (eds), *The Political Economy of Privatization*, London, Routledge, (185-202).

Stewart, R. (1967), *Managers and their Jobs*, Maidenhead, McGraw-Hill.

Strauss, A. et al. (1993), 'The Hospital and its Negotiated Order' in E. Freidson (ed), *The Hospital in Modern Society*, New York, MacMillan.

Strauss, A. (1978), *Negotiations*, New York, Wiley.

Strong, P. and Robinson, J. (1990), *The NHS Under New Management*, Milton Keynes, Open University Press.

Terkel, S. (1975), *Working: People talk about what they do all day and how they feel about what they do*, London: Wild House.

Watson, T. (1994), *In Search of Management: Culture, Chaos and Control in Managerial Work*, London, Routledge.

5 Some political and economic issues raised by privatization

Nigel Allington

This paper is based on an article by Samuel Brittan in the *Political Quarterly* of April/June 1984. This revised and updated version is the work of Nigel Allington, who bears sole responsibility for the present text.

Political Background

The sale of state assets to the private sector can now be viewed in retrospect as one of the key features of the Thatcher Government. Privatization, as such asset sales are called, fitted in with Thatcherite political beliefs but only belatedly rose to become a prominent theme. In the 1979 Conservative election manifesto, privatization was not a major issue beyond returning the recently nationalized aerospace and shipbuilding concerns to private ownership, selling shares in the National Freight Corporation and relaxing regulations on bus services. But Chancellor of the Exchequer Howe surfaced underlying Conservative thinking when he announced in the first budget of the new government that:

> (in reviewing)... the scope for reducing the size of the public sector it is already clear that the scope for the sale of assets is substantial. Such sales not only help in the short-term to reduce the PSBR. They are an essential part of our long-term programme for promoting the widest possible participation by the people in ownership of British industry. This objective - wider public ownership in the true meaning of the term - has implications not only for the sale of our programme, but also for the methods of sale we shall adopt (quoted in Lawson, 1992).

During the first Thatcher Government 'special asset sales' were on a very small scale, averaging £380m per annum compared with £2.6b in the second and £8.5b in the third government. Moreover the early asset disposals included portfolio sales of shares in companies in which the Government had a holding, but which were not state-controlled or treated as part of the public sector. Examples were BP, British Sugar Corporation, ICL and other National Enterprise Board holdings, netting in the case of BP, the most notable, £276m in 1979/1980 and £265m in 1983/1984.

Resort to BP disposals to reduce the Public Sector Borrowing Requirement (PSBR) was no novelty, having been pioneered under the Healey-Lever regime at the time of the IMF negotiations in 1976-1977. Moreover, even the genuine privatization measures carried out in 1979-1983 did not involve major state monopolies, but government-owned enterprises operating in a largely competitive environment, such as Britoil, Cable and Wireless, British Aerospace, Amersham International, Associated British Ports, and the National Freight Corporation. In these cases whether performance improved or deteriorated would certainly matter to the shareholder; but they were not important enough to make more than a marginal difference to the overall performance of the British economy. The success of the Amersham flotation however, twenty-four times oversubscribed, gave investors a large profit and changed the public's perception of the whole privatization project.

In the second government privatization took place of a much wider range of enterprises, including some enjoying monopoly or semi-monopoly positions. Enterprise Oil formerly owned by British Gas Corporation, British Telecom, British Gas itself and British Airways, on the whole had much bigger sales with BT capturing the public's imagination for the policy. (In addition to asset sales one and a quarter million council houses had been sold by the end of this Government in 1987, deregulation took place in the financial markets and contracting out progressed somewhat further in the NHS and the Local Authorities).

The third government saw further important sales, the second stage of British Telecom, British Gas, Rolls Royce, British Airports Authority, British Leyland, British Steel, the regional Water and Electricity companies and the power generators Power-Gen and National Power. In Table 1 a complete breakdown of asset sales is given, including the initial year of flotation, net proceeds to the Treasury and where available over (or under) subscription, where the Government holds a golden share and the discount on share price. Tables 2 & 3 list the remaining nationalized industries and public corporations at the end of May 1992, and what distinguishes most of these enterprises is that for either social or political reasons they cannot be set commercial objectives very easily and thus privatized. However, plans are now in hand for British Coal and British Rail, continuing the Thatcher policy and even the Post Office, ruled out by her, may follow although the precise form of its privatization is still uncertain (see Chapter 7).

In 1979 the nationalized industries accounted for 10 per cent of GDP, 15 per cent of total investment and 10 per cent of the RPI. They employed 1.2 million mainly unionized workers and completely dominated communications, steel, shipbuilding, transport and energy. But by 1992, 66 per cent of the public sector had been transferred to the private sector together with some 920,000 employees, many of whom had shareholdings in the newly privatized companies: by 1988 in fact there were more shareholders than trade union members in Britain.

The rise to prominence of privatization was due to a variety of forces. The theme was much discussed by Conservative policy planners in the years of opposition before 1979: but their assessment was that it might prove technically difficult and politically unacceptable. In the event it turned out a good deal easier than was supposed - in contrast to policies of targeting money supply growth, reducing public expenditure and raising incentives by lowering income tax. Public expenditure as a proportion of GDP rose 3 per cent from 40.5 per cent in 1978/79 to 43.5 per cent in 1982/83 and peaked at 45.9 per cent in 1984/85, only falling below 40 per cent in 1988/89, ten years after the Conservatives came to power. Unemployment rose without a break from 1979 to 1986 reaching 3 million or 11 per cent of the working population, before falling. The one clear achievement was a reduction in inflation to single digit level in 1982 and a low of 3 per cent in 1986 before it took off again.

Thus, privatization became a *de facto* ideological substitute for a set of economic policies that proved to be unattainable. In retrospect it came to represent greater efficiency through competition. Even where this was not immediately possible, it represented an extension of individual ownership that transformed public attitudes towards free market capitalism and an inducement for government to reassume its rightful regulatory function.

We leave assessments of competition and regulation until a little later, but first refer to an alternative explanation voiced by many commentators to the effect that privatization is a cosmetic device to reduce the PSBR - and of course the sums raised through asset sales at £42 billion by the end of 1992, are enormous. Nevertheless, it would be ludicrous to suppose that major industrial decisions such as whether to privatize the telephone system, gas or electricity have been taken to massage these figures. It would be questionable in any case to count asset sales as deductions from the PSBR instead of ways of financing it and Conservative Chancellors admitted that such sales ought not to count 'one for one' in the latter context. More plausibly, the financial benefits from privatization provided a basis for tax

Table 1: Asset sales 1979-1992[1]

	Yr. of flotation	*Net proc to HMG*	*Times over (under) subscribed*	*Golden Share*	*Discount on share price (%)*
Amersham Intl	1981/2	64	24	Yes	26
Assoc Brit Port Hldngs	1982/3	97	34	No	21
BAA plc	1987/8	1223	8.1	Yes	12
Brit Aerospace	1980/1	390	-	Yes	-
Briti Airways	1986/7	854	23	Yes	29
Brit Gas - sale shares	1986/7	5287	4	Yes	11
Brit Gas - debt redemptn	1986/7	2150	-	-	-
Brit Petroleum	1979/80	6083	-	No	-
Brit Steel	1988/9	2425	-	Yes	-
Brit Sugar Corp	1981/2	44	-	-	-
Brit Telecom(sale shares)	1984/5	3685	3	Yes	21
Brit Telecom (loan stock)	1984/5	451	-	-	-
Brit Telecom (redemptn preference shares)	1986/7	750	-	-	-
Britoil	1982/3	1053	(0.3)	Yes	N/A
Cable and Wireless	1981/2	1021	5.6	Yes	17
Electricity industries:	-	-	-	-	-
Sales of shares (Eng & Wales)	1990/1	5444	10.7	Yes	21
Sales of shares (Scot)	1991/2	1105	-	Yes	-
Redemptn of debt	1991/2	1105	-	-	-
Enterprise Oil	1984/5	384	(0.4)	Yes	N/A
Forestry Commission	1982/3	161	-	-	-
Gen Practice Fin Corp	1988/9	67	-	-	-
Harland and Wolff	1989/90	16	-	-	-
Insurance Services	1989/90	-	-	-	-
Land settlement	1983/4	22	-	-	-
Motorway Service Leases	1982/3	20	-	-	-
Nat Ent Brd Hldngs	1979/80	354	-	-	-
Nat Freight Con	1981/2	5	-	No	-
Nat Transcom	-	-	-	-	-
Prof & Exec Recruitment	1988/9	73	-	-	-

Table 1 (Cont'd)

	Yr. of flotation	*Net proc to HMG*	*Times over (under) subscribed*	*Golden Share*	*Discount on share price (%)*
Plant Breeding Institute	1987/8	65	-	-	-
Rolls Royce	1987/8	1032	9.4	Yes	25
Rover Group	1989/90	150	-	-	-
Royal Ordnance	1987/8	186	-	-	-
Short Bros	1989/90	30	-	-	-
Water	1989/90	3470	2.8	Yes	17
Wytch Farm	1986/7	148	-	No	-
Miscellaneous	-	2247	-	-	-
Total		41661			

Table 2: Nationalized industries and public corporations

Nationalized industries as at May 1992:

British Coal
British Rail
British Shipbuilders
British Waterways Board
Caledonian MacBrayne Ltd
Civil Aviation Authority
Nuclear Electric plc
Post Office
London Transport
Scottish Nuclear Ltd
Scottish Transport

Table 3: Public corporations at January 1992 are as follows:

Audit Commission
Bank of England
British Broadcasting Corporation
British Technology Group
The Buying Agency
Central Office of Information
Commonwealth Development Corporation
Companies House
Covent Garden Market Authority
Crown Agents Holding and Realisation Board
Crown Suppliers
Development Board for Rural Wales
English Industrial Estates Corporation
Her Majesty's Stationery Office
Highlands and Islands Enterprise
Housing Action Trusts
Independent Broadcasting Authority
Land Authority for Wales
Letchworth Garden City
National Dock Labour Board
National Film Finance Corporation
National Health Service Trusts
New Town Development Corporations
Northern Ireland Electricity Service
Northern Ireland Housing Executive
Northern Ireland Public Trust Port Authorities
Northern Ireland Transport Holding Company
Oil and Pipelines Agency
The Patent Office
Pilotage Commission
Royal Mint
Scottish Enterprise
Scottish Homes
Scottish Special Housing Association
Trust Ports
United Kingdom Atomic Energy Authority
Urban Development Corporations
Vehicle Inspectorate
Welsh Development Agency
Welsh Fourth Channel Authority

reductions and therefore quickly ousted monetary policy from the centre stage of government policy.

The supply side interpretation receives further support from the concomitant benefits that accrue from wider share ownership through privatization. Concessionary terms for small shareholders and workers in privatized concerns have enlarged the shareholder class and 'increased personal independence and freedom and ... have had an important effect on attitudes', (Moore, 1992). Various measures were introduced by successive chancellors to improve the tax treatment of shareholdings, culminating in Personal Equity Plans and these all served to reinforce the incentives for share ownership. Recent figures, however, suggest that only 40 per cent of original shareholders have retained their shares, although by 1988 the Government could claim that 20.5 per cent of the adult population owned shares compared with only 7 per cent in 1979 (although over the same period financial institutions raised their holding of equities by 50 per cent reflecting a world-wide trend). Many employees bought shares (in some cases 99 per cent did) but of course their aggregate capital value is extremely small, varying between 0.1 per cent and 4.3 per cent of the firm's capitalized value, except for the case of the National Freight Corporation. In effect share ownership has been widened but not significantly deepened (Bishop and Kay, 1988; Croft, 1990 and Veljanovski, 1990). But the symbolic significance of this positive argument for privatization remains compelling and as Nigel Lawson noted in his Maurice Macmillan Memorial Lecture of 1985: 'I give away few political secrets when I say that Governments are likely to be more concerned by the prospect of alienating a mass of individual shareholders than they are by the lobbying of half a dozen investment managers', adding that 'the widespread ownership of private property is critical to the survival of freedom and democracy' (Lawson, 1992).

Whilst privatization has not been overly popular with the general public (Crewe, 1988), those who have benefited directly from it, particularly by the sale of council houses, showed a greater tendency to vote Conservative (53 per cent) compared with Labour (14 per cent) and this was of strategic importance to the Conservatives (Veljanovski, 1989). However, what cause and what effect here is by no means readily apparent. But, certainly these new shareholders are a strong constituency against a future government renationalizing the industry at less than a fair price, if at all.

Another consequence of privatization appeared to be a reduction in the size, bargaining power and influence of public sector unions. Certainly contracting out has led to redundancies, lower wages and a deterioration in working conditions. But while there remains a dispute over the impact of asset sales in these areas, earlier findings that employment levels had increased are about to be shattered as Telecom, British Gas and the Electricity companies shed thousands of jobs. The state of labour relations in the newly privatized companies is much more influenced by industrial relations prior to privatization than by the process itself or the level of employment. Some, indeed, have argued that a private firm is less able to withstand industrial action than a public one having more limited resources at its disposal and more critically a narrower (shareholder) constituency to report to, thereby limiting the possible adverse effects arising from privatization on industrial relations, (Vickers and Yarrow, 1989).

In general terms, the membership of public sector unions has remained fairly stable, and any decline has been random, except in coal and the railways where labour losses have been large and privatization is now imminent. In the private sector, however, union membership has declined dramatically and not specifically in the newly privatized sector. Thus, whilst wider share ownership seems a plausible consequence of privatization, a direct impact on levels of unionization appears more problematical.

Finally, although privatization has reduced the role of the state, government involvement with its former charges is not eliminated. In addition to its regulatory function the Government retained, at least initially, a minority shareholding in BP, British Aerospace, Cable and Wireless, Britoil, Associated British Ports and BT. It also retained a 'golden share' (see Table 1) allowing a wide range of actions to block particular types of shareholding, variations in voting rights, further share issues and the disposal of assets. To date the Government has largely chosen not to interfere - it did allow BP to acquire Britoil and French water companies to acquire British ones - but the ability to do so exists and might engage a more interventionist party.

Nationalized industry problems

Privatization, therefore, emerged almost by default as the main theme of Conservative supply-side or structural policy. But it was also given a specific impetus from the growing difficulties experienced during the first Thatcher Government in handling the nationalized industries, whose performance in terms of a number of indicators including: rate of return on capital, prices, productivity, manpower costs and customer satisfaction, was derisory (Wharton, 1988). It was soon discovered that a genuine hands-off policy towards the nationalized industries represented a contradiction in terms. Nationalized corporations differed from their private counterparts, firstly through the statutory monopoly power which many of them had and, secondly, by the fact that the state inevitably stood behind their borrowing and made up any losses, making them hybrid organizations. Furthermore, the inevitable politicization of the nationalized industries meant strategic planning was compromized by short-term interference at every level from prices and salaries to the allocation of any new capital expenditure to marginal constituencies. Consequently commercial and national considerations were constantly subordinated to government interest or successful lobbying by pressure groups.

The impossibility of a hands-off policy came across to the first Thatcher Government in very practical ways. The large deficits of several of the state owned concerns, meant help for lame-duck industries and for achieving a massive turnaround in the financial position of all nationalized industries considered together, had to be abandoned. The most traumatic issue was the campaign by the nationalized industries to free their external borrowings from the constraint of the Government's PSBR limits; if investment in supermarkets or in North Sea oil was not subject to PSBR limits, why should investment in telecommunications be?

Investment in any sector of the economy must be subject to some rationing system. The question was whether it would be suitable for the nationalized industries to be rationed by public expenditure controls (in the shape of External Financing Limits and limits on capital expenditure) or by the prevailing rate of interest and equity yield in the private capital market? The arguments for the latter are superficially appealing, but wither away when it is realized that a state concern, which has the Government behind its debts, cannot help borrowing on privileged terms compared with privately owned companies. The Treasury also insisted that any loans raised outside the PSBR, must contain a genuine element of risk, a point on which it was not easily convinced. Here the most traumatic single event was the failure to devize a 'Buzby bond' which would enable British Telecom to borrow on the private market, an omission which played into the hands of those of Mrs Thatcher's advizers who were trying to bring denationalization onto the agenda. Another key event was the collapse in 1981 of the projected gas pipeline project to be built by private enterprise, but with government participation and guarantee.

The inference to be drawn from these protracted controversies was that an arm's-length relationship with nationalized industries was impracticable; and that if they really wanted to escape Treasury control the private sector was the best place for them. The same inference was drawn by some of the more predatory nationalized industry barons like those in British Telecom and British Gas, who focused their attention on a campaign to become privatized while retaining their monopoly privileges intact.

The intellectual background

The true *intellectual* background to the whole privatization issue is to be found in the debates on the possibilities of rational calculation under socialism held between the wars by economists such as Ludwig von Mizes, Oskar Lange and Abba P Lerner (see references under these names). In essence, that debate concluded that state enterprises could operate rationally to secure the best use of resources if they aped the competitive firms of economic textbooks: invested when prospective yield exceeded a given rate of discount (which might or might not be the market rate) and set prices equal to marginal costs.

These debates left many unanswered questions; but they did provide the foundation for the Buskellite consensus of the 1950s and 1960s, which downgraded ownership. Provided the Chancellor of the Exchequer set the right signals, nationalization or denationalization became irrelevant, despite the frequently changing position of the steel industry. The consensus was embodied in three White Papers, one in 1961 under Conservative Chancellor Selwyn Lloyd, a second in 1967 under Labour's James Callaghan and a third in 1978 under another Labour Chancellor, Denis Healey. Between them they established financial objectives for state industries, at least on paper, and inaugurated Discounted Cash Flow (DFC) rates of return and marginal cost pricing.

These White Papers engendered a great deal of enthusiasm and one professor suggested nationalized industries were the true home of competitive market economics because they were able to adhere to the textbook rules much better than imperfectly competitive private enterprises. And these theoretical rejoicings were backed by empirical research. Richard Pryke made a plausible, if controversial, claim that the nationalized industries had out- performed private industrial concerns; and the performance of the state sector did undoubtedly improve in the decade up to 1968, compared with the decade before (Pryke, 1971).

The theoretical snag in these otherwize optimistic doctrines became apparent with the development of the economics of both politics and bureaucracy and public choice theory in the United States, based on the insights of earlier continental writers (Mueller, 1979). The difficulties of mimicking private sector competitive performance in the public sector are essentially those of incentive and information. Even if Whitehall can persuade a nationalized industry chairman to price according to marginal cost, his executives have little incentive to make those costs as low as possible, since any cost-savings would not accrue to those making them and the threat of bankruptcy from poor performance does not arise. The key insight of the theory of bureaucracy is that state officials, deprived of the possibility of direct personal financial gain, will secure their benefits in the form of status, security and other in-house benefits. Every one of these temptations is present in large scale private corporations too; but the combination of the threat of take-over and greater personal involvement, via for instance stock options, acts as a mitigating factor.

There was another theme arising from problems at the macroeconomic level. Although each expressed it in different language, both Keynesian and more classical economists came to see union monopoly power as one of the emerging obstacles to post-war goals of high employment without accelerating inflation. The state sector was a stronghold of union power; and some change in that sector - whether towards smaller scale private enterprise or workers' co-operatives - seemed to be indicated. Perhaps because the early 1980s recession had reduced union power this theme, at least temporarily, fell out of the main debate, although the public sector unions have certainly not forgotten it.

The new developments in the economics of politics were ignored by nearly all politicians and by most economists in Britain, yet evidence accumulated which could not be so lightly cast aside. While the real return for the private industrial and commercial sector plummeted towards 3 and 4 per cent in the course of the 1970s and early 1980s, the average return in the state sector fell to about zero. Reviewing the period after 1968, Richard Pryke reversed his earlier conclusions after finding that nationalized industries had performed *less* well than private enterprises, even allowing for their different circumstances (Pryke, 1981). He backed his judgement by a detailed comparison of a few specific areas where state and private industry did compete: British Airways versus British Caledonian, cross-Channel ferries and hovercraft services, and the sale of gas and electricity appliances. As a further example, deregulation of express coaches reduced prices and improved the provision of services even before privatization of the National Bus Company had occurred. Lawson summarized the pre-privatization situation succinctly when he wrote that: 'what public ownership does is to eliminate the threat of takeover and ultimately of bankruptcy, and the need, which all private undertakings have from time to time, to raise money from the market', (Lawson, 1992).

There were signs, however, that a third phase was emerging. Nationalized industry losses in some cases began to decline rapidly and even changed into profits. The two principal remaining drains on the Exchequer were coal and rail, but even these were now held in check. Despite arguments about gas and electricity prices at the time, few argued that inflation was due to public sector prices running ahead and in 1983 the public sector section of the RPI rose less than the rest. During this phase preparation for privatization did as much to improve efficiency as privatization itself, even where the flotations had to await an economic upturn, since costs in the nationalized sector ran ahead in the recession of the early 1980s.

Competition and regulation

To gain full advantage from any privatization it must be accompanied by greater competition. And in the absence of adequate competition, regulation, the Gladstonian principle of an enforceable contract between the state and a private monopoly, has to be embraced, even though regulation has proved to be a highly inadequate mechanism. Most studies of regulatory devices have shown how very difficult it is to find a system which improves upon cost-plus (or minus) policies; and there is a wealth of US experience about the capture of regulatory bodies by the industries they are supposed to regulate. A formula has been invented for the regulation of telephone, gas and electricity prices - namely a maximum increase of x percentage points below the rate of inflation as measured by the RPI - and the level of x has been the outcome of hard bargaining with the Government. But it has the advantage that the company can benefit from its own cost-savings; and the application of the regime to a bundle of products avoids the worst rigidities of price control on individual items, although this flexibility could be abused as it was in the case of Telecom. It also avoids the gerrymandering that occurs in America where control is exercised over the return on capital and enterprises are tempted to adjust costs in a way that is most beneficial to them. Nevertheless, the inventors of the scheme are the first to emphasize that it is not a permanent method of control and that repeated bargaining rounds over the size of x in the light of past profit performance will inevitably cause the scheme to degenerate over time, (Beesley and Littlechild, 1983; Vickers and Yarrow, 1989).

If monopoly is really inevitable, it is a finely balanced question whether state or private monopoly is worse. State monopolies suffer from all the public sector disincentives already mentioned. In a private monopoly the forces of self-interest are given more pecuniary motivation, although this may merely mean that they would try to exploit monopoly power more fiercely than the less highly motivated state management had. But in any event it is more profitable to examine how competition may be extended; for an examination of state industry suggests that there is far more scope for competition than has been realized.

There is clearly no *natural* monopoly in steel, shipbuilding, aero engines, car production or bus services. In electricity and gas, natural monopoly (that is cost saving from avoiding duplication) arises mainly in distribution, but does *not* apply to production. Telecommunications bristle with high technology and a simplistic threefold classification of functions can be identified: a) terminal equipment in home and office, b) connection and local calls; c) trunk calls. The first and last are entirely suitable for competition. It is only in the second area, connection and local calls, that there are economies of scale which at the present time would make duplication costly. The sale of Telecom as a single entity was a mistake (although not beyond remedy, as the break-up of AT & T in the US demonstrates) but the entry of Mercury and six further operators has changed dramatically the operating environment and for the better.

State industries were heavily involved in certain obligations to provide loss-making services on grounds either of discrepancies between private and social costs (for instance in road versus rail traffic in the absence of road pricing), or of distributional considerations (for example fuel for old people or rural transport). Neither privatization nor the extension of competition, require changes in the boundary of these public service obligations, where the appropriate mechanism is an explicit public subsidy for non-commercial obligations. British Telecom charges an access fee to other networks that amounts to a tax to finance 'emergency' services, call boxes and rural telephone services - and this must represent a second best solution.

Artificial restraints on competition should be removed if privatization is to bring the maximum possible competitive benefits that the Government wants to see. But it will not have escaped notice that the nationalized industries were able to prevent too much competition occurring under privatization. Only one telephone competitor to British Telecom was envisaged initially, namely Mercury and the resale of leased capacity was restricted. British Airways sought assurances on limiting competitors' access to routes, when it would have been better for the regulatory authority to auction all routes if free entry had to be restricted because of limited airport capacity, or genuinely inescapable international agreements. British Gas pushed for privatization in its public monopoly form so that it could escape market discipline and got its way because of the tax payments it had previously rendered to the Treasury, and continued to price discriminatorily until forced by the Monopolies and Mergers Commission to desist. Again, many state concerns wanted debts written off or pension fund shortfalls made up to increase their attraction to investors. Too many concessions in effect were given to these companies to buy off union and management opposition.

Unfortunately the departments sponsoring privatization, if they were at all enthusiastic about the policy, usually backed the anti-competitive proclivities of their client corporations. Thus, the more highly protected the successor firms were against competition, the greater and more certain were the perceived and actual proceeds of privatization by which many departments measured its success. Competition would have brought more scope for guesswork and disagreement; and the more competitive the framework, the wider the range of views about the value of assets to be sold; and the greater the likelihood that issues would remain with the underwriters (as with Britoil, Enterprise Oil and BP) or take off into the stratosphere (as with Associated British Ports, British Airways, British Telecom and Amersham). A normal tender can guard against the former but not the latter, which requires the sale of shares in small trenches.

Many have argued that the structure of the various privatizations and thus the degree of competition at the time is not important (Pirie, this volume). Such arguments tend to emphasize the political importance of the process first and the economics second. Thus, given that competition is a government priority, after the expiry of the initial license period (usually seven years), the regulator can make the necessary changes to create more vigorous free market conditions in the industry. British Telecom has been subjected to enhanced competition and substantive revisions to the price formula and British Gas presently faces being broken up as the pressure for competition and structural change has grown. In the interim period, consumers can be protected by the combined efforts of government, regulators and if necessary the Monopolies and Merger Commission.

Even when an element of monopoly is unavoidable, competition can still be brought to bear by enticing contractors to bid against each other to supply a single service at the lowest cost compatible with appropriate quality guarantees. Many activities ranging from laundry services to refuse collection or the supply to motorway services can be contracted out and preferably by competitive tender.

As civil servants and government gained important experience from early privatizations, so later exercises have been more centrally concerned with competition. The most ambitious attempt was electricity supply, where to effect competition, workable relations between various parts of the industry, a process of interconnection or 'use of system', had to be worked out. Problems associated with interconnection cropped up again with possible rail privatization and led to its postponement in 1990. Present plans envisage a state monopoly confined to the railway track (Railtrack) that may subsequently be privatized, with private contractors providing or hiring the rolling stock and supplying services competitively. If a single supplier became necessary because of the need to co-ordinate the timetable or because the state wanted to provide a commuter subsidy, there could be competitive bids to provide the service.

The theoretical considerations here are reasonably clear. The benefits of any competitive tender have to be offset against the benefits of vertical integration between suppliers and final users where such benefits exist. The issues raised are similar to those discussed by Ronald Coase in his work on the firm, when he asked why the market principle should be set aside by people who come together inside a firm, where the alternative command principle obtains (Coase, 1937). Essentially it is because the benefits of competition and greater freedom are offset by the benefits from supervision, quality control and perhaps physical proximity.

Was liberalization an alternative?

The importance of competition and the likelihood that shareholders in a privatized concern will exert political influence to prevent it, as some boards did, raises the question of whether it would have been possible to remove those laws and practices that restrained competition (breaking up some state enterprises if necessary) without privatizing them? It would not have been easy.

Competition policy is often politically unpopular, but it stands a greater chance if directed against a privately owned company than a nationalized enterprise whose losses are borne by the state. Misallocation of resources stems from practices such as cross-subsidization and from pressure on state concerns sometimes to hold prices down for supposedly counter-inflationary reasons and sometimes to raise them for revenue purposes. To say that politicians should not indulge in these practises is to say they should not be politicians, but if they are willing to remove themselves from such temptation that would be the ideal.

Privatization has led to profit improvements within the vicissitudes of the business cycle and reductions in overmanning. Great reductions in manning levels since 1978-80 (20-40 per cent) have occurred in British Steel, Rover, British Airways and Rolls Royce. The main exception to this generalization was British Telecom where there had been a small increase in employment, perhaps attributable to the growing demand for the new technologies, but now here and in British Gas large reductions are in prospect, providing a ruling by the European Court on job protection does not make this a more expensive option.

While privatization without liberalization would yield disappointing results, so too would liberalization without privatization. Competitive behaviour will not be produced, by removing restraints on new entrants, in enterprises whose losses are covered by the state and where profits disappear into the Treasury coffers.

The political dialectics of privatization are important. The mere announcement of privatization schemes left the Government vulnerable to the charge of simply creating private monopolies; and in self-defence it was compelled to introduce some competitive element, admittedly far from enough, which would never even been on the agenda without the privatization debate. Privatization is one of the rare political controversies in which the arguments of both sides, taken together, have permitted considerable progress to be made in restructuring British industry. An analogy is the ICI bid for Courtaulds in the early 1960s which led to a take-over fight. ICI failed in its bid, but the result was to revolutionize and galvanize the whole management structure of Courtaulds, which would otherwize not have happened for many years.

A provisional verdict

Privatization is clearly only one issue in the challenge to improve the competitiveness and supply response of the British economy. A free trade policy, within an EU in which Britain took the open market side in every dispute, welcomed Third World products and abandoned 'Buy British' preferences would do far more to promote competition, consumer welfare, improved living standards and thus ultimately workers' welfare too, than even the best designed privatization programme. If a second plank in a genuine supply-side policy is required, it would be an onslaught on interest group privileges, ranging from farmers to pension funds and home buyers, which distort the British economy and where little progress has been made.

Nevertheless privatization, although less important than either of the above, is a good deal better than nothing. Without the privatization programme and union law reform, the first two Thatcher Governments would have been open to the charge of promoting 'monetarism without markets'. Political economists interested in strengthening the market should have supported more vigorously the programme of asset disposals if aligned with greater competition, for the programme had greater potential than the Government realized. Suitably reformed, it could have helped to change the structure of property ownership, and the distribution of income and wealth in a way which could also have had a bearing on the reduction of unemployment. It must be stressed that no profound distributional change resulted from the Government's programme, but that should have been all the more reason for political critics and independent observers to call for improvements to it rather than to stick to *centrist immobilism.* In particular, now that the programme has almost been completed, British experience might show how other countries, particularly those in Eastern Europe, might improve on the British result.

A different approach

Such a different approach would involve the distribution of shares to every individual chosen on a pro-rata basis rather than the sale of state assets to investors, much as Milton Friedman advocated in his 1976 lecture, 'Curing the British Disease' (Friedman, 1977). The 'handing over' approach eliminates at a stroke one political snag in privatization and that is that the privatized concerns may be subjected to renationalization and subsequent denationalization threats, according to the political colour of the Government. With widespread popular ownership, much wider than the Government has achieved, renationalization would be very unpopular, and would be inconceivable at anything less than fair market rates. The hand-over solution also abolishes the conflict between competitive efficiency aspects and revenue-raising aspects, by abandoning the latter objective entirely.

It must be admitted, however, that if state assets are given away there would be less scope for cutting taxes than if they were sold (or more need to increase taxes if fiscal developments proved adverse), but instead of obtaining tax cuts, citizens would instead have dividend payments on their denationalized shares that would have the following advantages over tax reductions:

(a) *Distribution.* Nationalized industry stock would initially be distributed equally to all citizens. Tax cuts inevitably benefit those who pay most taxes.

(b) *Capitalization.* Even more important: holders of the new stock would be able to realize their assets in the market, or borrow on their strength, and thus have the benefits of wealth ownership. There is not, on the other hand, and could hardly be, a market in rights to hypothetical future tax cuts.

Disposal problems

The distribution of wealth and property ownership is the suppressed question in the whole debate. If the owners of industries nationalized by Labour governments are fully compensated, as has been the official policy of virtually all democratic socialist parties everywhere, no change in the distribution of wealth can take place. For by definition the former owners have received titles to wealth, say gilt-edged stock, of equal present value to their former holdings. Similarly privatization at market values does not make the 'capitalist' classes any richer.

On the other hand, privatization which takes the form of handing over shares to all citizens without payment does help to make the distribution of capital assets less concentrated. If the Liberal Democrat party had been really radical, they would have sought to advance the debate in this direction, rather than to try to freeze the frontiers of state ownership.

What effect would widespread popular share holding have on the efficiency of formerly nationalized industries? It would undoubtedly create a widespread constituency against political pressures to hold prices below economic levels to massage the RPI, or to cross-subsidize to favour consumers of high cost-services, other than those that have been clearly identified as 'socially desirable' and paid for specifically from voted public funds. The populist agitation against energy prices which reflect long-term marginal costs and current market values may fall on much less fertile soil now that gas and electricity industries have millions of shareholders.

It must be admitted, however, that mass shareholders, like any others, have an interest in high profits and high prices arising from the exercise of monopoly power as well as from improved efficiency. Once trading in the new shares had got under way, there would be a relatively concentrated producer interest in monopoly profit and a relatively dispersed consumer interest in competition. A partial reply is that under conventional denationalization, shareholders are more concentrated still and thus have an even greater incentive to exert political leverage.

But the main moral is that the time to install a competitive framework and to break up huge corporations into smaller bodies is before denationalization rather than after, irrespective of whether the Government is contemplating conventional asset sales, the give-away suggested here, or any other disposal strategy. Another moral is the need to have a very firm monopoly and anti-restrictive practices policy, with much less political discretion than exists at present. This is a matter on which middle-of-the-road groups, whether consumer associations or other uncommitted organizations, whose support the Government would rather have than not in its privatization exercise, could exert some pressure.

Many other objections to give-away are less serious. There is for instance the moralistic objection that people do not 'deserve' to be 'given' assets for 'nothing' that in the words of Thomas Paine 'what we obtain too cheap we esteem too lightly'. Those who make this charge forget that nationalized industries are supposed to belong to the public already and that the Government holds them merely as a trustee on the public's behalf. Nor does the argument that most people would sell their 'free' denationalization shares cut much ice. It is irrational for a small investor to have all his eggs in one basket; and it would be highly rational for him or her to sell out to the institutions and invest the proceeds in a more broadly based fund such as a unit or investment trust. Those of a more paternalistic inclination might impose time limits before the newly issued shares could be sold, perhaps depending on the age and status of the holder.

Workers' ownership

A serious radical alternative to *pro rata* distribution of state industry shares to the general public would be to hand them over to the workers in the industries concerned. The two ideas are not mutually exclusive. Workers' ownership might suit some industries and general citizen ownership some others. Moreover, it would be possible to hand over some shares to workers and others to the general public; and the proportion can vary from one case to another, or from one country to another.

Worker shares have probably little advantage from the point of view of stemming pressures for political intervention to bolster monopoly and obstruct new entrants. If anything, workers whose jobs are at stake can exert more pressure for protection, and gain more sympathy than conventional shareholders whether dispersed or concentrated. It would be even more necessary in the workers' ownership case to fragment the industries as much as possible and strengthen anti-monopoly legislation. (Syndicalists have not on the whole been willing market socialists.) The great advantage of worker's ownership would be increased personal motivation from having a stake in the fate of the enterprise and an incentive to work harder and more efficiently, which was precizely the Conservatives motive in advancing share ownership for the employees of privatized companies. In addition, workers' objections to high profits would disappear since the distinction between pay and profits would be largely one of accounting convenience.

This is not the place even to attempt to add to the considerable literature on the micro-economics of worker's co-operatives. It seems reasonably clear, however, that the smaller the enterprise, the greater will be the link between an individual workers' effort and attitude and his own personal financial reward and other less pecuniary gains. Thus, the motivational argument reinforces the anti-monopoly one for the smallest feasible units, even more for workers' ownership than for the general give-away of shares.

There are, however, at least two snags about putting the main emphasis on workers' ownership. First there is the problem of equity. Workers in heavily capitalized industries such as electricity would gain disproportionately relative to those in labour intensive industries such as mining. The equity problem has a wider aspect. The majority of the adult population would not be eligible for workers' shares. Non-working wives, students, the retired and unemployed would not be eligible. Nor in practice would many footloose workers - some among the poorest - who would not have built up a long enough attachment to one place of work to qualify. Even among the regular workers, it is doubtful if even a bare majority work either for nationalized corporations or the larger limited liability companies. Workers' shares would not be feasible for civil servants, members of the Forces, small shopkeepers and small businesses generally, self-employed professionals, or probably employees in health or education, to take obvious examples.

A second and even more important objection is the undesirability of workers facing a double concentration of risk - their wage and employment prospects plus their capital assets - all in the industry in which they work. The more that ownership took the form of freely transferable shares to guard against this danger, and the more that workers took advantage of their opportunities to diversify their share holding, the fewer of the advantages, as well as the disadvantages, of genuine workers' ownership would be obtained.

The conclusion must be that there is everything to be said for piecemeal moves towards workers' ownership, despite the disadvantages, where units are reasonably small and where there is an initiative from, or at least obvious enthusiasm by, the workforce or even the managers. The worker-management buy-out of the National Freight Corporation is an obvious case in point. But for the majority of shares in the majority of cases, the preference would still be for a generalized give-away.

Relevance to stagflation

The relevance of popular ownership of the hitherto-nationalized industries for wider ownership of capital is clear. But let us look at the matter from the point of view of full employment. The proposition that, in the long run, demand for labour is inversely related to the real wage attracts a lot of misplaced hostility. The real problem about the proposition, however, is not whether it is true (the law of demand holds in the labour as in other markets) but that there is no guarantee that the market clearing real wage will be at any particular level, it could be much lower than today's pay and could, theoretically, for some categories of workers, be below physical subsistence.

The possible danger has been very clearly expressed by Professor James Meade in relation to new technologies and has added piquancy in the 1990s as the Asian economies with cheap labour and abundant capital press in on the west:

> It is possible, though it is by no means certain, that the nature of inventions is such as to make the new forms of capital equipment very close and very efficient substitutes for labour, in which case the office or factory would be able to produce its new output at a lower cost by dismissing many workers and replacing them with a small additional amount of capital equipment. In a free-enterprise regime in which labour became less productive at the margin relative to capital equipment, workers would be dismissed and replaced by the more productive equipment, unless the cost-price of labour (i.e. the wage rate) was lowered relative to the cost of employing capital equipment (i.e. the rate of return on capital funds), with a consequential shift of distribution of income from earnings to income on property (Meade, 1983).

Real rewards of labour relative to capital may thus need to be lower if full employment is to be restored and retained. Current unemployment figures suggest a substantial excess of labour relative to other factors at current factor price ratios. The recent world-wide trend rise in real interest rates may not all have been due to the US budget deficit or German reunification and could be a sign of a growing shortage of capital adapted to current technology and demand. It is thus at least a speculative possibility that to price workers back into jobs we may need a continuing fall in real wages relative to previous expectations and a rise in the share of the national income accruing to owners of capital.

Why is this so terrible a prospect? A shift in market rewards away from labour towards capital is a disaster only if capital is highly concentrated and many workers have very little, except for a stake in their own houses. If, however, income-earning assets were to be so widely distributed that every family derived a substantial annual amount from them, market-clearing wages would become more a political possibility; and the growing pressure for measures, such as 'job-sharing', to reduce the supply of labour would be somewhat less.

The main distasteful feature of investment or unearned income is that too few have it. Writers down the ages have sung the praises of a 'modest competence', i.e. a private income, and the sense of independence it brings. It would be worth extending this undoubted privilege more widely, and any help with the stagflation problem would be a valuable bonus. Popular ownership of shares in the formerly nationalized industries would only be a small step in shifting the distribution of capital ownership, but it would be a worthwhile start.

Measures to secure a broader spread of ownership of other capital assets outside the state industry sector would be necessary too, if the Meade fears materialize. But the give-away form of denationalization would at least point the way to a widespread popular ownership of capital. Thus with more imagination than has so far been shown in the political debate, privatization could both be given a more radical thrust and at the very same time contribute towards the policy combination required if we are to return to anything approaching full employment.

References

Beesley, M. and Littlechild, S. (1988), 'The Regulation of Privatized Monopolies in the United Kingdom', *Rand Journal of Economics*.

Bishop, M. and Kay, J.A., (1988), *Does Privatization Work? Lessons from UK*, London Business School.

Coase, R., (1937), 'The Nature of the Firm', *Economica*.

Crewe, I., (1988), 'Has the Electorate Become More Thatcherite?' in R. Skidelsky (ed), *Thatcherism*, London.

Croft, R., (1990), 'Deregulation and Reregulation of the Financial Services Industry in the UK', in J. Richardson, (ed), *Privatization and Deregulation in Canada and Britain*, Dartmouth.

Friedman, M., (1977), *From Galbraith to Economic Freedom*, Institute of Economic Affairs, London.

Hayek, F.A. von, (1935), *Collectivist Economic Planning*, Routledge and Kegan Paul.

Lange, O., (1937), 'On The Economic Theory of Socialism', in H. Townsend, *Price Theory*, London 1971.

Lawson, N., (1992), *The View from No. 11,* Bantam Press.

Lerner, A., (1937), 'Statics and Dynamics in Socialist Economics', *Economic Journal*.

Meade, J. (1983), *Different forms of remuneration and participation*, London: Public Policy Centre.

Mises, L. von, (1960), *Epistemological Problems in Economics*, Princeton (published originally in 1933 as *Grundprobleme der Nationalökonomie*,

Fisher Jena).
Moore, J., (1992), 'British Privatization - Taking Capitalism to the People', *Harvard Business Review*, January-February.
Mueller, D.C., (1979), *Public Choice*, Cambridge University Press.
Paine, T., (1790/2), *The Rights of Man*, R.S. Jordan.
Pryke, R., (1971), *Public Enterprise in Practice*, McGibbon and Kee.
Pryke, R., (1981), *The Nationalized Industries: Policies and Performance Since 1968*, Martin Robertson.
Veljanovsky, C., (1990), 'Privatization : Progress, Issues and Problems', in D. Gayle and J. Goodrich, *Privatization in Global Perspective*, London.
Veljanovsky, C., (1989), *Privatization and Competition : A Market Prospectus*, Institute of Economic Affairs, London.
Vickers, J. and Yarrow, G., (1988), *Privatization : An Economic Analysis*, MIT Press.
Wharton, R., (1988), 'Efficiency Reviews and the Role of the MMC', in C. Whitehead, *Reshaping the Nationalized Industries*, Policy Journals.

[1]Appendix 1: Excludes proceeds from sales of subsidiaries which are retained by the parent industry

The main sales in this category were:

		£ million
1982	International Aeradio (BA)	60
	BR Hotels	30
1983	BR Hotels	15
1984	Jaguar (BL)	297
	Sealink (BR)	40
	Wych Farm (BGC)	82
1985	Warship yards (British ship-builders)	54
	Sealink (BR)	26
1986	BA Helicopters	14
	Unipart (Rover) up to:	52
	Leyland Bus (Rover)	4
	British Coal subsidiaries	1
1987	British Transport Advertising	40
	Istel (Rover)	48
1988	National Bus Company subsidiaries	24
1989	National Bus Company subsidiaries	1
1990	Girobank P.O.	112
	National Bus Company subsidiaries	124
	Scottish Transport Group subsidiaries	27
1991	Scottish Transport Group subsidiaries	13

Section II

Privatizing Education

6 Recreating the past: The end of state dirigisme and the creation of a private university sector in Britain

Nigel Allington and Nicholas J O'Shaughnessy

Introduction

Privatization - an idea whose time has gone - is now much discredited, sometimes for good reason. There are now several examples of its dysfunctional consequences - 'private' water for example being one: the failure of private water companies to justify to the public price rises of up to 70 per cent and the complete disregard of public opinion in the award of enormous salary increases for chief executives. But our advocacy of independent universities has a different purpose, to shield them from a state hostile to the classic notion of a university. Independence is sought in order to preserve an ancient integrity in some format: but this is not to be confused with some of the less honourable reasons for privatization elsewhere, when state and taxpayer seek to disown certain of their core responsibilities.

It is the thesis of this chapter that there exists a political attack on universities under the guise of efficiency, and that this attack threatens to debauch the fundamental basis of what a good university is all about. A politically imposed ideology of competitiveness is being substituted for curiosity-led research. But why do we employ an emotive term like 'attack'? These policies constitute in the aggregate a political attack since they have been conducted at the rhetorical as well as operational level, have involved the continuous introduction of new and ever more detailed performance criteria, the steady attrition of financial support and vastly increased workloads. They are fed by an image of universities as inept and irrelevant.

And they have been sustained over a period of fifteen years (O'Shaughnessy, 1992).

This chapter is in two parts. Part one describes the current crisis and claims that no amelioration is in sight. It seeks to develop the claim that there has indeed been a political attack on education and to justify the demand for independence for the universities. It describes the deadweight of bureaucracy that has been imposed and also the consequences, not least in portentous sounding criteria that measure nothing.

The second part shows how our preferred solution - independence - would work in practice. Its detailed workings permit the presentation of equity, fairness and above all equality of access. We do not wish to diverge from a meritocracy in any sense. Since such a scheme could be misrepresented in this light, it is necessary to say at the beginning and as clearly as possible: *wealth should remain irrelevant as a criterion of entry to university.*

It is from the prevailing social climate that the politicians who ultimately control Britain's universities derive their attitudes and create their policies. It is from this very social climate that Britain's universities need to be protected. The British are possibly the worst educated people of the Organization for Economic Co-operation and Development (OECD) countries and their culture and values are hostile to theoretic abstraction: yet, in a democracy, they pass the ultimate judgement (OECD, 1993). By no means is this argument an anti-populist one, since the elites would appear to agree with them if the Confederation of British Industry's June 1994 report is anything to go by. It demanded from the universities a colossal 45 per cent efficiency gain over the next eleven years (*Times Higher Educational Supplement*, 1994). The fact that, after such travail in the universities, such a report can still be written by this influential body, is argument enough for independence - or at least for the critical attention of those to whom the concept of privatization is normally anathema.

Part One

The rise of state control

In theory British universities are private, self-governing organizations and subject to individual statutes and charters. In practice, however, university education is almost exclusively a state run monopsony with the universities exhibiting some of the same features associated with former nationalized industries.

Encroaching state control of the universities is an incremental process, beginning with government charitable donations and maturing into a generous but exclusive support system. Yet it was a long time before the latent potential for control was realized, for both partners subscribed to a gentlemanly if also dilatory establishment ethos where divisions of authority were dutifully respected: the profession, it was assumed, knew best what was good for it.

The first distribution in 1889 of £15,000 went to the English universities (excluding Oxford, Cambridge and London) and rose to £75,000 in the following year. Parliamentary grants accounted for 35 per cent of total university income in the inter-war period, but two years after the second world war topped 50 per cent, peaking at 78 per cent in 1974 when all UK universities were included (Allington and O'Shaughnessy, 1992).[1] Not until the mid-1970s and early 1980s however, did the universities discover the consequences of this umbilical relationship as the flow of funds was interrupted. Supervision of the system by the University Grants Committee (UGC) and later by the University Funding Council (UFC) gave way firstly to influence, then progressively to regulation and finally control from Whitehall, through the Department of Education and the three Higher Education Funding Councils for England, Scotland and Wales.

If we are to remedy the damage, particularly of the last two decades, we need the partial removal of the state monopsony. In the percipient words of the Earl Russell: 'the existence of a private sector (would be) a vital countervailing pressure to Government attempts to lower quality by increasing efficiency' (Russell, 1993). While such a proposal in the early 1970s would have been received with little enthusiasm, since academics then regarded the state system as axiomatic, today many would welcome a return to stable funding that independence would bring and the opportunity to regenerate the classic idea of a university (Johnson, 1993).

The political attack on universities

British universities are no longer sovereign and, despite the present Conservative Government's rhetoric, the 'market' plays no part in shaping their future (Thatcher, 1993).[2] It is the Government that tells universities what to do, and at the present time government looks beyond consumer demand to what it perceives to be 'national usefulness' in framing policy. Having once opted for cheap expansion through increases in arts and social science subjects, they now offer higher fees in science and engineering to shift the balance in favour of subjects where they see Britain's competitive advantage to lie (Department for Education and Science, 1985). Thus the universities are no longer able to respond to genuine market pressures, since the necessary prices (tuition fees) are determined by government, not as a result of the operation of the forces of supply and demand (Lall, 1989).

In Britain today fundamental research and scholarship on a broad intellectual front have been sacrificed for much vocational triviality. Additionally pressure has been applied to increase the output of science and engineering graduates in particular, when salaries in these areas do not indicate excess demand. British universities now represent a conflict between education on the one hand and the power structure of education on the other, between the cultured man and the expert as depicted by Weber (Gerth and Mills, 1947). The consequence is an American-style research conception of a university *à la* Humboldt but with the emphasis on applied and intermediate research rather than 'blue sky'.

Thus, for academics the longer term survival of a creditable university system must rest on removing the genre from government parsimony and control. The attitudes of all political parties have been ambiguous at the very best: to the Conservatives, universities are suspect. Labour has tended to see them as elitist and unresponsive, although this is more difficult to sustain as participation rates approach 30 per cent of the peer group. Despite this apparent disparity, much of the parliamentary agenda is common to both major parties. This was manifest in the political pressure to make universities more vocational, and to remove the binary line (even though the immediate result has been to create in the new universities poor imitations of the old). What is abundantly clear is the need for greater diversity, but at the present time a danger of homogenization emerges as the ex-polytechnics shed non-degree courses.

Again, all parties, including the post-Thatcher Conservatives, would like to use universities for social engineering, relaxing entry criteria to allow in larger proportions of favoured groups. They forget that universities are inherently filtering devices with consequences that are just as significant as the 11+ examination: 'universities have always played a role in social stratification, controlling access to highly valued cultural elements, differentiating the capacity of individuals to enter a hierarchy of labour markets and therefore being intrinsically inegalitarian institutions' (Halsey, 1992).

Funding controls

The political attack on universities is motivated by a belief in their inefficiency, a belief so powerful that it has become iron dogma, with the consequence that the budget of most universities in most years since 1979 has received an annual cut. Since 1980 higher education has expanded dramatically with the participation rate and student numbers doubling. But given that the unit of resource has fallen from an index of 100 in 1987 to a little over 70 in 1993, this should be viewed not so much as a rise in productivity, but rather as a reduction in quality (Department for Education, 1993).

Whatever the criticism of universities which might once have been made, this situation is clearly intolerable. A parsimony that began with the economic crisis of the late 1970s subsequently became a virtue and a fixture. As a strategy it is both crass, insensitive and destructive. But in the absence of any real possibility that this approach will change - and what evidence do we have? - the seeking of independent status should become high on the agenda of every university.

The quinquennial system of funding broke down in the late 1970s in the face of inflation and uncertainty about student demand. From 1978 financial constraints were imposed throughout the public sector and the universities themselves faced dramatic cuts of some 15 per cent in their income between 1981 and 1983, causing an urgent search for alternative funding and some insulation from the state's economizing. At this time the British system became the only one in the developed world to start contracting. Damage limitation, early retirements, natural wastage, short-term contracts, expansion of student numbers to maximize revenue, research selectivity, quality assessment, bidding for students, differential fees and so on were substituted for creative planning.

Baker's 1988 Education Act replaced the UGC with the UFC, the block grant remained differentiated between teaching and research allocations, but individual institutions were free to reward departments or faculties that performed outstandingly. Rewards for research were driven by selectivity exercises, initially rudimentary, rather than by student numbers. Generally, research funding through the Research Councils assumed greater importance than that provided through the UFC, reinforcing the impact of selectivity.

In the case of teaching, tuition fees were differentiated by subject (although remaining below average cost) and substantially raized in an attempt to create a market for students, but with the effect of reducing the block grant: in 1989/90 the block grant represented 90 per cent of teaching income, in 1991/92 only 70 per cent. Thus a more competitive grant system came into operation, but with the fatal flaw that it remained supply (state) driven. Genuine competitive tendering for student allocations (competitive bidding), subject to quality assurance, proclaimed in 1990, failed to materialize. The UFC scheme envisaged all places being competitively allocated. But universities used target prices as a guide to marginal cost, and very few subsequently bid below this figure, turning the exercise into a charade. Thus universities above the guide price were penalized as were those failing to meet the allocation of fully-funded places. High-cost institutions were protected by a safety net to allow an ordered adjustment to the new regime.

With the demise of the binary divide between universities and polytechnics in 1992, teaching allocations have been based on (essentially) the previous year's award, adjusted for inflation and with a margin to permit growth. Past performance very much dictates the distribution of the margin. With rising numbers the staff-student ratios have deteriorated, although these ratios are still generous by international standards of comparison and highly regarded by foreign students who are deprived of such intimate contact.

Typically the Government ordered expansion but failed to follow through on the financial implications. With a projected budget deficit of £50 billion looming, the Chancellor of the Exchequer ordered a period of 'consolidation' and an end to expansion in his autumn 1993 budget. The pretence of a market vanished as tuition fees were cut by 45 per cent and the resulting savings transferred to the funding councils for disbursement with the block grant. Hence the Government's dirigiste leanings are reinforced, and the advent of quality assessment widens the scope for more interventionist strategies from the funding councils that have even more financial power at their disposal.

Finally 'efficiency' gains are set by the Government and affect core funding, with the most 'efficient' institutions rewarded by a smaller cut. Ten per cent efficiency gains are required over the next three years. The mechanistic concept of 'efficiency gains' does not amount to a strategy. It is a bureaucratic reflex. The aim is control, but it is also to avoid the intellectual labour of research and thinking. Specific needs, the nuanced subtleties of particular situations, are replaced by what is, in addition to being a formula, a slogan. And the concept means little on its own. A better word would be effectiveness since that would suggest some notion of quality, which is not embedded within the idea of efficiency.

Research underfunding and selectivity

One important reason for seeking independence is that government has come to view university research in an instrumental light and sees no value in so-called 'pure' research.

Research, once the major motivating force for would-be academics, has suffered from underfunding. *Save British Science* found that the UK's poor performance in terms of investment in research and development between 1980 and 1992 arose from the reduction in the civil research budget, mainly as a result of the Government's decision not to fund 'near-market' research that they regarded as the responsibility of industry. Consequently the 0.2 per cent fall in such expenditure as a percentage of GDP, worth some £1.2 billion, pushes the UK down the research league table to eleventh position (from fifth) with spending at half the rate of that in Germany and France, our major competitors in Europe. The deficiency in 'near-market' research, in fact, marks the UK out from the USA, Germany and Japan, and ironically it is in the new universities that the potential in this area is greatest (*Realising Our Potential*, 1993).

Selectivity exercises

From the mid-1980s the Conservatives' drive for greater efficiency and accountability led to greater direction of research funds through an on-going process of assessment : 1986, 1989 and most recently 1992. Consequently the allocation of research funds has switched progressively from dependence upon student numbers to performance in selectivity exercises using performance indicators.[3] By 1992/93 the balance had swung 2:1 in favour of selectivity and a further element was based on the formula J-1 where J represents the 1 to 5 selectivity rating, so that a score of 1 meant no formula funding at all.[4]

Selectivity exercises are a legitimate way of rationalizing departments, but the problem with them is that performance indicators were crude. Even after three attempts, the weighting of inputs and outputs is imperfect. The evidence is that ratings depend on many different variables: research income, teaching loads, group dynamics, the size of the postgraduate body and so on. When all of these are factored out, *no noticeable difference exists between departments* (Johnes and Taylor, 1990). In the decision where to allocate research funds, past research performance has become the guiding principle, but there exists conflicting evidence concerning the opportunities for economies of scale in research, and thus the greater concentration of funding, is rendered doubtful. This would indicate that higher marginal returns accrue if more resources are given to weaker departments since the most productive are beginning to experience constant or diminishing returns. Thus, the political attack on universities is now often taking the form of a bogus managerialism in which various modes of measurement of teaching and research are put into place. There are simply too many subtle and conflicting variables to make accurate predictions and apply any form of universal criteria.

The result of the selectivity exercises has been the arbitrary and *de facto* division of universities into teaching only and teaching/research, a process somewhat expedited by the amalgamation of the two systems in 1992. Furthermore, in the same year some of the funding council's allocations were switched to the Research Councils, the second pillar of research support. Essentially the Research Councils became fully responsible for equipment and overhead charges for their own sponsored research, but the overall result left institutions financially worse off since the transfers did not balance.

Why is research freedom necessary?

Despite level funding for 1994/5, research in the universities remains in a precarious state. By leaving decisions to politicians, long-term research capabilities are being sacrificed to short-term voter preference. The present Conservative Government fails to understand that the discovery of new knowledge, and hence ultimately competitive advantage, cannot be preordained. The Nobel economist, Arrow, has shown that research is costly to undertake, but cheap to replicate since information about it becomes public through published results (Arrow, 1962). Therefore, a pure market mechanism would be unlikely to yield the correct volume of appropriate research without a substantial state contribution. Indeed, the higher the demonstrable public good from research output, scientific and cultural, the greater the case for public support. The freedom for an academic to pursue a research topic of his or her choice and to publish perhaps controversial and unpopular opinions is essential and fundamental to academic freedom. To have to apply to a Research Council or similar body lessens the autonomy of the researcher and endows the assessors with unrealistic power of foresight in the quest for projects of commercial value. No academic would question the need to ration highly expensive capital equipment in the sciences, particularly astronomy, but much significant research in the humanities and social sciences can be achieved with small sums of money. Certainly our research successes as a nation in the past have not been the result of government foresight programmes. Moreover, the value of commercial research conducted by commercial companies, where financial incentives are of major importance, does not seem to have led to results of greater economic significance. Therefore, the private university's research efforts require public support and the most efficient allocation can be achieved by the funding councils, but below that level decisions should be left to individual universities.

Teaching audit

The term 'audit' is not neutral. It comes from the accounting profession (only in Britain is effective management so closely equated with the skills of the accountant). Implicit in this term is an ideology of measurement and control; the expression of achievement in qualitative form may make sense in business where profitability is the chief aim and a certain clarity of judgement can be achieved. Even here an accountancy-driven approach may miss the nuances and subtleties of situations. In the context of education, objective-sounding terms are used to describe a highly subjective process.

Auditing the teaching of universities has largely managed to miss the core criteria, the consumers of knowledge themselves: the reference to market forces simply becomes, in this context, a rhetorical strategy. The reality is a bureaucratically driven process using arbitrary criteria so that the permanent aim of cost-cutting can receive some spurious management-speak legitimacy.

In teacher auditing the key is the quality of the assessment personnel: they must be highly acclaimed university teachers themselves who are familiar with the mission and goals of the institutions they audit. None of this has happened.

The concomitant of teaching allocations is quality assurance to ensure the standard of education given meets as yet rather ill-defined and subjective standards, with excellence rewarded. In the past quality had been assured by a combination of professional ethics and a system of external examiners in the old universities and Council for National Academic Awards (CNAA) validation in the ex-polytechnics. The UGC had a subject review system and the UFC utilized a single subject advisory system. Now external assessment takes place through a quality review committee. In effect teaching is to be rendered into statistics with a full audit of every subject completed by 1998. Auditing teams are dominated by assessors from the new universities and the process has manifested itself in the old universities as a conflict between the values of the auditors and those assessed, with the ex-polytechnics and not the universities carrying the definition of what constitutes a university. The absurdity of the situation is demonstrated when minutiae concerning pastoral care triumphs over the intellectual content of courses and the interface between teaching and research as a key performance indicator. Beyond the process itself much damage will be done to the external constituency of overseas students and sponsoring governments, who equate anything less than excellent with being markedly inferior and therefore unsupportable.

Academic salaries

It is in the area of salaries that the political attack on the universities has been particularly strong, illuminating how far the profession is entirely dependent on the prejudices of the government of the day. As a union, lecturers have little power and have always been difficult to organize. Since 1979 average non-manual salaries have risen by 54 per cent (and the average salary of a schoolteacher by 52 per cent) while academic salaries have increased a paltry 9 per cent. In 1993 the average starting salary for a 21 year old graduate was £14,000; in comparison the average starting salary for a 27 year old academic PhD was £15,186. A 1992 survey by the OECD examining the percentage growth of real academic pay between 1980 and 1988 recorded that in fourteen countries rises of between 0.4 and 9 per cent were found whilst in Britain the comparable figure was -3.8 per cent, the only negative registered (OECD, 1992).

Beyond real cuts, the salary structure is overly rigid and fails to provide realistic incentives with performance pay derisorily low and its distribution subject to a myriad of academic abuses. There should be regional variations in salary to reflect market conditions and meaningful increments for tangible achievements and service as in America. But as long as the public demands, and the state accepts that free tuition in higher education is a public right, then low academic salaries, poor recruitment, demoralized staff and a real brain drain will all continue. During the present recession recruitment has been easier, but by mid-decade more than 50 per cent of staff will be over 50 so that this fact, coupled with recent expansion, will require a massive recruitment exercise. This will prove difficult in the sciences where the output of PhDs has fallen dramatically, but more generally academic penury in the UK makes overseas academic posts or city jobs much more attractive.

It is unlikely that opposition parties, even those in whose ideological defence so many academics have written eloquently, will be more generous should they come to power. The natural tendency of all politicians is to give more to those groups having greater sway over public opinion like health, social security, law and order or secondary education. Looking at what the state has promized academics in comparison with what it has given, the time has come for all academics to ask fundamental questions about their relationship with it and to seek a solution in real, rather than paper, independence.

Another reason for seeking independence is to escape from the judgement made by politicians of the individual academic's worth. They would treat academe as an artisan skill and pay them about half the earnings of the lumpen professions of law, medicine, accountancy and so on.

Part Two: how independence would work

Private universities

It would be foolish, however, to expect any government to fund the expansion or revitalization of higher education. There are stronger political constituencies making competing demands on finite resources. Conservatives still aspire to cut personal and corporate taxation and reduce public sector expenditure, and at the same time both parties promise to improve the health and welfare of an ageing population. There is also the problem of the low participation rate of 16-18 year olds in education, a priority which would preoccupy Labour and will increasingly concern this Government; indeed attention to this problem is a prerequisite for building up higher education. Thus while the Government proclaims a massified system, increasing numbers in higher education to one-third of the age group, it offers no promise of increased resources.

In Britain, we have what has become virtually a hereditary higher education system. Many undergraduates are the children of sixties graduates, most are middle class, and by having a method of total state tuition support, with some living cost help, high per capita costs have been created such that places are rationed. Rationing also favours the best educated which is not always the same thing as those with the best intellectual potential, so the working class is largely excluded, while there are, in addition, consequences for academic freedom in total state funding (Russell, 1993). We therefore need a system of university finance that allows students, parents and employers as well as government to make a contribution. The aim should be to make universities more prosperous and more independent by variegated finance. To do this requires a new charge mechanism and the activation of capital market resources.

Australia has provided an inspiring example by charging tuition fees since 1989, but providing maintenance through means-tested grants (although each one dollar of grant can be exchanged for two dollars of loan up to A $2000). To summarize their system: fees were differentiated by the cost of courses, in bands of 1,500, 2,000 and 3,000 Australian dollars, but are now set at a uniform 2,328 or £1,100 (1993) irrespective of subject: with a zero real rate of interest this adds an average of 2 per cent on graduates' income tax and the revenue obtained is hypothecated to fund universities' expansion (Wran Report, 1988). Graduates do not begin to start paying the tax until they are receiving above the average pay of A$21,500. Most pay within ten years.

Twenty-seven per cent paid immediately in 1992, and therefore obtained a 25 per cent discount and the state recouped £62.5m through up-front and voluntary payments, plus £25m collected through the tax system. After graduating in 1992 a number of students elected to make accelerated repayments and this amounted to a further £6m. The Students' Union took the Government to the High Court to challenge the validity of the graduate charge, but did not proceed with the case since after a twelve month acclimatization period had elapsed all opposition had dissipated. The scheme had no negative effect on a students' decision to attend university either: Australia had 415,000 university students in 1988, 540,000 in 1990 (Chapman, 1994).

The import of such a tax to Britain should not prove to be a disincentive either, especially when set against the tax benefits many graduates have enjoyed over the past decade, with progressive reductions in the highest rate of tax from 98 per cent to 40 per cent. We are *not* suggesting that there should cease to be significant state funding of universities: merely that other sources should be brought into play to yield a degree of independence. The system proposed would improve participation ratios amongst under-represented groups and allow universities to expand further. This would substantially reduce state funding in the long run: the state would act as an administrative agency between producer and consumer, regulate the quality of degrees awarded and underwrite defaults, (the only open-ended financial commitment with a PSBR implication) in order to guarantee the participation of long-term lenders from the capital markets.

The Higher Education Contribution Scheme (or Higher Education Users Payment Scheme-HEUPS), developed by us, incorporates features of the Australian system, but has a unique repayment strategy to minimize student resistance by minimizing the burden (Allington and O'Shaughnessy, 1992 and 1993). Its aims would be manifold and include: widening access to higher education, raising the quality of buildings and equipment, better motivating those who work in it and enabling new recruitment into subjects which have become ossified as their teachers age. *A further, and perhaps more fundamental aim, will be to make universities less dependent on the state by creating a direct consumer-issued stream of financing.* The core idea will be that the universities, the producers, would receive direct funding from the Government in the form of a voucher for each student, since many of the benefits of higher education are societal and not exclusively personal. But, because of the extensive element of individual benefit, most vouchers would not cover total tuition costs. Any difference between the vouchers and full cost fees (including a research funding component) would be covered by groups of universities issuing University Bonds through holding companies on the long-term capital market. Such an arrangement reduces the Government's spending on higher education and the student-as-consumer would pay the difference through the medium of subsequent enhanced tax appropriations, but incur no interest payments, marking this scheme out from most in Europe and America.

The new mechanism in summary

Private universities would operate as follows: (1) universities will recruit students directly and signify the full cost of a degree course that incorporates a charge for research (this is justifiable on the grounds that best practice teaching benefits from active research) and reflects the prestige, teaching and research profile of individual universities; (2) a decision to opt for maintenance support represents an additional charge (currently 14-27 per cent of the cost of a degree) and this is administered by the university and advanced from the new capital pool; (3) universities receive a voucher from the government, the number and size of the vouchers to be determined by the state; (4) upon graduation the university notifies the Inland Revenue of the net advance to the student and repayment commences when income exceeds the national average wage; (5) repaid sums are held in accounts designated by the university partnership for the repayment of bonds and interest; (6) the government meets any default or forgives payments in areas of its choice; (7) the government funds the Research Councils and thus some university research; (8) industry provides universities with endowments and teaching/research contracts, with the possibility of a recruitment fee or profits tax to fund endowments.

Repayments through enhanced income tax represent an administratively efficient way of collecting higher education user payments and maintenance advances. We have provided illustrative costs of such a scheme elsewhere, but that original scheme envisaged considerable state pump-priming (Allington and O'Shaughnessy, 1993). In this development of that earlier scheme the capital market provides the necessary resources. However, repayments would operate as in the previous scheme where the average cost of a degree was £4,220 per annum or £14,092 in total, and where appropriate maintenance raized this to £21,592.

Staged annual repayments might start at £125 per annum and rise to a maximum of £1500 per annum, much depending on the value of the voucher and the need to keep the repayment period as short as possible. Repayment periods of between 6.5 and 24 years could be envisaged, considerably shortened if students elect to pay upfront and receive a discount. If 20 per cent, for example, choose to pay up-front, the holding companies would benefit by some £330m in, for example, a full year of operation of the entire scheme. Overseas students would continue to be charged full cost fees as they presently are, payable in advance, but since EC students are treated as home students a system of safeguards and precautions is needed to guarantee their payments.

As the scheme matures, several things would occur. Repayment of the user payment would be phased so that the impact on the marginal rate of tax is minimized. Charge scales would be indexed for inflation so the real value of the cost of a degree will be maintained, and the income level at which payments commence rises as average incomes rise. The scheme could be tidily maintained and adjusted and since it charts a new *demesne* there can always be modifications as problems arise in practical application.

Postgraduate funding, however, should continue as it does at present. Postgraduates would not of course pay the charge but be fully funded through industrial or state scholarships with realistic fees. Taught courses would be charged at full cost as now and probably not attract scholarship support, but scholarships will continue to benefit postgraduates doing M.Phil and PhD research.

The role of the long-term capital markets

The most radical part of this scheme embraces the findings of the Pearce Committee to both ease the burden on state funding and to give a number of universities their independence (Pearce Committee, 1992). Pearce recommended that Exchequer funded assets should be available as security for institutions to raise capital, primarily for building accommodation. We would extend that proposal. Those universities with a similar profile and outlook would declare their intention to seek independence. To do so they would form themselves into a partnership and establish a joint holding company, to issue University Bonds on the long-term capital market, to finance student user payments, research and capital projects. Partnerships are essential to make the issue sufficiently large to minimize costs and maximize the amount of capital raized. Necessary security would be available through the pledging of capital assets, now vested in the independent university. It is anticipated that pension funds and life assurance companies would want to invest to raise the human capital stock on the one hand, whilst receiving an adequate return on the other.

Perhaps twenty universities, forming themselves into four partnerships of five, would form a private sector in higher education. These would inevitably be the most prestigious and intellectually able since there would be no cross subsidy from the strong to the weak. They would be research and teaching institutions conserving the original 'idea' of a university. Many of the rest would probably become teaching only higher education institutions, offering advanced training in a few areas and opportunities for scholarship rather than research in just a few disciplines. This is an inevitable projection of current trends but under the new scheme the vitality and integrity of the major institutions would be preserved. Mass higher education of the traditional British kind is a nonsense, as the United States testifies. That does not mean that higher education for many more is illusory or unnecessary, simply that it must be different and certainly not a three year honours degree. Public sector teaching institutions might offer a combination of two year, three year and postgraduate courses, designed with a much wider intelligence group in mind, and probably much broader in scope and vocationally orientated.

Why vouchers?

The voucher scheme outlined here will increase competition between the private universities for students and make them more market orientated; but 'market' must never imply diminution of standards. Academic integrity should ensure that standards are maintained, but such a view may be complacent, and if necessary the system should be surveyed using the Academic Audit Unit.

With such a voucher plan, students will enjoy much more flexibility in their choice of universities than the present UCAS system, with its lottery element, permits them. Since the voucher under this scheme has both an allocative and a financial, but not primarily a remunerative function, the objections normally associated with voucher proposals do not apply. That is that they restrict access, bear no relationship to the ability to pay, and raise little revenue. The vouchers can, however, be used for fine tuning by subject, sector, region, course, gender/ethnic or social group.

The scheme would be administered by the universities. An offer to the student will be signalled to the DES as a commitment to recruit if an appropriate qualification is obtained. The voucher's value would be agreed in advance: government may alternatively give an overall sum to each department in a university, with any over-spend absorbed by that university (the difference between endowment plus voucher minus full-cost fees and maintenance will be covered by a special disbursement). If a student is drawing maintenance, it would be channelled to him or her from the holding company through the university administration and into their bank account.

If the student is resident at home no maintenance is claimed and there will be positive incentive to do this. At the beginning of the student's final year, the university administration informs the Inland Revenue of the size of the user-payment and any maintenance: the Inland Revenue will tag the student and collect a tax supplement as appropriate. This is a simple matter in a computerized tax collection system.

University revenue will be boosted by the repayments after interest payments on the University Bonds have been made - an expansion of numbers and the reduction in course costs will be a concomitant, since revenue is linked directly to the student. A recruitment fee could also be added: but employers may avoid this by not using university careers offices. However, if a fee of £1,000 per graduate were taken, an income of £85 million would have been generated in 1992 (given the 85,000 who graduated in that year).

Vouchers are an important development, which provide more certain tranches of funding and raise the level of competition between universities, top-up loans, currently the present government's solution to the cost of maintenance, have been a disaster (Woodhall, 1993).

Top-up loans

The White Paper, *Top-Up Loans for Students*, published in 1988, aimed to increase resources available to students so that the real value of the maintenance grant returned to its 1978/79 level (the average for the 1970s). However, the withdrawal of social security benefits, that were actually well targetted and rather modest, had the effect of reducing the increase to 11 per cent rather than 18 per cent. In fact, 40 per cent of the value of top-up loans in 1990/91 was removed by the change in social security provisions. The burden of provision will change dramatically between 1990/91 and 2007/8. The parental contribution and net grant were frozen in cash terms from 1990/91. Assuming inflation averages 3 per cent per annum (as the Government did), both will fall in real terms and loans will assume greater importance (15 per cent of total finance in 1990/91, but 49 per cent in 2007/8). The net grant in 2007/8 will represent 29 per cent of total support and the parental contribution 22 per cent (a 40 per cent reduction in real terms of both for the average student). Thus student numbers can rise, but parents and government will both spend less: 'top-up' becomes a misnomer, since a fully fledged loan scheme is created with none of the safeguards with respect to minimum income offered by our user payment.

Top-up loans were initiated because of the serious fall in the real value of grants - in the ten years after 1979 their real value fell 20 per cent (Top-up Loans, 1988). Thus, in 1989 it was estimated that the income of 10 per cent of students fell below the long-term supplementary benefit level and parents were expected to make a greater contribution. Between 1979 and 1989 the parental contribution actually rose 209 per cent, but some 40 per cent were failing to make their full contribution. In 1989 the cost of grants to the Government had risen to £761m and with the impending rise in student numbers this figure would have escalated.

In 1992, the Government agreed to raise top-up loans to £715 in a full year for students outside London and to £830 for those studying in London. Grants remain frozen at £2,845 in London and £2,265 elsewhere. The minimum parental and government contributions remain at £45 and £58 respectively - hence, parents earning residual income of £15,630 to £17,419 contribute £1 for every £11 of grant; those earning residual income of £17,420 to £25,599 contribute £1 for every £6.30 of grant. In 1993 the Chancellor of the Exchequer raized the value of the top-up loan again whilst lowering the maintenance grant by 10 per cent, causing general consternation.

Top-up loans attracted general hostility from the student body, and the commercial banks, asked to operate them, considered them too expensive to administer, and the whole concept damaging to their image amongst students. In the event the Government had to establish a separate company to organize them and until recently, when student indebtedness has soared to new levels, they have not proved popular. Now need, rather than acceptance, ensures greater levels of take-up. Our own scheme demolishes both direct maintenance grants and loans, so that parents are no longer expected to provide maintenance support for their children. Those electing to study away from home are automatically eligible for a full maintenance payment, indexed for inflation, and repayable after graduation as a manageable addition to income tax.

Who benefits from higher education?

Since the benefits of higher education are private as well as public, there should be some kind of personal payment involved while seeking to avoid the negative clutter associated with the idea of debt. Graduates, in general, secure better jobs, experience less unemployment and have higher average incomes (those in their twenties earn incomes equal to those of non-graduates in their thirties). They also achieve greater personal fulfilment, and enhanced promotion prospects. Their comparative polish and ability to articulate means that they ascend to all kinds of positions of social, business and political leadership: though it may be fanciful to suggest they enjoy life more through greater awareness of its possibilities, they undoubtedly live lives which are substantially different from those of their contemporaries. Of course, there are also costs to the individual in studying for a university degree - the opportunity cost of income foregone - but those costs are relatively low by comparison. Although the student does forego income, he or she gains much at university which peers in work do not have - more cosmopolitan acquaintance and experiences, sporting and other opportunities, an enhanced social life, freedom from many of the constraints of working life.

Employers, the other 'customers' of the universities, also gain - a skilled and adaptive workforce, access to university research, lower training costs, management capable of absorbing new ideas faster and conscious of broader horizons, the possibilities of in-house R and D. In France and Hong Kong, by comparison, education and training levies give industry a more benevolent attitude to higher education. These levies are an addition to the wages bill and are not based on profits. There is also support for training programmes for employees through unions and so on, government provided matching funds for joint industry/university courses, and tax off-sets of up to 100 per cent, particularly for equipment donated by industry. While British industry does pay taxes already, many enterprises pay comparatively little corporation tax: there is, in fact, no correlation between those that pay and those that employ graduates.

At present taxpayers sustain nearly all of the costs of universities: the block grant, fees and maintenance. They receive few of the benefits since most are not privileged members of society and do not participate in higher education. There is currently no concept of the user costs that are essential to our scheme, and while there are solid benefits from universities - they provide training for engineering and many of the professions and other social returns - such a contribution is often difficult to quantify, and this is at the root of the universities' dilemma.

Conclusions

Under present funding arrangements the future that awaits universities is mediocre indeed, partly because the funder, the British Government, itself suffers ideological confusion - between contracts and per capita funding, between the tensions of market dynamics as against central planning. The one neglected support source is the future wealth of students themselves:

their compulsory contribution would save the universities from quiet but inexorable decline. Recourse to the capital market would provide the funds to support independent universities at the lowest possible commercial cost.

Currently the goal is to create retail mass higher education, at relatively little cost. Our proposals would permit a populist system without destroying the ethos and quality of higher education, because it would enable the substantial expansion envisaged to be properly financed and split between private and public institutions. There comes a point where good management ends and parsimony begins: the scope for efficiency gains is not limitless, and it is a perception of many in universities that such a point was reached some time ago. Moreover, the mechanism we advocate provides long-term dividends from a mixed economy in higher education with enhanced competition.

All international models of universities are flawed. In the United States the standard of living of the middle class has been sabotaged by uncontrolled medical and higher education costs. Higher education is also a burden on individual states as they struggle to honour their social commitments. In Japan, private higher education pressures parents and ensures that the salaryman's strenuous labours will receive limited reward. In Europe, the slow-burning mixture of work and study is the optimally inefficient combination, with a consequent postponement of tax yields until graduates start serious work in their late twenties or even early thirties. Yet Britain, at various times, has been exhorted to emulate these bogus models. The distinction of our domestic alternative is that it achieves what other systems achieve without the ridiculous costs.

British higher education represents a unique transfer of resources from the state to the individual. The only legitimate comparison is with major surgery such as a heart transplant, a contingency that is accidental and neither foreseeable nor universal, or likewise a long period of confinement in state care. Our scheme establishes a more equitable balance of responsibility between funder and consumer: the benefits of universities to most of the population are currently too abstract to justify their monopoly of the funding burden. In any case, the current government is unwilling to spend more on higher education. Unless we have a more strategically determined approach to public spending priorities, economizing in some areas to finance better those that contribute to national competitive advantage, or increased taxation, the only hope for the universities is either to charge their 'customers' or benefit from some scheme similar to our own. Ours is probably not the perfect answer, practice would probably modify it: but conceptually it is surely a *potential* solution.

References

Allington, N.F.B. and O'Shaughnessy, N.J., (1992), *Light Liberty and Learning: The Idea of a University Revisited*, Institute of Economic Affairs.

Allington, N.F.B. and O'Shaughnessy N.J., (1993), 'Grants, Loans or Vouchers?: An Alternative Funding Mechanism for British Universities', University of Cambridge Judge Institute Discussion Paper.

Arrow, K.J., (1962), 'Economic Welfare and the Allocation of Resources for Invention', in *The Rate and Direction of Invention Activity : Economic and Social Factors*, NBER, Princeton University Press, pp.609-26.

Chapman, B.J., (1994), 'Income Contingent Charges for Higher Education: Theory, Policy and Data from the Unique Australian Experiment', Discussion Paper 307, Australian National University.

Department for Education (1993), *Departmental Report*, HMSO, Cmnd. 2210.

Department of Education and Science (1985), *Higher Education Into the 1990s*, HMSO.

Gerth, H., and Mills, C.W., (1947), *Essays from Max Weber*, London.

Halsey, A.H., (1992), *The Decline of Donnish Dominion: The Academic Profession in the Twentieth Century*, Oxford University Press.

HMSO (1993), *Realising Our Potential*, Cmnd. 2250, para. 3.16., p.27.

Johnes, J. and Taylor, J., (1992), *Performance Indicators in Higher Education*, Society for Research Into Higher Education.

Johnson, N., (1993) 'Time for a Declaration of Independence', *Oxford Magazine*, pp.12-16.

Lall, D., (1989), *Nationalized Universities : Paradox of the Privatization Age*, Centre for Policy Studies.

O'Shaughnessy, N., (1992), 'Ourselves As Others See Us: Journalists and the Universities', *The Cambridge Review*, pp.165-68.

OECD, (1993), *L'Ensignement dans les pays de l'OCDE*.

OECD, (1992), *Public Education Expenditure : Cost and Financing*, Tables 3E14 and 3E13.

Pearce Committee (1992), *Capital Funding and Estate Management in Higher Education*, University Funding Council.

Russell, C., (1993), *Academic Freedom*, Routledge.

Thatcher, M., (1993), *The Downing Street Years*, HarperCollins.

THES, (1994), 'CBI Report on Universities', 10 June.

Top-up Loans for Students (1988), HMSO, Cmnd. 520.

Woodhall, M., (1993), 'Financial Support for Students in Higher Education', in the *National Commission on Education*.

Wran Report (1988), *Report of Committee on Higher Education Funding*, Australian Government Publishing Service, Canberra.

Footnotes

1 The 1705 Act of Scottish Parliament provides the earliest example of state aid in Britain, when modest support for the Scottish universities to secure the Protestant religion was established. In 1831 these endowments were switched to an annual parliamentary vote. London (1820s); Manchester (1850s); Aberystwyth (1880) received small, one-off grants before annual awards commenced in 1889 for English universities. See N.F.B. Allington and N.J.O'Shaughnessy, *Light, Liberty and Learning: The Idea of a University Revisited*, Institute of Economic Affairs, 1992, especially chapter 2.

2 It would appear that just before Mrs Thatcher's demise she actively considered radical decentralization for the 'leading universities' by allowing them to opt out of Treasury control 'raising and keeping capital, owning their assets as a trust', M. Thatcher, *The Downing Street Years*, HarperCollins, 1993, p.599.

3 Performance indicators seem to be subject to a version of Goodhart's Law. Indicators are open to distortion through the impact of outside research funding and it has proved possible to 'manufacture' indicators to gain advantage.

4 Individual funding councils choose variants, so that a department scoring 3 in Wales received formula funding of J-1 + 0.5 to boost research development.

7 Privatization: Some implications for education

Peter Morgan and Marsden Preece

Introduction

The current world wide concern about 'privatization' may be seen as part of a general reappraisal of attitudes towards society consequent upon the apparent economic and political failure of regimes committed to state control of, and participation in, the economy. Such failure has been universal and has been experienced by regimes on both the left and the right of the political spectrum as typified by the collapse in recent years of the socialist governments of the Soviet block and of the corporatist/militarist right wing governments of South America. One consequence of this collapse has been that most countries have been re-examining the areas in which the state may be unhelpfully interfering in the economy and one of the key areas being examined in this way is education. This examination has focused on two particular and separate aspects of education, one being what role if any the state should play in the provision of education and the other being concerned with whether the content of education is such as to encourage innovative and enterprizing attitudes in students which are seen as being essential prerequisites of a successful market economy.

Privatization and education provision

A wide ranging discussion has been taking place on the degree to which education should be provided by the state system or alternatively by private providers. This discussion has often been predicated on the assumption that the state is the natural and universal provider and that attempts to encourage private provision in some way represent an attack on the education process itself. This assumption ignores the historical reality that education provision at all levels was initially a consequence of private initiatives, provisions and endowments and that this state of affairs pertained, by and large, until the late nineteenth century. It is only in comparatively recent times that the state has concerned itself in educational matters, and in the UK, state organized erosion of the autonomy of universities is a very recent phenomenon indeed.

In all the advanced industrialized countries that make up the membership of the Organization for Economic Development & Co-operation (the OECD), present educational provision is a mixture of private and state with state provision generally tending to dominate the market. Before discussing the way in which this mixture is currently being subjected to change it would be as well to note that there are various ways in which the state may and does make use of public money in order to support the educational system. In the extreme case, formerly prevalent in the old communist block, the state may take responsibility for all aspects of education including the infrastructure, buildings, real estate of all kinds, staff training selection and emoluments, research, commissioning and publishing textbooks, and etc.

Other totalitarian regimes have attempted to emulate this model but such 100 per cent state control has never pertained in any of the industrial democracies of the west. At the other extreme, schools colleges and universities may be privately owned and run (in many cases by trusts and foundations) with the state paying the institutions on a per capita basis for students enrolled and making an arbitrary contribution towards research costs either directly or via research funding councils. There are many variants and different mixtures of state and private funding between these two extremes, in the UK for example, funding for university research may frequently depend upon a mix of research council and commercial funding. It is evident that, whilst the state may respond to the will of its electorate, from whom it collects monies in the form of taxes etcetera to use a portion of such public monies to support the education process, there is no compelling obligation, either by historical precedent or some natural law, for the state to take upon itself the onerous task of administering controlling or initiating the institutions which deliver such education. There are many alternative means and methods by which the state can ensure adequate provision of appropriate education to its citizens, some of which can themselves refer to a long and successful tradition.

The recent emphasis on the ethos of privatization - spurred on by the evident failure of excessive state interference by regimes of both the extreme right and left to create enduring economic success, has led to a growing interest in and research associated with, exploring various alternative methods of state funding of the education process. A recent example of such research is an OECD report entitled 'School: a Matter of Choice' (Hirsch, 1994) which examined current funding practice in six countries, namely the US, England, Sweden, the Netherlands, Australia and New Zealand. It was discovered that all six countries are experimenting, in their own different ways, with policies to expand parental choice. Sweden for example is currently offering parents who choose to send their children to private schools a subsidy equivalent to 85 per cent of the cost of education in the public system and Australia, Denmark and Holland have strengthened their long standing policies of using public money to pay for private schools. In the USA various experiments are taking place including the recent establishment of 'magnet' schools and the setting up by a philanthropic association of privately run schools whose cost per pupil is deliberately controlled to match current spending in the state (i.e. State rather than Federal) sector. Similar experiments are also taking place in many countries in the funding of higher education. Germany and France are both currently formally examining the funding of the higher education sector and similar reviews of education funding are taking place in countries throughout both the developed and developing world.

In commenting on the OECD report referred to above, a leading article in the Economist magazine has examined some of the main arguments put forward in objecting to the concept of applying market theory to education. It has been suggested that 'Education differs from other commodities in that it is irreducibly social. The choice of each person affects the choices available to all, and the supply of desirable positions is necessarily rationed. In choosing a school, parents are choosing the society of fellow consumers (parents and children) as much as the services of producers' (Economist, 1994). Comments of this type clearly indicate a subjective social aspect to educational choice quite separate from the debate on effective educational values. Central government domination of education provision consequently implies not only control over strictly educational matters but also a degree of social engineering which may well reflect the social attitudes of the party in power. The same article takes note that 'The report also emphasises that, in practice, educational markets have found it difficult to match supply with demand. In ordinary markets, the two reach equilibrium through adjustments in the price and quantity of goods available'.

In education, on the other hand, most 'buyers' (parents and children) are not subjected to a price constraint because education is 'free', and most 'sellers' (schools) have limited room to increase the number of places available. (ibid). Arguments of this type are clearly related to the way in which the present market is dominated by central government control and might well prove irrelevant if the market was arranged in some other way. What becomes evident from the nature of the present debate is that there appears to be an increasing concensus that a degree of parental choice, particularly from diverse suppliers, would be of benefit to the students and might well meet the aspirations of parents.

Moves in this direction are however inhibited by the reluctance of governments to abandon central planning and a general agreement in the more advanced countries that basic school education should be freely available to all young people, irrespective of parental income, which will inevitably entail provision of education funding via central government tax collection and re-distribution. In suggesting how this dilemma might be resolved, the Economist recommends that 'Instead of managing schools, politicians should try to regulate markets. They should make sure that everybody has access to the same opportunities, subsidizing transport and disseminating information, particularly to the poor.' (ibid). Idealistic solutions of this type would imply a degree of market friendly, altruistic, egalitarianism and a relinquishing of central control way beyond the aspirations of any allegedly market friendly modern political grouping. It seems far more likely that resistance from professional groups with a vested interest in the status quo combined with the electoral timidity of politicians is likely to result in more of the fudged mix between centrally imposed policies and a sprinkling of individual initiatives which our present generation of students have to patiently endure.

Privatization and education content

> It is important to recognise immediately that the imparting of inappropriate or irrelevant education, even of the highest calibre, would equally lead to a poor and ineffective product. Thus university education has to be relevant not only to the people but also (to) the culture and environment in which it is being imparted (Makgoba, 1994).

This comment by Professor Makgoba of Witwatersrand University, Johannesburg, commenting on future directions for education in the newly democratic Republic of South Africa, neatly summarizes the second strand of the debate on the implications of the current trend towards privatization for the education sector. It is almost a tautology that the content of the education process, both at university and pre-university levels, ought to be relevant to the subsequent working and social lives of those students experiencing that process. In the debate surrounding such implications it is often either forgotten or ignored that the content of education has been subject to continuous change over the centuries in order to provide a reasonable match between societal exigencies and educational inputs. The extent to which the trend towards privatization has had implications for educational inputs at all levels and has led in recent years in the UK to a plethora of national and local initiatives would require at least one thick volume of its own. What follows therefore is a brief look at some of the major initiatives and an attempt to assess the effects, reactions and possible future directions that the trend of these initiatives implies.

Education, by its very nature, acts upon societal *mores* over a much longer life cycle than that of most goods, services and political expedients.

In this sense, the educational time scale aligns with the cultural changes taking place in society complicated by a built in time lag of anything up to twenty years before the effects of educational changes impact upon the society in which they occur. Education has been described as:

- A means of passing on cultural heritage;
- Initiating the young in worthwhile means of thinking and doing;
- A fostering of an individual's growth (Hodgkin, 1977).

Whilst the first definition, 'passing on a cultural heritage' and the third, 'fostering an individual's growth' have a certain worthy, apple pie, motherhood aura to which most would pay pious lip service, it is the second definition which tends to dominate discussion about education policy, particularly if 'worthy' is understood to mean educating young people to make a positive contribution to society's future economic well being, including, of course their own success in society's labour market. At its most basic level this means equipping young people with fundamental literacy and numeracy skills sufficient to make them useful participants in the industrial/commercial world. This basic approach was the original motivator in the spread of universal education in the western world at the time of the industrial revolution and could well be perceived as the reason for the stress on these basic skills in the recently introduced National Curriculum in the UK where there has been much navel gazing about the reasons for a perceived blunting of the economy's competitive edge. It can and has been argued that it is by improving the delivery of these basic literacy and numeracy skills and raizing them to a higher level via their education systems that has led to the surge of economic success in the so-called 'dragon' states of South East Asia. (It is incidentally germane to the overall discussion that these 'dragon' states tend to have a mix of private and public education provision with a much greater proportion of private provision than is currently normal in western democracies). These 'dragon' economies have however been engaged in a catching up operation and therefore it should not be a source of surprise that the education policy that they thought appropriate to this catching up operation shows a similar emphasis to that adopted in western industrial nations a hundred years ago.

There has been a general consensus among the more serious thinkers about education policy in the OECD countries that if their economies are to maintain and/or improve their (not necessarily fair) share of world trade then there is a need to ensure that their workforces at all levels are educated in a manner that will increase their innovative and high technology skills and potential. It is self-evident that the alternative of attempting to compete via the low labour unit cost route will inexorably lead to a downward spiral in western living standards which would almost certainly, in due course, lead to social unrest. The problem of enhancing high technology skill levels is compounded by the accelerating pace of technological change consequent upon which the life span of such learning grows increasingly shorter. An approach which was seen by Professor Charles Handy (Handy, 1984) and other luminaries as providing a coping response to this dilemma was to encourage via the education process the development of skills and attitudes which would facilitate the students' ability to cope with change. Handy labelled this change in emphasis in education content as 'education for capability' (ibid) but despite support from the Royal Society for Arts and Manufactures (the RSA) and the high esteem in which Professor Handy is generally held, this initiative has received only limited support from the educational establishment.

Thinking along similar lines seems to have informed the UK governments' encouragement and financial support for that which has been labelled 'Enterprise Education' - a heading which has been attributed to a wide variety of initiatives the most important of which have included the Technical and Vocational Education Initiative (TVEI) aimed at secondary schools and the 'Enterprise in Higher Education' (EIHE) programme aimed at the university sector. The response to these two major initiatives by the educationalists varied. Initially it was negative because of the perceived political intent. Eventually it was accepted because of the inherent extra financial resource implications and at the present winding down stage, a grudging admittance that some measurable benefit to students is difficult to ignore. The debate has to some extent been confused by a plethora of local and national initiatives generally grouped under the same heading although very frequently pursuing quite disparate objectives. In a recent internal research report to the Wales Chamber of Commerce (Richards, 1994), seventy separate initiatives of this type were mentioned, and this was by no means an exhaustive list.

In recent years, practicing educationalists in the UK, i.e. the teachers at the chalkface and the lecturers in the overcrowded lecture theatres, have consequently been faced with a multiplicity of competing and conflicting pressures. They are being asked on the one hand to concentrate on what are fashionably considered to be 'basics' and on the other to involve themselves in a confusing welter of initiatives which themselves are unfocused and aimed at various objectives determined without apparent reference to pedagogic theory, and tending rather to pander to a particular fad or fancy which currently obsesses the sponsoring body. This is not to say that such sponsoring bodies, whether they be private companies, local bureaucrats, civil servants, politicians or some mixture of any or all of these, are not well meaning, but there is very little evidence to suggest that the boosted initiatives are suitably grounded either in economic or pedagogic theory, rather they give the impression of being a rushed and panicky reaction to a perceived if somewhat hazy notion that the education system is failing to meet the needs of a post-industrial society.

These concerns with the suitability of the existing education system are not peculiarly a UK phenomenon. Evidence of similar concerns throughout the advanced industrial societies are apparent in the recent OECD report on 'Schools: A Matter of Choice' (opp. cit.) listed above and in previous OECD work in the same area. A consensus appears to be forming that some degree of priority should be given to encouraging in young people at all levels their inherent aptitude for innovative skills and attitudes and, whilst some practical steps are beginning to be taken at the higher education level, there is very little evidence of any positive action being taken at the pre-higher education levels. A typical example of the increasing importance being attributed to the development of innovation can be found in the recent Economic and Social Research Council statement on management research which states unequivocally that its new programme of action will focus 'particularly on those (researchers) contributing to understanding and improving innovation, which the Council has adopted as its strategic priority (ESRC)'. Additionally, in the same bulletin, the ESRC council announced that it is proposing to introduce new Innovation Research Fellowships as part of the Council's Fellowship Scheme with effect from 1995. (Ibid). At a more micro level one typical example of the increasing importance being attributed to innovation was the setting up in 1989 at the University of Wales, Cardiff Business School, of a Centre for Research in Innovation Education one of whose main aims was and is to develop programmes specifically intended to integrate innovation into mainstream curricula.

A relevant example of the kind of work carried out by this Centre has been the development (by the authors) of a module called 'Managing the Innovation Process' (Preece & Morgan, in press) aimed specifically at postgraduate students. This module has already been taken up by postgraduates in Engineering and in the Life Sciences and negotiations are in progress to make it available to postgraduate students in all subject disciplines. The ready acceptance which this module has found is perhaps indicative of the growing awareness by academics across a wide range of studies of the importance that a knowledge of concepts of innovation should play in preparing students for the challenges arizing in the modern post-industrialist world.

At the pre-university level however the main focus of attention has been of late on the strengthening of basic numeracy and literacy skills as may be observed in the recently proposed amendments to the National Curriculum. Whilst there may well be a need to restore the level of the teaching of these skills to perceived previous higher levels and whilst there will no doubt continue to be attempts, however unfocused, to create in young students a better understanding of industry and commerce, there is little, if any, in the way of evidence of a concerted attempt to instill in our younger students an awareness of the importance to the future success of our economy of innovative attitudes and innovative people. Equally absent from the present agenda is any thought-through attempt to develop in pre-university students (the majority of whom will not have an opportunity to move on into higher education) a basic understanding of the innovation process and the knowledge of how to harness constructively their own inherent innovative skills.

Privatization and future education trends

As discussed at the beginning of this chapter, consequent upon an apparent lack of credible alternatives there is currently a world wide trend towards establishing competitive market economies as the preferred form of societal organization. The only competing form of organization seriously discussed is the mixture of the authoritative centralized state coupled with a developing market economy which has been adopted by the Peoples Republic of China and the neighbouring South East Asian 'dragon' states which have utilized this mixed economy format with a degree of success during their catching up phase. Even these successful economies are displaying trends towards a greater degree of private enterprise and a diminishing amount of state economic activity as the newly adopted market economies result in upward trending living standards and a consequence of this change in emphasis has been an increasing amount of privatization of previously state owned companies. In the older industrialized states in Europe and North America, in the old socialist states of the Soviet bloc and in the previously corporatist states of South America, a similar flurry of privatization is currently taking place, and even in Africa and the Indian sub-continent, privatization is currently one of the primary concerns of the various state governments.

This major shift in societal emphasis and social attitudes necessarily gives rise to a period of questioning of the appropriateness of the existing educational structure and content to society's needs. Education does not exist in a vacuum but rather in a dialectical relationship with the societies in which it takes place and therefore any major change in the structure and activity of a society ineluctably brings about change in the education process. In the first section of this chapter, attention was focused on the present manner of education provision - particularly in the UK.

It was noted that this was currently a mixture of private and public provision with centrally controlled state provision overwhelmingly predominant. Whilst centrally controlled state provision predominates in both the university and pre-university sectors, there is a noteworthy difference in which this similarity has come into being in the different sectors. At the school level in the UK the original private provision of education has to a large extent been replaced by state provision since the state took an interest in basic education in the latter half of the nineteenth century. A residual private provision still exists at preparatory and secondary level although this is largely utilized by the wealthier sections of the community. These include the majority of members of parliament, irrespective of their party labels and publically proclaimed policies, although a limited amount of scholarship funding does provide assisted places to a small number of pupils from less wealthy families. This lack of synchrony between the manner of provision of school education and the trends that predominate the industrial and commercial life of society is much more pronounced in the UK than in most of its economic contemporaries and the use of state funding to finance pupils' attendance at private schools, as is the case in Sweden, Holland, Denmark *et al* is conspicuous by its absence, both from current practice and from the political agendas of any of the main political parties.

The provision of university education in the UK has evolved from a markedly different historical background although the outcome of predominant central state control of provision in this sector at the present time is remarkably similar. The earliest universities in the UK were funded from a mixture of various private sources including royal patronage and church support. There was a surge in the number of universities in the eighteenth and nineteenth centuries as the industrial revolution took effect, a colonial empire was established and the need for educated citizens increased. This second wave of university building was again funded by a mixture of endowment by wealthy private individuals with support from the increasingly wealthy municipalities and it wasn't really until the twentieth century that central government became directly involved in the establishment of seats of higher learning.

Central government has always been able to influence the higher education system by various means, including the favouring of graduates from particular establishments or in the disbursement of research funding, but until comparatively recent times the universities were able to maintain a degree of autonomy which enabled them to explore a variety of innovative approaches to learning without the fear of central sanctions. This autonomy has recently been severely curtailed and the establishment of new funding councils for higher education with the associated quality assessment boards has given central goverment an unprecedented stranglehold on the higher education sector. As any one with a familiarity with the work of Max Weber will be aware, a concomitant of central administration is a bureaucratic structure with an affinity for rules and regulation which is the antithesis of the innovative climate necessary for competitive success in free market economies.

There appears to be at the present time no official policy in any of the major political parties in the UK to encourage the growth of an independant higher education sector, although it is almost a commonplace that in the world's three most successful economies, i.e. the USA, Japan and Germany, often cited as exemplars of succesful practice, such private provision of higher education is normal practice. Such a conspiracy of silence seems to be a consequence of entrenched attitudes rather than a reflection of political ideology.

There can be little doubt that it is well within the compass and abilities of government ministers and civil servants to develop ways and means of funding students pursuing higher education without the government needing to involve itself in the control and administration of the institutions which arrange the provision. Such funding arrangements, could with no great difficulty, be ordered to meet the political priorities of whichever political grouping held the reins of power at the time and 'political' opposition to the concepts seem to be founded on vested interest in the status quo and normal reactionary resistance to change rather than grounded in any substantive political theory.

Privatization and the worldwide move towards free market economies implicit in the notion, may be seen as having created in the UK at the present time an asynchronous relationship between the manner of education provision and the economic trends in society at large. It would therefore seem not inappropriate that appropriate research and pilot initiatives should be encouraged in order to explore the various ways in which the future provision of education can be made appropriate to the society which it seeks to serve.

In addition to ensuring the maintenance of basic literacy and numeracy skills, it is argued that one of the factors having a bearing on the content of education is that, if the UK economy is to improve or at least survive, then there is an urgent need to nuture an innovative, high value added industrial and commercial base. A prerequisite for such an industrial and commercial base, in a world in which free market economies predominate, is a highly skilled and innovative workforce. The content of present day education programmes in the UK has emerged from a culture in which the administration of an empire was a priority and bureaucratic and administrative skills were at a premium. As has been pointed out in an earlier OECD research document 'Until recently, society has required, in the bulk of its citizens, qualities of conformity, with social cohesivness thus secured through individuals applying their skills and knowledge to particular tasks and social roles' (Ball). These skills were successfully developed in the UK by an appropriately bureaucratic education system within which conformity was highly valued and innovation was considered the private preserve of an idiosyncratic elite. The present economic imperative implies a need to examine new ways in which the content and process of education can help to develop innovative skills and attitudes in our young people. For such research to produce initiatives which will have a lasting effect, they will clearly need to be of the kind that can be integrated into the curricula and enter into the ethos of the education system. Such integration will in due course require a wide ranging re-evaluation of not only curricula but also teacher training and graduate programmes and may well entail in-service training for existing teaching and lecturing personnel.

An, as yet unidentified, willingness to challenge deeply entrenched shibboleths and an uncommon degree of political boldness will be required to undertake the root and branch review of the existing education system and initiate the research, programme development and staff training implicit in changes of the kind signalled in this chapter. Major structural changes of this type will no doubt have considerable cost implications but in the longer term the cost of such change in the education system will be insignificant compared to the alternative of doing nothing or tinkering at the edges and allowing the UK economy to continue its present slow but inevitable drift towards third world levels. There can be no doubt that privatization and the widespread trend towards market economies is one of the major influences in the world outside education.

For educationalists and others concerned with education policy the trenchant comment made in a recent leader in the Times Higher Education Supplement seems particularly apposite when considering the likely effects of the trend towards privatization on the education process.. 'The one option not available to anybody is acting as though the outside world does not exist.' (*The Times Higher Education Supplement*, 1994).

References

Ball, Colin, (1989), *Towards an Enterprizing Culture,* OECD/CERI Educational Monograph No.4., O.E.C.D., Paris, France.

E.S.R.C. Bulletin (1994), based on *The Report of the Commission on Management Research,* The Economic & Social Research Council, Swindon, England, January.

Economic Focus (1994), 'Parent Power', in *The Economist* (pp.95), May, 7th, 1994. The Economist Ltd; London.

Handy, Charles, (1984), *The Future of Work,* Basil Blackwell Ltd., Oxford, England.

Hirsch, Donald (1994), *School: A Matter of Choice,* O.E.C.D, Paris, France.

Hodgkin, R.A. (1977), in *The Fontana Dictionary of Modern Thought,* (pp. 191), eds A.Bullock & O. Stallybrass, Fontana Books, London.

Leading article, *'Shifts in Emphasis' The Times Higher* (1994), (pp.11), May 27th, The Times Supplements Ltd., London.

Makgoba, Malegapuru, (1994), *'Africa's big challenge' The Times Higher* (pp. 16); May,13th, The Times Supplements Ltd., London.

Preece, M. and Morgan, P., 'Developing an Innovation Programme for Higher Education' in *The British Journal of Education & Work,* Trentham Books Ltd., Stoke on Trent, England, to be published spring 1995.

Richards, J.W. (1994), *The Structures of Enterprise Support in Wales 1994,* Internal Document, Wales Chamber of Commerce, Cardiff.

Section III

Privatizing Services

8 The question of privatization in the British Post Office: A discussion

Miguel Martinez Lucio

Introduction

The case of privatization and organizational change in the Post Office is complex due to the recent changes in public policy. As a public organization, the Post Office had successfully prepared itself in anticipation of privatization. In addition, it had begun to respond in a positive manner to what can be considered to be very real changes in the external markets delivering mail throughout this and other countries. Its dominance in questions of quality service and cost effectiveness in international comparative terms are unanimously regarded as being unquestionable. In what has been a very short space of time the Post Office has undertaken some very successful and ambitious reform projects in the areas of technological development, performance measurement, and structural change. The Post Office has also taken on board contemporary developments in managerialism in an innovative and effective manner. However, the political context of change, the constant uncertainties surrounding such developments, and the subsequently forced pace of reform (however inevitable) has provided Post Office managers and employees at every level with a range of questions and even enigmas.

The chapter begins by outlining some of the broader economic and political reasons for privatization and its centrality within New Right discourse. This chapter then continues by outlining the salient and relevant characteristics of the postal services regarding its organizational transformation and preparation for privatization. Next, it discusses the obstacles to privatization and how the Post Office was becoming steadily 'reorganized' in its preparation for competition and to act as a source of further revenue for the government: this new strategy corresponds to a new logic of privatization developed later on in the Thatcherite years based on the 'decentralization' of public services.

The discourse of privatization

Privatization has become a feature of Government policy in many European countries since the early- to mid 1980s. In Britain, privatization policy has developed within a political context based on the discourse of the free market, the sovereign consumer, and the inefficiency of the state sector. The pulling back of the frontiers of the state has been tied to a set of Conservative political projects that have had very peculiar ideological characteristics. These have been summarized by Hall, who defined the political discourse of Thatcherism as 'authoritarian populism': the Conservatives developed a language of the people to turn the tide of 'creeping collectivism', undermining Keynesian illusions (Hall, 1988: 49). They connnected with anti-statist sentiments which legitimized their objective to undermine the social democratic state from within.

It is a project that was both at the same time populist, in that it referred to and drew in the subject of the consumer and the individual, whilst also being 'authoritarian' because it was uncompromizing and unaccountable in its reform of the state which is seen as negating the consumer. Gamble therefore considered this to be a strong state approach to the free economy, i.e. that market orientations are not given but have had to be institutionally and ideologically constructed in an assertive manner (Gamble, 1988). Assertive management practices were therefore developed at the level of the state and were integral to this strategy.

These changes are seen as emerging as a response to three contradictions within the development of the modern post-war welfare state:

(i) the structural crisis of the Keynesian interventionist and welfare state, i.e. increasing demands for resources and the fiscal limits that are emerging in a market economy (O'Connor, 1973);
(ii) the increasingly dysfunctional features of the state bureaucracy which has assumed finite resources as its organizational context and culture; and
(iii) the increasing expectations and demands of the consumer which has

become more critical and demanding in the last few decades (Piore and Sabel, 1984) even in the public sector (Murray, 1991).

Consequently, privatization, along with other related policy developments, was considered a viable alternative to the predicament outlined above as far as the Conservative Government were concerned. It was seen as being an effective response to the three problems outlined above because it would:

(i) avoid the crowding out of the private sector by the public sector;
(ii) force bureaucrats to reform themselves in the face of new market realities and pressures, and
(iii) eventually allow for the privileging of market and consumer interests over other more political and sectional interests.

Regardless of a range of 'successful' privatization programmes in other services (Marsh, 1991), the British Post Office has experienced extensive delays, reconsiderations, and U-turns that tell a different story with regards to the politics of privatization. The government has had to constantly refashion and remake its policies in the light of obstacles and problems. Furthermore, the way in which these problems have been 'solved' in the case of the British Post Office led to a fundamental reconsideration of the policy of privatization and a need on behalf of observers to understand its ideological and obsessively political characteristics. This has created a climate of uncertainty for both Post Office managers and employees who have had to continuously predict and preempt ministerial decisions.

Some background

The Post Office consists primarily of three key divisions: letters (Royal Mail), parcels (Parcelforce), and retail (Counters Services). In 1990 it employed 205,000 employees. In 1991-92 the Post Office, of which Royal Mail is by far the largest part employing over 170,000 employees, had a turnover of just over £5 billion and delivered 16 billion items of mail per year. It had been in profit throughout the entire period of the Conservative government since 1979 and had actually contributed £74 million to Government funds in 1991 bringing the total to £750 million for the previous ten years (*The Post Office*, 1992). The scale of the operations are such that it is considered to be the largest employer in the country with operations that cover every single town and household. Part of the mystique of this organization is not just its sheer size and coverage, but the fact that it has been a pivot, along with the police and the army, of the creation of the modern nation state. This is the case in many other countries where postal (and telegraphic) services were one of the fundamental bed-rocks of the modern state. At one point, when it was responsible for telephony, this organization was actually a ministerial department and therefore on a par with education and defence, for example.

Symbolically, it is significant too. The presence of the rural sub-post office as an outpost of the central state, keeping communities in touch with each other, has proved to be an important feature of its services. With reference to the recent closures of some of these offices, the then Post Office chairman Sir Brian Nicholson was more than aware of this aspect:

> If a packet of margarine changes in price it doesn't make newspaper headlines. If the price of mail changes, it does. If the margarine supplier decides not to supply someone in Cornwall, we don't hear a dickybird. If we close a rural sub-post office there are headlines (*Enterprise Magazine*, 1988).

Furthermore, the uniformed postman or postwoman delivering mail early in the morning, working in varying and even hostile locations, and carrying out their duties in a range of weather conditions has contributed to their positive image. Since the 1900s this has been the basis of many Post Office advertizing campaigns emphasizing the broad activities and scope of the organization.

In addition, a salient characteristic of this organization has been its unquestionable success in financial and service delivery terms when compared to the Post Offices of other countries. This argument could be validated with respect to official measurements even before the registering of the extremely high levels of end-to-end letter delivery registered in 1992-1993 which exceeded 90 per cent for first class post received on the following day. Furthermore, recent public opinion surveys have proved that this organization is considered by far to be the most popular amongst all the public services.

All these characteristics have provided Conservative Government reformers of the organization with a fundamental problem. The discourse of privatization rests on a belief that the public services are ineffective, inefficient, and basically driven by bureaucratic inertia. In the case of the Post Office many would argue, along various points of the political spectrum, that regardless of certain problems this assumption is highly questionable.

The initial obstacles to privatization

A strong lobby for postal privatization began to emerge linked to the Institute of Economic Affairs. It was argued that 'liberating the letter' would improve services (Senior, 1983):

> The Post Office is a provider of services. It does not require the crutch of an archaic and near-obsolete monopoly. It requires the spur of rivalry as a privately owned company competing with others (Senior, 1983: 49).

Later on, more subtle arguments for privatization were presented by key observers:

> Privatization would free the Post Office from political interference, notably in pricing and investment.
> It would remove the time-consuming process of agreeing corporate strategies with government.
> It would allow the Post Office to enter more freely into joint alliances, undertake acquisitions and, where necessary, sell off peripheral activities and outlets....
> Wages would be freed from current constraints on public sector pay....
> The Post Office would be opened up to scrutiny by the private capital market.... (Parker, 1994: 19)

Yet, in the early Thatcherite years privatization of the Post Office was not central to the political agenda. During the 1980s Prime Minister Thatcher herself, initially opposed the idea of privatizing the postal service. The monarchic symbolism incorporated within the organization (the 'Royal' in Royal Mail along with the image of the crown) made the idea of its privatization somewhat politically sensitive; and, opponents of privatization were not slow in using such symbols in their campaigns to keep the Post Office in the public sector.

Secondly, the very pricing structure of the organization made the opening of competition within postal services difficult due to the consumer equity built into its pricing policy and the sheer cost of market entry that emerged as a consequence. Whether you live in London or the Hebrides there is no difference in price. Yet, the actual cost of moving and delivering mail around the country varies from under the price of a standard second class letter to, in some cases, over £7. This matter of equity actually impregnates the economic logic of price with a 'national' identity. This peculiar form of standard pricing has its own historical origins. And the very same question of consumer equity and national logic applies to the coverage provided by the Post Office counters services (especially with rural areas), hence the limits to privatization of this part of the service.

This peculiar ideological context within which the pricing of postal services had developed appeared so immutable to the extent that the 1984 Monopolies and Mergers Commission Report on the Post Office barely touched on the issue while referring extensively to everything else (Monopolies and Mergers Commission, 1984). When the relevant issue of cross subsidies was discussed it was done in the context of the relationship between the distinct functions of the business and not the geographical scope and coverage of the services. Neo-classical economists, many of whom are the mainstay of New Right economic thinking, are, for reasons related to their particular paradigm, incapable of, or uninterested in, understanding the social and political logics that give meaning and significance to economic mechanisms such as pricing. Consequently, they fail to recognize how such historic constructions are not easily transformed and changed.

Thirdly, the industrial relations and personnel management system of the Post Office could be classified as being highly regulated. Furthermore, the government during the 1980s was unable to play one of its key hands with regards to the restructuring of the state's system of employment. In many cases the government has symbolically and/or materially gratified core professional groups which it has seen as potentially damaging its political image (for example the police and, at times, the nursing profession), whilst in other cases the government has stigmatized and politically isolated key groups of workers, such as social workers and miners, which are seen as peripheral to its interests and being highly politicized in their intentions. This 'strategy' was not so straightforward when it came to the Post Office's workforce. The less than extravagent pay rates of this workforce, improved only by bonuses and overtime, along with the kind of mythological identity outlined above has made its stigmatization very difficult. What is more, the Royal Mail workforce was already a fairly 'flexible' workforce tending to do jobs throughout sorting and delivery offices. There has been a tradition of workers moving between the delivery, distribution and processing functions. This tended to create a fairly wide and experienced pool of multi-tasked employees with the relative skills necessary to be moved around in response to changes in mail traffic and labour turnover. On the other hand, the desire for greater profit levels in order to eventually attract buyers to the organization has restricted the chances of increasing relative rates of pay in the organization over the past decade. Hence, with regards to the Post Office, the Conservatives were unable to either coherently incorporate or marginalize postal employees, being forced instead to develop longer-term reforms to the industrial relations and personnel management system of the organization.

What these range of obstacles eventually contributed to was a significant delay in the decision to privatize, except for the Post Office's banking services which were sold off in 1988. The organization therefore presented the Government with a series of anomalies as far as its intention to privatize public services was concerned. In large part this was not so much due to the inefficiencies of the organization, a questionable assumption, but its popular imagery, and the way it had historically and successfully provided services to the public.

Decentralization and privatization

There were a range of reforms in the 1980s regarding, for example, the measurement of mail traffic, the productivity of employees, and the restructuring of certain key departments. These were rather piecemeal activities and one could not detect any dramatic break with the past as was evident with the distinct cases of the telecommunications and mining industries.

Nevertheless, what began to emerge in the mid 1980s was a strategy of 'decentralization' based on the government demand for terminating cross-subsidies across the different sections of the organization along with a clearer set of internal divisional structures. Any eventual sell-off would not involve the entire Post Office, only distinct parts of it. Restructuring in the area of counters would present different challenges to management when compared to restructuring in letters or parcels. And it was new 'market threats' which were at the centre of the Post Office's official rhetoric regarding the need for organizational change (Dearing, 1986).

It would be unwise of any observer to reduce such changes to purely political considerations. In the case of the parcels section, the growth in competition in the delivery of parcels was forcing this particular part of the Post Office to systematically restructure in the face of these international markets and actors. In the case of the London postal market, specialist firms dealing with business mail began moving into Royal Mail's local market quite successfully even if they were charging substantially more for their services. Declining costs of entry and the prospect of further competition were very real developments (Parker, 1994: 22). In more recent years the European Community has launched a range of proposals aimed at introducing competition into postal services, which has acted as a further spur to change. Thus Post Office management were confronted with a very serious set of developments in their external environment and market, which in turn had to be communicated to the public and to employees.

In internal and organizational terms, the 1988 Royal Mail dispute on the decentralization of pay and the use of casual labour during the months of conflict contributed to an internal organizational awareness that any further changes in the structure of the Post Office would require a more carefully prepared decentralization. In addition, there was a belief that the political, market and technological impulse for change would intensify during the 1990s (Martinez Lucio and Noon, 1995). This would require a more systematic approach to these issues of decentralization and employee commitment as well as its internal marketing. The latter led to the adoption of a Total Quality Management-type project which exposed all employees and managers to the demands of the customer from both within and beyond the organization.

But why the further decentralization? And how did it occur? The Business Development Plan agreed with most of the organizational stakeholders in 1991 took decentralization even further within core operations, i.e. Royal Mail. This new project reorganized Royal Mail along two lines. First, nine regional divisions were created which were to critically co-ordinate key features of operations. Secondly, within this structure a set of different functional divisions were created that, for example, split the letter function into three separate units: distribution, processing/sorting, and delivery. These in turn would be co-ordinated at the regional level. This represented a drastic reorganization in the form of a functional and regional decentralization. In turn the industrial relations system, beyond formal collective bargaining, was reorganized (as were the unions) in relation to these new structures.

One could detect two rationales within a project which had to be executed in a comparatively short space of time and during likely government changes. The first related to the 'functionalizing' of Royal Mail which at one point it was thought would allow for a type of privatization that would involve specific parts of Royal Mail operations. The processing/sorting function with its automated sorting offices could be a part of a network that did more than just official Royal Mail work; the distribution section could be used for more than just the transporting of mail traffic; the delivery section could be franchized at the local level with, as was suggested, postmen and women 'buying out' their work and setting up businesses. The new decentralization would, it was believed, allow for greater options within the type of privatization that would eventually be considered. The second rationale was one of creating regional divisions in order to remove substantial decision-making power from the local districts. New reforms and changes would require a more strategic and co-ordinated approach from higher levels of the organization and this would be facilitated by the new regional structures. For some this was tantamount to a centralization of Royal Mail and an undermining of traditional managerial authority and trade union roles at the local level.

In the case of the counter services the principal strategy was to restructure it steadily over time pushing some of its services into other retailing units. This has been seen with the sale of stamps and at one point the proposed changes to social security payments. Although political opposition from even within the Conservative Government was substantial.

The preparation for privatization and commercialization has therefore involved a more systematic reorganization of the Post Office. The Post Office as a unified organizational entity began to be questioned within higher governmental circles that were preoccupied with plugging the public deficit and maintaining some lineage with their Thatcherite antecedents in the form of further privatizations. This was the political logic at the heart of the reorganization of Royal Mail.

There have been other imperatives for change (related to the market, the demands of organized business customers, and the range of sorting technology on offer to the organization within the international market) but with relation to the organizational restructuring of the Post Office, and Royal Mail in particular, it has been the desire to privatise that has inspired the type of 'decentralization' that has eventually been developed. That is why discussion concerning privatization per se, both academic and political, does not address the real long-term organizational issues.

Privatization and some problems with late Thatcherite ideology

As with other public services such as British Rail, interest in privatization developed in a way that differs from early forms of privatization. The levels of cross-subsidies and the varied success of different parts of the organization brought to light a desire within certain political circles to *disaggregate and reorganize* the service in question. Whether Royal Mail, and the other parts of the organization, were sold off in one piece or not is not really relevant. What has been set in motion is a series of developments that will create the basis for franchizing, organizational separation, and the further restructuring of various aspects of postal services.

> Privatization coupled with competition seems to be the best solution, but if this should prove to be politically unacceptable, then a form of

> franchise arrangement established by periodic competitive tender would be a second best option (Parker, 1994: 23).

This raises some very serious and strategic issues for discussion. Some of the main points will briefly be dealt with below.

The first issue is that of quality. Regardless of the rhetoric of continuous improvement which has been developed and some very successful outcomes in service delivery standards, are further and substantial increases in the quality of the service provided by Royal Mail conceivable? Furthermore, while being a fairly low skill industry in comparative terms, the sorting and delivery of mail has been organized through a workforce that has, for reasons outlined above, been 'multi-tasked' and, according to many observers, both relatively skilled and trustworthy in the delivery of personal and business mail. This issue of trust was at the centre of the organization's employee profile due to the confidential status of mail. Yet how will the prospect of franchizing and the development of cost centres affect this tradition? This becomes a particular problem when one considers that the casualization of employment may be an outcome of such types of decentralization. This is an interesting problem because high levels of employee commitment are not always compatible with high levels of casualization (Blyton and Morris, 1992). In addition, will such changes require an even greater amount of organizational surveillance and detailed and costly forms of measurement? How will levels of trust and organizational commitment be maintained, or even improved, when extremely high levels of demoralization amongst the organization's workforce have been recorded due to the prospect of potential redundancies and casualization that new employment systems tied to decentralization have been percieved to bring in other sectors? Seventy per cent of the Royal Mail workforce claimed they were unhappy at work in 1993 according to the findings of an internal employee survey (*Financial Times*, 8th June 1993). The uncertainty as to how to eventually privatize the organization was contributing to such developments, even amongst higher management tiers of the organization.

Furthermore, the new working practices being developed in conjunction with the organizational changes discussed above were seriously eroding a traditional system of work which could not be easily labelled as archaic and inflexible. As mentioned above, this traditional system of work had actually evolved quite high levels of internal worker mobility between different sections, albeit at a cost. What divisionalization and de-centering were likely to do was focus this mobility around specific areas and teams within the distinct sections of Royal Mail, for example. Even when workers were heavily and fairly consulted by management through participative communication programmes on matters relating to such changes in shift patterns and task rotation many were perceiving such changes as potentially unsettling the right to mobility and overtime payments. This may appear to be a minor problem but, as one union representative stated to the author in London, it was as if the organizational changes were forcing management into re-establishing the demarcation lines that existed in British industry in the 1960s. On the other hand, management would argue that real enhancements of skill levels would eventually emerge within different sections. However, the relevance of this is that the nature of politically led change was disturbing the internal role of employees both collectively and individually which had, strangely enough, coexisted with and actually contributed to a very successful period for the Post Office both financially and in terms of service quality levels.

Another related point is that the issue of demoralization cannot be seen purely as a worker problem. Managers had, through their union organizations, registered high levels of grievance and demoralization themselves. They found themselves having to manage the new internal structures and systems without the resources, pay and support that they were clearly aware existed in other organizations. At the higher levels of the organization, managers were developing strategies in a context of political uncertainty and this led some at these highest levels in 1993 to call on the government to eventually decide the fate of Royal Mail one way or another. Throughout the 1980s and early 1990s a range of key national managers were very explicit about how government interest in using the sector's resources for financing its political projects were starving the organization of key long-term investment funds. Aspects of New Right strategy were ironically undermining attempts at competitive and technological innovation within the organization in question.

Finally, one must assess the possible outcomes of the strategy of reorganization mentioned above. In their quest for new and international markets are the German and Dutch Post Offices, for example, pursuing similar strategies? Or are they entering into these new arenas as highly co-ordinated, unified and, in monetary terms, publicly supported entities that have very clear strategic objectives? This raises the issue as to how private companies have historically achieved results within market economies, something which appears to be strangely absent from the privatization discourse. The problem is that the new style of privatization has latched onto the rhetoric of, and obsession, with decentralization. This discourse has ignored that this new panacea is ridden with contradictions. Many organizations have reassessed and modified similar ventures in the face of unexpected and contradictory outcomes (Colling and Ferner, 1992: Kirkpatrick et al, 1992: Blyton and Turnbull, 1992). This leads us to conclude that whereas the privatization strategy has been complex and diverse in its development over the last two decades, the significance of political and ideological factors should not be ignored.

Given the constant changes in policy of the last few years the ability of the Post Office to continue with its success story will very much depend on *both* the support and autonomy it is provided whilst remaining in the public sphere. Even the leadership of the Union of Communication Workers began to address and support these two issues in the wake of postponements in privatization in 1994. The negotiation of political autonomy is something Post Office management have had to concern themselves on almost a daily basis due to a range of factors beyond their control. Commercialization and organizational change will continue. No one is disputing that a new logic of reform has emerged, as discussed above, and that further changes are inevitable given the commercial challenges facing this organization from foreign competitors. How these are managed and developed within what is now an even more complex political and economic environment will provide keen observers with a need to study such an organization in a more detailed and independent manner.

Acknowledgements

I am grateful to my colleagues Phil Morgan and Paul Stewart for their useful advice and support.

References

Blyton, P. and J. Morris (1992), 'HRM and the Limits of Flexibility' in Blyton, P. and Turnbull, P., *Reassessing Human Resource Management*, Sage: London.

Blyton, P. and Turnbull, P. (1992), 'Introduction', *Reassessing Human Resource Management,* Sage: London.

Colling, T. and Ferner, A. (1992), 'The Limits of Autonomy: Devolution, Line Managers and Industrial Relations in Privatized Companies' *Journal of Management Studies* 29,2 209-227.

Dearing, R. (1986), *The Commercial Public Sector: A Changing Face,* London: Post Office.

Gamble, A. (1988), *The Free Economy and the Strong State,* London: Macmillan.
Kirkpatrick, I. Davies, A. and Oliver, N. (1988), 'Decentralization: Friend or Foe of HRM' in Blyton, P. and Turnbull, P. (1992) *Reassessing Human Resource Management,* Sage: London.
Hall, S. (1988), *The Hard Road to Renewal,* London: Verso.
Monopolies and Mergers Commission (1984), *Report on Royal Mail.*
Murray, R. (1991), 'The State After Henry', *Marxism Today,* May: 22-27.
Martinez Lucio M. and Noon M. (1995), 'Organizational change and the Tensions of Decentralization: The Case of the Royal Mail', *Human Resource Management Journal*, March, 1995.
O'Connor, J. (1973), *The Fiscal Crisis of the State,* New York: St Martin.
Parker, D. (1994), 'The Last Post for Privatization? Prospects for Privatizing the Postal Services', *Public Money and Management*, July-September.
Piore, M. and Sabel, C. (1984), *The Second Industrial Divide,* London: Basic Books.
The Post Office (1992), *Report and Annual Accounts,* 1991-92.
The Post Office (1993), *Report and Annual Accounts,* 1992-93.
Senior, I. (1983), *Liberating the Letter,* London: Institute of Economic Affairs.

9 Privatizing the Police Force: Issues and arguments

Roy Wilkie, Colin Mair and Charles Ford

Introduction

This chapter may seem oddly out of place in a book concerned with privatization, as both historically and in much contemporary writing the necessarily public character of policing and law enforcement, along with defence, tends to be taken for granted. In a tradition that begins with Smith, and stretches through to contemporary writers on public economics and government, at minimum three reasons are recognized as to why a ***core*** of Government and public provision is necessary even within a market economy :

(1) Elements of legislation, regulation and provision that are preconditions for free and efficient private transaction are necessarily public as they are anterior to market operations themselves.

(2) Major infrastructural investments that would exceed the scale and capacity of the private sector, but provide the basis for market transactions, are also allowed to be necessarily public. This might be viewed as a special application of the principle embodied in (1).

(3) Services and goods of social, cultural or economic importance but which, for technical reasons, would be subject to market failure are also viewed as necessarily public goods. This was argued by Samuelson, in the *locus classicus* on this issue, to reflect the 'non-excludable' and 'non-

rival' characteristics of the benefits of such provision, or more generally their 'non-appropriability' by private individuals (Lane).

It is clear that at least points (1) and (3) above would apply forcibly to policing. Not simply legislation, but law enforcement is needed to provide the integrity of private property, integrity of contract, and freedom from assault or imposition that free market operations require. Equally, if private individuals pay to secure their own safety by providing a street patrol in their area, or a watchman service, it is hard to exclude others living in the area from deriving benefit, although they are paying nothing towards the cost. Where benefits are 'non-excludable' in this way, it is argued that a market cannot evolve. As safe streets and a secure community are also 'non-rival' - one person's benefit from them does not diminish any other person's - and rivalness is central to price-based allocation on a market, then again it is argued that markets are not possible.

If we add to these essentially economic arguments, the political consideration that law enforcement may involve the use of force or coercion that requires the public empowerment, control and accountability of those who exercise it, then the case for legal institutions such as 'the office of Constable' and accountable public organizations such as police forces becomes apparently overwhelming.

The first argument of this chapter is that, while sound points are captured by the above arguments, they are incomplete and confused, and as a result confuse what it is that is necessarily public about policing - the broad function of law enforcement and community protection itself *or* the present legal, institutional and organizational arrangements for fulfilling that function. We examine this in Section 1 below.

The second argument of the chapter is that 'privatization' comprises two related elements :

First, a concern, both at the level of the State and public provision as a whole and at the level of particular services, to distinguish the *core*, that which is necessarily public, from the *ancillary*, that which has been publicly provided but need not be so. At the whole State level, the privatization by sale of public companies, the encouragement of 'private markets' in security, health, education and pensions, etc., and the emphasis on the 'duties of family' represent attempts to redefine the role of the State and public activity within the economy and to reduce it to the necessary core.

At the level of particular services, a core-ancillary distinction is implicitly being drawn as well. Thus across a range of services functions like catering, cleaning, vehicle maintenance, etc. are defined as clearly ancillary and contracted out or exposed to CCT. Indeed, the client-contractor (policy-implementation) split in all its various forms and guises (Next Step

Agencies, NHS Hospital Trusts, DLOs, DSOs) represents a core-ancillary distinction in operation. The public core becomes setting objectives and standards, and financing provision, but service delivery within that framework becomes ancillary and open to being 'hived off', 'contracted out' or 'market tested'. It is evident (see Section 2 below) that similar thinking has applied to the police service. Civilianization initiatives implicitly separate off what is core and ancillary within the 'office of Constable', and seek to substitute lower cost civilians for higher cost constables in ancillary areas. CCT for cleaning, catering and vehicle maintenance is predicated on the same distinction, as is real cost charging for customized provision such as policing football grounds or pop concerts where such provision is clearly deemed to lie outwith the core public service.

The second element is that of securing the most economical and efficient achievement of public functions and objectives either by creating pressure for improvement within current arrangements, or by exploring alternative arrangements. The former approach has typically involved financial constraint and emphasis on performance, quality and VFM. The latter, more radical, approach has viewed market pressures as essential to economy and efficiency and has therefore sought to create a market or quasi market framework for public service delivery (via CCT, agency contracts, the internal market in the NHS). This second theme is intimately bound up in both rationale and practice with the core-ancillary distinction.

Our concern is not to argue against the view that the scope, scale and affordability of public provision should be periodically reviewed against the significance of the public interest advanced by it. Nor is it to argue that questions of cost, efficiency and effectiveness of public provision should not be considered. Our worry is that, if this whole development occurs against a background of conceptual inarticulacy and confusion about the publicness of public services, there is a profound danger that the core-ancillary distinctions drawn will be driven by cost considerations, rather than considerations of cost and efficiency being framed within a clear understanding of the core public character of the services concerned. These issues are explored in Section 1, and their application to and implications for policing discussed in Sections 2 and 3 below.

Section 1 : A Necessarily Public Service?

As noted above, 'law and order' services have been largely taken for granted as necessarily public services, even by committed advocates of free markets and small government (see, for example, Buchanan, 1986; Mueller, 1979) As a framework of law and order is a precondition for market operations, and non-appropriability of benefit applies, then the argument runs that market failure would necessarily occur, and therefore public provision is required. Three major issues are raized by establishing the necessarily public character of policing on this basis, and we explore these below.

First, arguments based on non-excludability and non-rivalness *per se* establish the need for *collective* provision but not necessarily *public* provision. While services such as street protection and community patrol could not be marketed to individual consumers because of these factors, given the territorial character of such provision excludability could apply at a community level, that is a given community employing a private company for such services would derive benefits that would not be available to neighbouring communities. Indeed, assuming that some displacement of criminal activity might well happen from the protected community to its non-protected neighbours, benefits would not only be excludable, but potentially rival as well. Thus markets could operate, and indeed do operate, for collective consumers such as communities, companies or public authorities (see Mason, 1991). For example, 'neighbourhood watch' or resident financed community patrols provided by private security companies are examples of the provision of policing-like services on a 'pool' rather than 'public' basis.

The clear problem with these developments is that provision of policing services on a collective but not public good basis undermines some of the key requirements placed on public policing, particularly impartiality, equality of provision and public accountability. Any marketed and privately acquired service is necessarily partial in the interests of its customers, unequal in its provision due to price rationing, and accountable largely to the purchaser, albeit public accountability through regulation and inspection might be secured. It is noteworthy that the development of public policing services in London under the Peel reforms was precisely motivated by concerns about the partiality and non-accountability of collectively financed private police forces in the City (Johnston, 1992). In the contemporary period considerable concern has been expressed about these issues with reference to the private policing of docks, harbours and parks and the private security industry more generally (see Mason, 1991; Eastwood, 1989; George and Watson, 1992; Johnston, 1992).

What this suggests is a second major issue in the establishment of the case for a necessarily public police service on the basis of market failure, and that is the precise definition of the service being provided. The various arguments about public service privatization across the last decade have crucially assumed that, whether public or marketed, the service remained the same basic service. But suppose what we wish is not property protection per se, but *'universally available protection'*, then market failure would inevitably occur as market pricing rations availability.

Equally 'impartial and accountable' attributed to a service changes its characteristic, not merely its context : it becomes a different service altogether, and one for which market failure is inevitable, even on a 'pool' basis. This follows as collective private provision would still be partial, non-universal, and questionable in terms of its public, as opposed to consumer, accountability. This is no mere semantic quibble because upon it hinges the issue of whether 'publicness' is *inherent*, a characteristic of the service provided, or *extraneous*, a question simply of the ownership and management of the delivery system.

Clearly the above analysis seems supportive of a necessarily public police service on all counts. However, a third issue is that all the above establishes is the necessarily public character of a given *function* - law enforcement and community protection. It tells us nothing about the institutional or organizational arrangements appropriate to fulfilling that function, or the scale of investment and activity necessary to fulfil it.

Clearly, the public interest in law enforcement and community protection of a universal, impartial and accountable kind might be achieved in a variety of ways. For example, the legal frameworks, policy guidelines, service levels and performance criteria could be publicly determined and financed, but the actual service delivery contracted to private organizations within that framework. Existing police forces could undertake such work on an agency basis ***or*** it could be opened to competition from private interests. Assuming appropriate specifications, monitoring, and contract enforcement, the collective interest would be in theory just as well satisfied on this basis, as with current institutional and organizational arrangements. The necessarily public character of law enforcement and community protection, therefore, implies only that :

(a) Such provision is publicly financed as public, not individual, interests are to be secured;
(b) Such a provision occurs within a publicly legislated and regulated framework; and
(c) Such provision is rendered publicly accountable for both its propriety and performance.

In thinking about privatization, therefore, it is important to note that it is the function - law enforcement and community protection - that is necessarily public, not existing institutional and organizational arrangements. Any alternative approach that meets conditions (a)-(c) above is in principle a feasible policy option.

To sum up this section, we have argued that conventional analyses of market failure and public goods do establish that law enforcement and community protection are necessarily public, not simply collective, functions. This follows from the recognition that universality, impartiality and public accountability are inherently part of such functions, not extraneous values. We have argued, however, that the necessarily public nature of the function does not imply that forms of contracting or partnership with private interests could not be adopted as long as basic public criteria are satisfied. Nor crucially does it establish the scale and scope of provision necessary to fulfil this necessarily public function.

Section 2 : Privatization and the Police

The OED offers a useful starting point for this section by defining privatization as 'the advocacy or exploitation of the private sector by Government'. The first merit of this definition is that it captures the common element of 'advocacy and exploitation' in any as yet identified 'type', 'form' or 'mode' of privatization, at the same time as allowing that this 'advocacy and exploitation' may take different forms for different purposes. The second merit is that it makes clear that privatization, often assumed to be the reduction or elimination of Government, is everywhere and always an act of public policy - conscious advocacy or exploitation of the private sector.

Within such a broad definition, we can differentiate levels of definition or privatization, and distinctive concepts. Figure 1 below summarizes a range of definitions and levels of definitions that exist.

Figure 1 : Privatization, Concepts and Definition

1. The sale of public companies and assets to private interests;
2. The elimination of government control and involvement or the move from more to less intensive forms of involvement;
3. The imposition of 'business-like' management on public sector (e.g. competition; PRP; short-term contracts; VFM; TQM; resource substitution;
4. Whole economy level: 'liberalization', structural adjustment
   Reduction of government spending as per cent GNP
   Elimination of regulatory controls
   Reduction of tariffs/subsidies
   Elimination of labour market rigidities and encouragement of private sector/market-led development

Tax reform.

The first, and most obvious, definition of privatization is simply the selling of publicly owned assets to private interests, either individual or corporate. As noted in Section 1, 'lock, stock and barrel' type privatization could not possibly apply to law enforcement and community protection, given the function is necessarily public, even if current policing arrangements are not. This version of privatization is, therefore, in principle irrelevant to the context of policing.

As important, an emphasis on sale of assets misses the various other ways that markets, competition and the private sector can be used to achieve the *'transformation'* of public management (for example, management contracts, compulsory competitive tendering, market testing). What we need, therefore, is a definition of *'privatization'* that allows that modification, not elimination, of public control and involvement may be the norm, and that market mechanisms can be deployed within the context of public control. Definition 2 in Figure 1 provides such a definition.

What this definition indicates is that 'pure' privatization, that is the elimination of all government control and involvement, is the limiting case, and that transition between forms of control and involvement is the more plausible meaning of privatization. Given the range of ways in which governments become involved, there is equally scope for a variety of modes of privatization.

Figure 2 provides a summary list of the major forms of government control and involvement in ascending order of intensity, illustrating the potential for privatization by moving to lower intensity involvement.

Figure 2 : Government Involvement Levels

1. Legislation and regulation.
2. Subsidies for private production/consumption.
3. Public production of marketed goods and services (ie charged).
4. Publicly financed privately produced goods and services.
5. Publicly financed publicly produced goods and services.

Although, in the UK, level 5 involvement is assumed to be the natural organization of public services, in theory all health, educational and social objectives of government could be achieved by legislation, regulation and selective use of subsidy. Rather than a publicly financed, publicly owned and publicly produced education service, we could in theory legislate that people must pay to educate their children for a minimum period, with selective subsidies or vouchers to help those with low incomes. A less dramatic and more prevalent approach is to move from level 5 to level 4 involvement by contracting out aspects of service delivery to private or independent organizations through competitive tendering or agency contract arrangements. In this case, policy remains publicly determined and financed, but the delivery system is privatized.

Clearly this is a definition of *'privatization'* that both follows from our broad definition in that the private sector is 'exploited' for service delivery purposes, and also one that is directly relevant to policing. The core public police service represents level 5 involvement, but a variety of initiatives across the last decade have sought to diminish that level of involvement. McLean notes the increasing use of charging by the police for services that were previously either not charged for at all (for example, registration of burglar alarms) or were marginal cost priced rather than full cost priced (for example, policing of football grounds). This move from level 5 to level 3 involvement has been encouraged by the Audit Commission as a mechanism for generating revenue from private and other public bodies (Audit Commission, 1990a).

A second example is the growth of the private security industry as a service provider to the corporate private and public sectors, with the incentive for the private sector that the costs of such provision can be set against tax. This suggests a possible future scenario of diminished public provision with tax incentives to utilize private provision, that is, a move from level 5 to level 2 involvement.

By far the most important transition between levels of involvement to date in relation to policing has been from level 5 to level 4 involvement via contracting out and competitive tendering. A wide range of ancillary services has been contracted out including catering, cleaning, vehicle maintenance, facilities design and management, building maintenance, laundering, publishing and equipment repair (Johnston, 1992). McLean notes, on the basis of a survey of English and Welsh forces, that 37 areas of service have been placed out on contract. Most of these areas are relatively non-sensitive, but contracting out has moved into some operational areas such as police building security, clamping and storage of illegally parked vehicles, and computer and information services. These do raise questions of confidentiality, police-public relations and accountability.

Perhaps more fundamental, although not yet an example of changed level of involvement, is civilianization, by which we mean the replacement of constables by lay civilians in areas of administrative, clerical and even operational duty. Civilianization has been official policy since Home Office Circular 114/83, 1983. This circular stipulated that bids for increased police establishments would not normally be accepted if existing officers were filling posts that could *'more economically and properly be filled by civilians'*. A subsequent circular, 105/88 (1988), specified twenty-five areas of work appropriate for civilianization, and emphasized that it was *'accountable civilians'*, those doing work that would otherwise be done by constables, not *'unaccountable civilians'*, those that were doing catering, cleaning and ancillary work, that would be considered in the assessment of force establishments. Civilianization has been prominent in administrative and clerical work. Indeed, Johnston estimates that over two thirds of police forces have administrative support units, largely staffed by civilians. These units undertake all routine clerical and administrative work, including the preparation of prosecution files, thus releasing police staff for operational duties. Other areas of civilianized posts includes scenes of crimes officers, careers officers, photographers, press officers, counter assistants and personnel staff. As with contracting out, much of this is relatively uncontroversial, although work as gaolers or control room operators has been seen as encroaching on basic police functions.

Civilianization is not directly a change in level of involvement as civilians remain police employees, but it does establish the basis in principle and practice for a massive extension of CCT or contracting out. Once it is accepted that (a) the whole range of duties above need not be fulfilled by police officers, and (b) security, confidentiality and other anxieties about deploying civilian staff in important duties in a police milieu are not necessary, there seems no reason why CCT could not be required for those functions. Indeed, there is every reason to believe that it will be. First, if the replacement of police staff by civilians is concerned with reducing costs, competition seems a logical next step to take that process further for civilianized work. Second, the 1992 White Paper *'Competing for Quality'* reiterates the government's view that *'competition is the best guarantee of efficiency'* and gives a commitment to extending CCT to managerial, administrative, clerical and technical activities across central and local government. Given the 'foot in the door' provided by civilianization, it is most unlikely that CCT would not be extended to, at least, already civilianized areas of police operations.

'Privatization' as modification of the form of public involvement involves the implicit, and sometimes explicit, drawing of a distinction between the core service and ancillary matters, both in terms of areas of provision, the separation of policy and finance from service delivery, and what is and is not chargeable. It is also clearly motivated by concerns with both the economy and efficiency of service provision, and the use of competition and contracts as the basis for improving cost structures and output. Real concerns exist, however, about the basis of the core-ancillary distinctions being drawn and about the impact of the pursuit of efficiency in this way on the effectiveness of police forces. We return to these in the next section.

'Privatization', as modification of the nature of public involvement, broadens the definition, but still fails to capture the possibility that fundamental changes in approach to governance, management and operational practice are brought about without modifying the form of public involvement. The third definition in Figure 1 - the imposition of business-like management practice - allows that the 'privatization' of management practice may happen without more fundamental change.

A wide array of initiatives of this sort have affected public policing across the last twenty years, from the vogue for MBO in the 1970s to the more radical structural and managerial reform proposed in the recent Sheehy Report. The public police service has been the subject of VFM review in a number of reports by the Audit Commission and the National Audit Office since 1980, and as with other public services, considerable time and effort has gone into the development of a matrix of performance indicators (National Audit Office, 1991; Audit Commission, 1988; 1990a; 1990b; 1991). Since 1988 the Police Inspectorate has been active in undertaking 'Efficiency Scrutinies' of both administrative and operational police work, and advises individual forces on areas of work where internal efficiency scrutiny should be undertaken. The results of such initiatives have identified variations in force performance, and identified areas where cost savings could be achieved, but the current state of the art has been viewed as inadequate by both Government and academic commentators. A National Audit Office report on 'Promoting Value for Money in Provincial Police Forces' concluded:

> Despite substantial and increasing expenditure on the police over the last ten years or more, it is difficult to establish with any certainty how far there have been commensurate benefits in terms of improved policing and greater efficiency (National Audit Office, 1991).

Carter, in a cross-sectoral study of performance measurement in public and private organizations, concluded that the approach to police performance measurement was *'promiscuous'*, that is far too many indicators; *'off the peg'*, indicators simply drawn from existing information, and used indicators that were question-begging rather than question-answering in relation to performance (Carter, 1991).

A second key area of 'business-like' management, as noted above, has been 'resource substitution', the substitution of cheaper civilian resources for more expensive police resources across a range of functions. The tying of increases in police establishment to the extent of civilianization achieved by a force has brought significant external pressure to accelerate civilianization. While resource substitution clearly improves economy of resource acquisition, there is little evidence available about the impact of changed resource mix on the efficiency and effectiveness of the police service. However, its impact can be seen from the evidence that almost all the growth in overall manpower between 1980 and 1990 is in civilian staff (National Audit Office, 1991, Figure 2).

The apotheosis of the 'business-like management' philosophy has come more recently in May and June 1993. In May, the Home Office announced proposals that, in future, Police Committees should cease to be made up primarily of elected representatives, these would comprise only 50 per cent, and that 25 per cent of their membership would be appointed by Government on the basis of their (business) management experience and expertise, with the other 25 per cent being local magistrates. These bodies would take policy as laid down by the Home Office and be responsible for its interpretation and implementation in their areas. This emphasis on technical or managerial expertise rather than representative legitimacy moves the local governance of the police from the political committee model to that of a Board of Directors.

The thrust of the Home Office proposals was reinforced by the publication of the Sheehy Inquiry into Police Responsibilities and Rewards in June 1993. That 'business-like management' was the order of the day was evidenced by the fact that the Chairperson, Sir Patrick Sheehy, was a top business executive and that the Committee included no serving or ex-police officer. The Committee recommended *inter-alia* :

(1) The simplification of the rank structure of the police force by the elimination of three ranks (Chief Inspector, Chief Superintendent, and Deputy Chief Constable). This recommendation was based on a 'span of control' study that assessed the police structure against assumed norms of management practice.
(2) The employment of police officers on the basis of short-term contracts, initially ten and subsequently five year contracts, to improve 'flexibility'.
(3) The remuneration of police officers on the basis of performance related pay, though interestingly the Committee noted it was not for them to suggest how this would actually be done, or how performance would be measured.
(4) The pay and conditions of new entrants should be reduced to the market norms for employees of that age and stage of their careers.

Although the distinctiveness of the police service is acknowledged in the Report, the recurrent thrust is that this does not preclude the adoption of management practices that have been shown to work in the private sector. The implications of this 'business-like management' approach will be discussed below, but the point to note is that it fits well with our broad definition - the exploitation or advocacy of the private sector by Government. In this case, as a source of management approaches or techniques.

The final definition - privatization at the whole economy level - clearly does not directly impact on the police, or any other public service, but has long range implications for them. It might be felt that the police escaped reasonably lightly within the process of controlling and reducing public spending, to the extent that spending rose by 50 per cent in real terms between 1980/81 and 1990/91, and police force strength rose by 10 per cent across the period, albeit the actual police establishment remained fairly static (National Audit Office, 1991). However, as the evidence on police establishment indicates, the increased spending was on increased input costs, not more officers, while the workload in relation to crime rose by 40 per cent, and in relation to traffic by 25 per cent across the same period, that is, the ratio of manpower to workload deteriorated (National Audit Office, 1991).

Of key concern here is the relationship between that and the second part of the liberalizing agenda, the stimulation of private activity and markets in areas hitherto dominated by public provision. As police resources become stretched in relation to workload, 'load shunting' through incapacity or perceived ineffectiveness may occur, to the benefit of the private security industry. It is certainly clear, though estimates vary, that the scale of the private security industry greatly expanded during the 1980s, with turnover increasing three-fold to almost £1 billion per annum, and the workforce expanding to possibly 250,000 staff (George and Watson, 1992). This covers not just industry and property related services, but also residential patrols and community security. Boothroyd's 1989 survey showed that there were 241 non-police patrols in the UK funded by local authorities or residents. Government departments have also actively adopted private security, with Ministry of Defence expenditure on this rising ten-fold between 1985 and 1990. By 1990 46 contracts, covering 56 establishments, and employing 500 guards were in operation at a cost of £4.4 millions (House of Commons, 1990). More recently (1993), the Home Office has awarded a contract for escorting prisoners from prison to court to 'Group 4 Security'.

The basic idea underlying 'privatization' at the whole economy level is that of restricting public provision to a core of service, and allowing market provision to provide above and beyond that. The dynamic is of an often stretched public core service, possibly perceived as limited or inadequate, providing the opportunity and the impetus for the development of private marketed provision.

We have reviewed the various definitions of privatization, and their application to the public policing to illustrate two basic points. First, although the essentially public character of law enforcement and community protection as a function has not yet been challenged, a wide range of options for 'privatization' have been identified and applied. Second, insofar as all imply that some core-ancillary distinction has been drawn, the basis for drawing such a distinction, and the principles informing it have not been clearly articulated. For example, how are core requirements of equality of protection, impartiality and public accountability to be fulfilled if community and property protection is increasingly the province of unregulated private security companies? It is to these issues we turn below.

Section 3 : The implications and paradoxes of 'privatization'

As noted in Section 2, in relation to the public police service privatization has largely meant the contracting out of ancillary services and the encouragement of growth in the private security sector.

While the contracting out of cleaning, catering, laundry and other genuinely ancillary services raises few issues of principle, the extent of civilianization, and the potential extension of CCT to civilianized work most certainly does. Already key points of contact between police and public have been civilianized, such as station reception and switchboard services, meaning that police/public contact is diluted and mediated by non-police staff. Furthermore, civilianization has been argued to be leading to fragmentation and a two-tier service, with public order functions remaining the preserve of trained police officers, and most other functions, such as crime prevention and community relations becoming increasingly civilian operations (Mason). If CCT were extended to civilianized work, as it might logically be, not only would important aspects of the police mandate be fulfilled by non-police personnel, but they would be fulfilled by personnel employed by an entirely separate organization.

The removal of elements of the police mandate from the framework and duties of the Office of Constable raises issues of the image and reputation of the police being substantially influenced by the actions of non-police personnel, but also raises more fundamental issues about the definition of the core police service itself. On one definition at least the core character of policing is its reactive, multi-functional and flexible capacity to adopt and fulfil a number of roles simultaneously or as and when required - maintenance of public order, crime prevention and detection, twenty-four hour social service, conciliation and arbitration, etc. (Wertheimer, 1975). Deeming some of these roles to be ancillary and essentially non-police is clearly possible, but such a modification of the nature of police work and qualification of the role of police officers requires a reasoned and articulate basis that has not been provided. It also ignores the likelihood that these roles are closely interrelated and that authority in one role confers authority in others that civilian staff would lack (Dance, 1990). The underlying question is whether processes of civilianization and CCT improve the efficiency of policing, or whether they fundamentally modify the nature of policing itself, without explicit and reasoned argument as to why this should be the case. It is not that a core/ancillary distinction cannot be drawn, if wished, but that it should be principled and purposeful, not an accidental by-product of cost containment initiatives.

Similar issues are raized by constraining the core public service, and increasing dependence on private security services for property and community protection. By definition, the incidence of private protection will be uneven, dependent on ability and willingness to pay, and the service will of necessity be partial in the interests of the paying clients. Furthermore, there are fundamental unresolved questions about the deployment of private services which are *almost completely unregulated, with no statutory licensing systems, codes of ethics or obligatory guidelines* (Bailey and Lynn, 1989). As George and Watson note, the only statutory regulation presently in force is the Guard Dogs Act 1985, and, to date, attempts to persuade the Home Office to introduce a system of public regulation of the industry have been unsuccessful (George and Watson, 1992). Clearly, issues of impartiality, propriety and accountability exist, but more fundamentally it is evident from the growth of private uniformed patrols that the industry has encroached substantially on traditional police duties. While, again, drawing an explicit core-ancillary distinction in relation to public and private responsibilities is perfectly possible, it is (a) unlikely that anyone would explicitly define community beat patrol as ancillary; and (b) the distinction implicitly drawn is arbitrary and driven by the budget constraint and resource position of the public police service. Again, therefore, the issue is not whether some such distinction and division of roles are possible, but rather the unprincipled and implicit way they are being drawn. As with civilianization, and CCT, whether this is about the more efficient deployment of public police on core activities, or a fundamental modification of the character, policy and practice of public policing is a question that requires urgent review.

The same issues arise again in relation to the recently proposed reconstruction of police committees and the recommendations of the Sheehy Report. Is the more business-like committee structure, and the related proposals on structure, pay and conditions a way of improving efficiency or a modification of the police mandate to whatever specific emphasis the Home Office wishes at any point in time, and the modification of performance requirements to those that can be measured as a basis for pay and contract renewal? As Waddington has noted :

> Instead of doing those things that reassure victims of crimes - arriving quickly, taking statements, conducting forensic examinations - a cost effective police force will tell them to clear up the mess and impose an administrative charge for reporting the burglary for insurance purposes.

How do we measure reassurance, re-establish a sense of security?

Again the danger is that an arbitrary core-ancillary distinction is drawn on the basis of the measurable and the non-measurable aspects of policing, with the non-measurable becoming secondary. A similar concern follows from VFM studies and the adoption of the 'performance matrix' in policing. The indicators adopted implicitly define what public policing is 'really about', even if this covers only limited aspects of the legal and social mandate of contemporary police forces.

The above analysis in no sense denies the view that the public police force cannot do everything, and that resources will always be limited (Dance, 1990). Nor would it challenge the view that a partnership has always necessarily existed between public police and private interests (Mason, 1991) - police advocacy of private physical crime prevention and sponsorship of neighbourhood watch schemes indicate this. What it does question is allowing the definition of core police duties to be driven solely by cost consideration and resource constraint and without reference to questions of equity, impartiality and accountability in law enforcement and community protection. The fundamental danger is that we end up with a two-tier system, with those, corporate or individual, who are able and willing to pay receiving better service and protection than those dependent on the public service, with disadvantaged and deprived communities most in need almost certainly falling into the latter category. If this would be unacceptable as explicit policy, it should also be unacceptable as the consequence of cost containment and budgetary constraint.

A second issue is the paradox inherent in the way police privatization has proceeded in the UK. Privatization implies markets and decentralized decision-making (Pirie, 1993), yet quite the opposite has applied in this case. Initiatives such as civilianization and CCT have been required by central government not voluntarily adopted by local police committees and forces. Extensions of CCT following the 'Competing for Quality' paper will also be statutorily required. As 50 per cent of police funding is directly provided by the Home Office/Scottish Office and a further 20 per cent comes through the revenue support grant system, local forces have little power to resist central requirements. The adoption of the proposals for streamlining police committees, and the recommendations of Sheehy, would greatly increase the centralization of policing. As Waddington argues :

> Limiting the size of police committees to 16, reducing local representation to a half, who will have precious little influence even over the budget, will seal the process of centralization.

Furthermore :

> The Sheehy recommendations further extend central control in the name of managerial efficiency and flexibility. Denied a "job for life", officers of all ranks, but especially those in senior positions, will be beholden to the Home Office for the renewal of their contracts. Careers and remuneration will depend on the achievement of "performance indicators" set by the Home Office. This will enable the Home Office to set policy by remote control (Waddington, 1993).

Again, in terms of accountability, a core-ancillary distinction is being drawn, with accountability to central government being core, and to the local community ancillary. This fundamentally modifies police-community relations and redefines the concept of 'policing by consent' as policing by central consent. There may be an arguable case for such centralization, even for a single national force controlled by central government, but it should be explicitly argued for as policy, not disguized as business-like management reform.

Finally, in the spirit of the 'privatization mentality' itself, the evaluation of privatization should be on a balance sheet basis, examining costs as well as benefits. To date, abstracted data on savings have been produced without any reference to the costs of those savings in terms of managerial time, dislocation and force morale. How much has it cost to establish, specify, monitor and review contract systems. What have been the financial and performance costs of the very high turnover amongst civilian staff? (Johnston, 1992) What has been the value for money of VFM studies?

What are the costs of centralization on local accountability and policy community relations? At present, privatization initiatives proceed apace without any detailed review of the impact of earlier initiatives, which scarcely seems business-like management. This is not an argument against change, but an argument against a flood of discrete unintegrated and largely unevaluated initiatives, at least in cost/benefit terms.

Conclusion : where do we go from here?

In this chapter we have demonstrated that a variety of concepts of 'privatization' would legitimately apply to initiatives to change and reform the police service over the last ten years. We have not argued for or against such initiatives per se, but rather argued that they have tacitly redefined policing, police work and police performance without explicit debate or consultation. The core-ancillary distinctions underpinning privatization are at minimum questionable and at worst such that they would never survive explicit policy discussion. As we approach the millennium, the questions become *'how do we secure forms of law enforcement, property and community protection appropriate for the next century?'*, and *'what is the role and function of public policing within that?'* These questions need to be addressed in a principled way and in the round, not by a selective focus on privatization or management reform in isolation.

Our view is that the time is ripe for a Royal Commission on the future of the public police service. This Commission should be charged with reviewing and redefining the role and function of the public policy force for the next century, specifically with reference to the core-ancillary distinction and the principles that inform it. This should include consideration of the balance of public and private activity desirable in property and community protection, and the forms of regulation and accountability pertaining to both. Within the public service, it should explicitly consider the role and extent of civilianization and privatization of service delivery possible and desirable, and thus define the core role of public police officers. Within the framework established by the conclusions of these enquiries, it should subsequently consider appropriate structures, management approaches, and reward systems to achieve the role and objectives of public policing. Finally, it should review issues of performance and accountability in that light.

The alternative to such a commission is alarming: creeping privatization, driven by resource constraints, based on core-ancillary distinctions that are arbitrary, implicit, and unrelated to policy, and increased dependency on an unregulated private industry as a response to the perceived limitations and resource constraints of the public service. If what is ultimately sought is an equitable, impartial and properly accountable system of law enforcement and community protection a fundamental review of the ad hoc, often opportunistic, innovations of the last fifteen years and a clear restatement of the principles and role of public policing are urgently needed.

Only a body with the status, resources, and independence of a Royal Commission is likely to achieve this.

References

Audit Commission (1988), *Footing the Bill: Financing the Provincial Police Forces*, Audit Commission Police Papers, No 5.

Audit Commission (1990a), *Taking Care of the Coppers : Income Generation by Provincial Police Forces*, Audit Commission Police Papers, No 7.

Audit Commission (1990b), *Effective Policing - Performance Review in Police Forces*, Audit Commission Police Papers, No 8.

Audit Commission (1991), *Reviewing the Organization of Provincial Police Forces*, Audit Commission Police Paper, No 9.

Bailey, S. and Lynn, G. (1989), *The Private Security Industry - Towards 1992*, Northumbria Police.

Boothroyd, J. (1989), 'Nibbling away at the bobbies patch', *Police Review*, pp. 64-65.

Buchanan, J.M. (1986), *Liberty, Market and the State*, Brighton : Wheatsheaf.

Carter, N. (1991), 'Learning to Measure Performance : the use of indicators within organizations', *Public Administration*, Vol 69 No 1.

Dance, O.R. (1990), 'To what extent could or should Policing be privatized?', *Police Journal*, Vol. LXIII, No. 4, pp. 288-293.

Eastwood, A. (1989), 'Put another record on', *Police Review*, pp. 9-10.

Economist (1990), 'An old force on a new beat', 10th Feb, pp. 27-38.

George, B. and Watson, T., (1992), 'Regulation of the Private Security Industry', *Public Money and Management*, Vol. 12, No. 1., pp. 55-57.

Home Office (1993), *The Government's Proposals for the Police Service in England and Wales*, London : HMSO, CM 2281.

Home Office (1993), *Inquiry into Police Responsibilities and Rewards*, London : HMSO, CM 2280.1

Johnston, L. (1992), *The Rebirth of Private Policing*, London : Routledge.

Lane, J.E. (1992), *The Public Sector*, London : Sage.

McLean, A. (1990), 'Private Coppers Saving Pounds', *Police Review*, pp. 2016-2017.

Mason, C. (1991), *Private and Public Policing : improving the service to the public through co-operation*, Brookfield Paper, No 6.

Mueller, D. (1979), *Public Choice*, Cambridge : Cambridge University Press.

National Audit Office (1991), *Promoting Value for Money in Provincial Police Forces : Report by the Comptroller and Auditor General*, London : National Audit Office.

Pirie, M. (1993), 'Police Plc?', *Police*, Vol xxv, pp. 12-14.

Waddington, P.J. (1993), 'The case of the hidden agenda', *Guardian*, 1st July.

Wertheimer, R. (1975), 'Are the Police Necessary?' in Viano C. and Reiman, J.M. (eds), *The Police in Society*, Mass : Lexington Books.

10 Franchise operations, competition and consumer welfare: The privatization of British Rail passenger services

Charles C Okeahalam

Introduction

Some of the literature on privatization; for example, Vickers and Yarrow (1988) and Vickers and Yarrow (1991) identifies three major types of privatization. Firstly, the privatization of competitive firms, i.e. the transfer to the public sector of firms operating within competitive product markets with low market failure. Secondly, the privatization of monopolies, i.e. the transfer to the private sector of firms with significant market power and third, the contracting out of public services to the private sector.

What are the prospects for British Rail? The first step is to decide on the objectives and type of programme to pursue. When privatization via state asset disposal takes place the government has to decide what the objective of the exercise is. The objective might be to dispose of a loss making enterprise to reduce the negative impact on tax payers. On the other hand it might be to place government managed concerns within a true market environment without government subsidy, and in so doing increase efficiency and potentially, ex ante financial rates of return in a competitive market environment or to improve the quality of management via the market for corporate control.

Although reference is often made by some writers (e.g. Pirie (1990)) to the experience, and by all indications relative success, of privatization it should be obvious that such results are the occasion not the rule; and that the results of any privatization policy may not be the same. The empirical issues at work are much too numerous and diverse for there to be a homogenous 'optimal' privatization policy.[1] Privatization policy will then be, as it should be, determined by the problems which it seeks to address and by the environment within which it is being implemented. For example, (on the contentious premise- to be touched upon later in this paper- that privatization would improve efficiency and generate higher revenues) a government may undertake privatization of an inefficient monopolistic state-owned company. It might also choose to minimize the probability of market failure and loss of the benefits of the market mechanism such as higher rents and revenues. If the objective of the privatization is to maximize revenue from the disposal of the utility then the social cost of government intervention, i.e.; the impact of government failure will reduce the financial returns. If however a flotation is carried out which maximizes the revenue explanatory variable in the governments public asset disposal utility function (at a cost no doubt to the welfare variables) then some provision must be allowed to address this issue.

There is agreement- see Hartley, Parker, and Martin (1991); Vickers and Yarrow (1991), and Parker (1992) - that the nominal change of ownership does not in itself guarantee increased performance. What appears to be important is the impact that the movement to the private sector will have on rail operations provided by the new franchises.

Furthermore where there is a change of ownership from the public to the private sector, if government has to continue to play a major role within the organization or the regulatory environment within which the firm operates in, then the actual difference which privatization may make is limited. The paradox is that government need not intervene in truly competitive markets unless there are obvious signs of market failure. Government intervention in the form of regulation will only be necessary where government has privatized a corporation which is likely to generate market failure. This is likely to be the case with British Rail. Yet in itself the initial privatization of a monopoly supplier is evidence of government failure. The need for strong regulation is a manifestation of this fact. Without competition rail transport market failure would continue to be present irrespective of the transfer of ownership from the government to franchise operators.

Privatization policy for British Rail

Hopefully one of the central points that should have emanated from the above discussion so far is that determining the exact nature of appropriate privatization policy is difficult, best practice changes from industry to industry, and should be influenced by the underlying objective behind the particular privatization process.

But it is necessary to state at the onset that the type of, and use of rail privatization policy should be seen as part of an overall strategic plan to improve the performance of rail services in the UK. Furthermore privatization affects many different issues. With the above in mind three important factors that should be considered in the privatization process of British Rail are identified for further discussion in this paper. They are as follows:

a) The difficulty of calculating and creating appropriate financial incentives for private sector interest;
b) The impact of private sector entry on efficiency and competition; and
c) the impact on fares and service quality.

Railway economics and difficulties of the government railways franchise programme

There are three facts which should be borne in mind in any discussion of the economics of railways. Firstly, there are positive effects of economies of scale on rail services. Higher passenger miles per train mile implies higher revenues in relation to costs and lower net losses per train mile. It may not necessarily imply lower net losses per passenger mile. Secondly, fixed costs in railway operations are high. Financial returns in the short run are therefore usually higher if the decision to incur these costs is delayed and average costs of operation do not decline infinitely. As a result of the above, the third factor is that there are at least two methods of measuring the financial performance of the passenger services of British Rail (e.g. InterCity); the proportion of expenses which are covered by revenues, and net loss per passenger mile.

Uncertainty in the franchise scheme

With the above in mind it appears that there is no exact principle as to how the franchising scheme for passenger services is expected to work. Indeed the white paper 'New Opportunities for Railways - The Privatization of British Rail' -has statements in it which might lead one to reasonably conclude that the government is still not sure as to how to price, or structure the franchise contracts - see paragraph 26 of the White Paper. Furthermore there will be no universal template for a franchise contract indeed the White

Paper states that;

> There will be no standard duration for franchise contracts.' Yet further paragraph 36 states that ' The precise manner in which InterCity services will be franchized will have to be decided in the light of private sector interest ...

The only clue of substance is that the Government's general intention is to franchise the routes and services on a line or route basis, e.g. the East Coast Main Line. In principle the White Paper proposes to divide British Rail into 25-30 separate franchises. The private sector will be invited to bid for franchises to operate passenger services. To reduce the probability of bids focusing concentrating on profitable routes (sometimes referred to as cherry picking) loss-making lines will receive government subsidies.

Possible private sector evaluations

While the government appears confused, the private sector is probably more certain of the role and opportunities that may arise. So it is not unreasonable to assume that the prime motivation for private sector investment in railway operations is financial gain. This might be in the form of profits or it may be in the form of revenue. There may also be strategic reasons such as growth and (horizontal and vertical) integration which might provide an incentive for franchise investment.

But what will the private sector consider of interest in operating railway franchises on a route or line basis? Given that there is considerable uncertainty on the part of government it would seem reasonable that the prime private sector considerations will be; firstly, the contribution to their asset value of the franchise investment, and secondly the level of expected returns achievable. This will be used to compare the opportunity cost of investing in a passenger route or service franchise, given the existence of other potential investment. But the private sector is only likely to bid for the franchises if the financial costs are slanted more in its favour (than espoused at present) at increased cost to the Exchequer. This same point has been made in a different context by Gomez-Ibanez *et al.* (1991). Furthermore some routes are not contestable (Baumol, 1982). Since subsidies will be payable to franchises which operate less profitable routes it may be sound private sector strategy not to bid for apparently 'profitable' routes given the opportunity cost of capital employed, but to bid for subsidized routes, or delay their bids to a later point in time; in the hope that they can benefit from a distress sale or discount price for the franchise. This strategy is dependent on the size of subsidy to be made available (as of yet undisclosed) and the asset value and expected residual value of the assets that come with the franchise. However given the economics of railway traction (see Majumdar (1985) for further details) this might only be best determined by experiences gained from the first series of franchises.

Yet further Nice (1991) has shown that there is a short run financial profit incentive to delay capital expenditure in railway infrastructure. This is an important point because the government is attempting to sell franchises to operators primarily motivated by the desire to make a profit on the franchises which they purchase. This raises a variety of questions. To what extent are the operators aware of the capital expenditure requirements necessary to make their franchise profitable? To what extent are they driven by short run considerations? Will they be able to sell their franchises on? Will the government realize anything like the true asset value for British Rail passenger services ? Is the government better-off improving the value of the rolling stock and assets of passenger services in the belief that the new market it creates will enable it to realize the full financial return on investment; or is it better-off reducing the overall level of investment in rail infrastructure in the hope that the operators will take on the franchises as they are and generate their own investment?

Costs of restructuring and subsidies

It could be argued that the Government is not 'privatizing' the railways but is restructuring railway services and therefore what is actually being planned is 'semi-privatization'. Yet restructuring the railways is complex and the existence of government subsidies does not make it easier.

There has been speculation (particularly by the pressure group Transport 2000) that to restructure the service and account for the removal of government subsidies will lead to an aggregate fare increase of 18.5 per cent. On top of that there are the huge costs of the bureaucracy of the regulatory body- Railtrack, which will have to cope with the formation of more than 80 new companies. As a result it is difficult to estimate the true overall cost-benefit of privatizing British Rail passenger services.

Furthermore the private sector has not been provided with the type of information which might enable potential operators to bid effectively for a particular franchise;[2] and although it is not difficult to establish which routes or services are the lemons in the bunch, the use of shadow franchises (as proposed by the White Paper) does not help much since they are likely to be managed by ex-British Rail employees aware of the operational difficulties on particular routes, at certain stations, and with various make of rolling stock type etc.[3]

A Transport 2000 study also suggests that even if government subsidy were held constant then the net effect of privatization would be an approximate £498 million or 14.9 per cent reduction in the financial revenue of British Rail. In addition there is likely to be an increase on premiums for train operator insurance (see Ignarski, 1992)[4], safety, leasing facilities and legal arrangements. On the plus side the major likely benefit is that there might be savings in overall track maintenance and operating costs[5] and the private rail sector might, through skilful marketing, develop increased total transport market share.

Efficiency

The second major area of British Rail privatization which this paper addresses is to do with efficiency. Vickers and Yarrow (1988) have suggested that privatization of public sector organizations such as British Rail might increase efficiency and Pirie (1990) suggests that this increase in industrial efficiency may be realized by an increase in worker commitment.[6]

However others (e.g. Parker and Hartley, and Parker (1992)) argue that a plethora of cumulatively significant factors may impact on the success or failure of privatization when measured on an efficiency criteria. This is particularly so when the incentive to increase efficiency, through the introduction of competition is lacking or in this instance improperly planned. It is also very relevant when the organization is a large monopoly supplier of services such as British Rail[7] with high capital intensive products, and by definition high market entry costs. Indeed while the rigours of the market may make the operational environment more dynamic, there is debate as to the exact impact privatization will have on the efficiency of rail operations. Furthermore the problems of identifying and differentiating the exact effects on performance of change in ownership and competitive market conditions is well illustrated by Pryke (1982). This will have to be examined carefully particularly because franchise operators are likely to operate in different market conditions and face different levels of competition.

Indeed, De Fraja (1991) has shown that the privatization of a broadly inefficient public sector enterprise such as BR into an oligopoly market can have an adverse welfare effect. The argument is that entry by an inefficient (social service motivated) public enterprise such as British Rail into an oligopoly private sector profit maximizing industry such as passenger transport may reduce the profit of the market incumbents.[8]

This would contradict some of the earlier efficiency arguments and as Parker (1992) suggests is at odds with the hype which privatization has been accorded in political economy. It also has implications for British Rail privatization. Firstly, it may reduce the incentive for transport entrepreneurs (who might in some cases already be employees of British Rail) to put capital at risk. The skills of these operators should not be overlooked and getting full employee participation may make the vital difference since margins are likely to be very tight. Secondly, it shows that total welfare will be reduced by the short-run reduction in industry profit combined with the relatively more long-run reduction in consumer choice. Since the equilibrium market price achieved would be the result of quasi-competitive market interaction the true welfare optimum would be actually achieved if this were the outcome of full competition or as close to this as possible.[9]

Competition and regulation

A well managed privatization programme can be effective as a method of revenue generation. Although a relatively banal point it is worth noting that monopolies are worth more all things equal than competitive industry firms. Consequently a government concerned with maximizing the revenue derived from the sale of public assets is unlikely to implement competitive liberalizing policy at the same time. Some of the evidence from the earlier privatization in UK is fairly instructive. This is the reasoning that led to the disposal of British Telecom and British Gas as monopolies. Yet Kay and Thompson (1986) put it like this;

> If as we have argued the privatization of large dominant firms is at best pointless and possibly harmful in the absence of effective competition, the result is that no benefits to economic performance are likely to be achieved. Privatization of this type would not be the first ineffectual restructuring of relationships between government and the nationalized industries ....it is potentially more damaging than the others because privatization makes it more difficult to introduce competitive incentives in the future.

More information to ensure effective competition

Yet the present government has always maintained that the privatization policy it has chosen for British Rail is that which realizes for the taxpayer the most reasonable value for the assets of British Rail and which at the same time allows it to reduce dependence for investment on the public sector and the impact of financing constraints. However the exact nature of the rights and obligations of the franchisees is still unclear. What will different franchise operators have to pay for the right to use the track infrastructure. Who will have responsibility for maintaining the track? Nominally this would be Railtrack. But how will track costs be evaluated since some track infrastructure is of a newer vintage than others, and as such, is less likely to be subject to failure.

If the government is interested in effective economic railway service management it has to ensure that there is a level playing field and equal opportunity for all franchise bidders to use their entrepreneurial skills to provide the necessary level of service to the consumer and dividends to their investors. A failure to do this might lead to financial instability and bankruptcy of some franchise operators and will greatly affect the quality of service on some routes. The rate of potential entry by franchise operators will decline. The rate of entry is then only likely to rise if demands for higher levels of government subsidy, lower rates of payment to Railtrack for railway infrastructure and other concessions are met.

Marsh (1991) and Fenn and Veljanovski (1989) suggest that the best way to overcome this problem is not through draconian regulation but by ensuring the presence of competition. Of course this will be easier to achieve where cost of entry is low. By definition this is more difficult in capital intensive industries such as railways, with high sunk costs. With this in mind the government is therefore to be commended; in that by separating the high capital costs involved in track infrastructure from the variable costs of operating rail services it has reduced one of the major barriers to entry. Yet it still has the problem of ensuring there is a sufficient level of competition; reducing entry barriers for potential franchise operators may not be enough.[10]

Franchise operators will have to be fairly convinced that Railtrack's commitment to maintain the espoused charging and regulatory policy as set out at the time of investment will be guaranteed at least in the short run; i.e. for more than the seven years which the government feels is the appropriate length of time for a franchise. This will be conditioned by a range of factors. Firstly, franchise operators have to have reasonable expectations of the probability of re-nationalization in the event of a change in government or policy. Secondly, while the probability of regulatory failure is less likely in industries with competitive contestable markets it is up to the government and Railtrack to ensure that the industry is truly contestable. In this regard the government's hands are fairly well tied since attracting franchise operators will not be easy unless they are given the opportunity and sufficient time to make a reasonable return on their investment.

A profitable or potentially profitable passenger service, such as InterCity; is likely to be evaluated at premium by franchisees. However monopolistic profitability is perceived differently when it takes place in the public sector and profits accrue to the government exchequer, than when the profits accrue to private franchise operators. Both profits are achieved at cost to the consumer.[11] Yet profit should be a composite of the welfare function of both the public and private sector; indeed the welfare function is not fully maximized without profits. Nevertheless there is strong probability that consumers will campaign vigorously against the new transport rail service operators if they believe that they are deriving monopoly profits.

The extent to which the cost of capital dictates the level of expected returns necessary for potential franchise operators to participate cannot be overlooked. This will not be intra-industry homogenous. Various routes and services have their own particular costs and price limits.

Unless the franchise operators self-finance for example, National Express Coaches is interested in the Victoria-Gatwick (Gatwick Airport Express) service they are likely to encounter high financing and leasing costs unless the government gives potential creditors clearer guidelines with which to be able to evaluate projected income streams e.g. Railtrack track infrastructure charging structures and the specific length of time of each franchise. This applies particularly to bids for subsidized routes; where size and payment arrangements of subsidies will be evaluated keenly by creditors. Potential financiers are unlikely to participate unless their risks are underwritten or diversified away. It would therefore appear, at least on face value, that there is still a role for government to play. Government has to decide whether or not to hold on to the loss making passenger services and routes. Yet if it does so, there is likely to be difficulty in explaining the policy. It may be argued that government has simply sold the most profitable parts of the railway to the private operators and for political reasons is using the tax payers funds to continue subsidizing the loss making routes and services. As a result selecting the routes and services to stay open and those to be closed may in the end be more of a political than economic decision.[12]

The regulatory contract and service quality.

So in truth the government has to compare the cost (via fiscal measures, differential rates of tax for start-up franchises, other transport companies etc.) of providing true competition with the social welfare costs of the consumer. Although high levels of profitability or prices are not in themselves pure evidence of monopolistic or lack of competitive behaviour they are often referred to when discussions of consumer welfare take place.

An example of this can be derived from the experience of Network South-East. There has been much debate on methods to improve service quality on Network South-East. (For example, see Okeahalam (1994)). The main constraint is that this requires higher capital investment. To overcome this problem the government implicitly agreed that price controls would be such that it allowed for returns on new track and other railway related infrastructure investment to be made. In effect, as Vickers and Yarrow (1991) put it, 'regulatory contracts' were struck with Network South-East to enable it to obtain infrastructure finance via price increases.[13] However after privatization, the railway franchise companies will have to make different levels of investment (in leased rolling stock etc.) to achieve acceptable standards of service. Those that have to invest the most to meet the required service standards are not necessarily those that have the largest revenue, number of passengers, or highest mean unit financial return per passenger. So the regulatory contract may create price differentials and further muddy the consumer welfare price argument as it becomes easier for the franchise companies to explain price rises with the cost of improving service quality to meet regulatory standards. Those that can not meet the standards even with subsidy will withdraw and as explained by Stafford (1993) their exit may create financial instability. Furthermore marginal improvements in service quality might not compensate for marginal price increases and intra-industry price/quality increases will not be linear.

Railtrack regulation or market failure

However there is a problem of government failure and the role of Railtrack bureaucrats. If government plays a significant role in underwriting the financing or subsidizing of the franchises then there is the possibility that a bureaucratic or political agenda may interfere with optimal private sector management decision making. The bureaucrats' individual utility function may begin to override the optimal market derived social welfare function, i.e. a form of government failure may develop. Furthermore what might the effect of government subsidies on the loss making services have on the distinction in ownership of the firm? This question is important because earlier research (Parker and Hartley (1991) and Hartley, Parker, and Martin (1991)) has shown that nominal change in ownership is unimportant. What appears to be most important vis-a-vis this issue is the perceived allocation of risk and ultimate managerial control.

Overt government intervention (government failure) in the provision of direct or indirect subsidy to the franchises may muddy the ownership distinction.[14] But there is a problem of market failure. Two forms come to mind. Firstly, the price of the franchises are so high and the perceived potential returns so low; that very few operators actually participate in the bidding process, and if they do their interest ends at the profitable services. Secondly, where the market price and financing (for those not equity financing) is such that the institutions play a bigger role in the financing of the franchises than the operators. Even if the franchise operators are the majority shareholders there is the difficulty that a significant group of shareholders do not take the same view with regard to the management of the company. This type of division may decrease the hypothesized benefits such as motivation, increased efficiency productivity and profits which this form of privatization is hypothesized to bring. There may therefore be a temptation for the mispricing of some of the franchises to ensure the success of the overall privatization scheme. Menyah, Paudyal, and Inyangete (1990) illustrate that this form of mispricing has occurred in earlier privatization schemes - particularly where this has involved share flotations. Brittan (1986) has suggested that this was carried out to achieve not only financial objectives of the transfer of ownership but also political objectives. In any event, apart from the issue of who pays for the difference between the market price and the socially optimal privatization value there is the problem of deciding on how to reach the appropriate price valuation for the service franchises. Sophisticated differential pricing will be needed to resolve this issue. See Meirnadus and Walz (1991). However even such methodology will not answer the following type of questions. What will the financial cost be of discounting the franchise price to existing British Rail management and employees interested in bidding for routes and services? Will the governments financial losses be covered by efficiency gains on routes and services ?

We should also recall that for the government, the privatization of parts of British Rail is akin to the selling of equity. Since the actual railway assets are not going to be sold then the government objective is to attempt to establish the net present value of revenue that would be derived from British

Rail operating a particular route or service in comparison to the revenues derived from leasing the rights to operate the route to the franchise operator plus fee income to, and costs of Railtrack. Irrespective of the accounting method used this does not help in deciding on what discount rate to use to price the franchises prior to privatization. However, if government gets this calculation wrong, it leaves itself open to the criticism that the railways have been privatized for dogmatic rather than economic reasons. [15]

Service quality

Firstly, franchise operator strategic and operational decision making will affect consumer quality of rail transport. The quality of decisions taken will be dependent on the ability of the operators to evaluate the market efficiently.

Secondly, there may be indirect costs to passengers as a result of the changes in the national network. Typically on British Rail passenger services, the average price per mile decreases as the origin-destination distance increases. The London-York-Scarborough line serves as a good example. At it's origin it is an InterCity service but after York it comes under the control of Regional Railways. A through ticket to Scarborough costs less than the total price of the two parts of the trip. Deciding the correct prices to charge consumers for such services after privatization will not be easy because the franchise operator on the York-Scarborough service is unlikely to agree to less than the market price for its part of the service. This will not be helped by the proposed reduction in subsidies.

Since rail passenger demand is fairly price elastic increases in fares may not lead to increases in franchise operator revenues and as a result dramatic fare increases are unlikely. However franchise operators may try to minimize costs by operating skeletal services, or only services which have synergy with their existing transport products. This would reduce consumer choice.

Service quality will also be influenced by the particularities and industry practices of the new operators. Given that the level of entry and type of private sector entrants is unknown, it is at best conjecture, vis-a-vis the nature and direct impact these practices may have on passenger service quality experiences.

Conclusions

Establishing a framework with which to effectively introduce private sector investment and management into British Rail is complicated. The method which the government has opted for is likely to increase the complexity of the privatization process. Furthermore short-term financial gain to government is likely to be greater if British Rail were to be privatized in a stepwise manner as a whole. However this would have had to be offset by greater long-run price regulation costs.

Yet the overall hypothesized private sector benefits e.g. (increased efficiency, productivity, etc.) may not cover the social costs (the choice of potential increases in fares/or closure of some services and routes) and may be less than the costs of regulating the franchise operators and subsidizing routes which the private sector would otherwise not bid for.

The experience from earlier privatization has illustrated the need to ensure adequate competition so as to reduce potential welfare costs to consumers. In this regard the government has to be more specific, and has to provide greater guidelines to potential rail transport market entrants. Nevertheless the experience from earlier privatization (particularly British Telecom) has also illustrated that greater private sector management input can have a beneficial impact on service quality.

Finally, earlier on it was suggested that privatization should be seen as part of an overall strategic plan to improve British Rails performance. Accordingly the true acid test should come from a transport policy perspective based on whether privatization will lead to greater utilization of passenger railway services (particularly by commuters), reduce the demand for private car travel, and reduce the environmental costs of transport. (See Appendix 1). Given this, the issue is not whether or not; the government should attempt to increase the efficiency, productivity and quality of British Rail passenger services; but whether it is doing this in the correct manner.

References

Baumol, W. J., (1982), Contestable Markets: An Uprising in the Theory of Industry Structure, *American Economic Review,* Vol. 72, pp.1-16.

Brittan, S., (1986), Privatization: A Comment on Kay and Thompson, *Economic Journal,* Vol. 96, March, pp. 33-38.

Buckland, R., (1987), The Costs and Returns of the Privatization of Nationalized Industries, *Public Administration,* pp. 241-257.

Button, K.J., and Keeler, T.E, (1993), The Regulation of Transport Markets, *Economic Journal,* Vol. 103, pp.1017-1027.

De Fraja, G., Efficiency and Privatization in Imperfectly Competitive Industries, *Journal of Industrial Economics,* Vol. XXXIX, No.3 March, pp.311-321.

Fenn, P. and Veljanovski, C.G. (1988), A Positive Economic Theory of Regulatory Enforcement, *Economic Journal,* Vol. 98, No. 393, pp.1055-1071.

Gomez-Ibanez, J.A ., Meyer, J.R., and Luberoff, D.E., (1991), The prospects for Privatising Infrastructure, *Journal of Transport Economics and Policy,* Vol. 25, 3 pp.259 -278.

Hartley, K., Parker, D., and Martin, S., Organizational Status, Ownership and Productivity, *Fiscal Studies,* Vol. 12, No. 2, May 1991, pp.46-60.

Haskel, J., and Szymanski, S., (1992), Privatization, Liberalization, Wages and Employment: Theory and Evidence for the UK, *Economica,* Vol. 60, pp.161-181.

HMSO Department of Transport (1992), 'New Opportunities in the Railways', *The Privatization of British Rail.*

Ignarski, J., (1992), The Privatization of British Rail - A Unique Organization Will Make Demands on the Insurance Industry, *Journal of the Institute of Risk Management*, pp.7-11.

Jenkins, H., (1993), 'Oh ! Mister Porter , What Shall I do ?' *The Comedy of Misdirection and the Prospects for Railways after Privatization,* Inaugural Lecture as Professor of Transport Management, University of Salford, May.

Kamien, M.I. and Oren, S.S., and Taumen, Y. (1992), Optimal Licensing of Cost reducing Innovation, *Journal of Mathematical Economics*, Vol. 21, No. 5, pp.483-492.

Kay, J.A., and Thompson, D.J., (1986), 'Privatization: A Policy in Search of Rationale', *Economic Journal,* 96, pp.18-32.

Kazuhiko, O., (1991), A note on Terminal Date Security Prices in a Continuous Time Trading Model with Dividends, *Journal of Mathematical Economics,* Vol. 20, pp.219-223.

Majumdar, J., (1985), *The Economics of Railway Traction,* Gower Publishers.

Marsh, D., 'Privatization under Mrs Thatcher: A Review of the Literature', *Public Administration,* 69, Winter pp.459-480.

Menyah, K., Paudyal, K.N., and Inyangete, C.G., (1990), 'The Pricing of Initial Offerings of Privatized Companies on the London Stock Exchange', *Accounting and Business Research,* 21 , pp.50-56.

Meirnadus, G., and Waltz, G., (1991), 'On the Zeros of Gauchy Polynomials with Application to Optimal Depreciation', *Journal of Mathematical Economics,* Vol. 21, No. 4 pp.343-346.

Nice, D.C., (1991), 'Financial Performance of the Amtrak System', *Public Administration Review,* March- April, Vol. 51, No. 2, pp.138-144.

Okeahalam C.C., (1994), An Econometric Analysis of Perceptions of Service Quality in British Rail Network South-East. Forthcoming in *International Journal of Service Management.*

Parker, D., (1992), 'Agency Status Privatization and Improved Performance: Some Evidence from the UK', *International Journal of Public Sector Management,* Vol. 5, No. 1, pp.30-38.

Parker, D. and Hartley, D., (1991), 'Do Changes in Organizational Status Affect Financial Performance?', *Strategic Management Journal,* Vol. 12, No. 8, pp.631-641.

Pirie, M., (1990), (ed. Yul-Kwon, O.), 'Principles and Techniques of Privatization' in *International Privatization Global Trends, Policies, Processes, and Experiences.*

Pryke, R., (1982), 'The Comparative Performance of Public and Private Enterprise', Fiscal Studies, Vol. 3.

Sen, A.K., (1987), *On Ethics & Economics,* Basil Blackwell.

Stafford, L., (1993), 'Rail Privatization: Efficiency, Quality and the Consumer', *Consumer Policy Review,* pp.17-21, January.

Vickers, J., and Yarrow, G., (1988), *Privatization: An Economic Analysis,* Cambridge MIT Press.

Vickers, J., and Yarrow, G., (1991), 'Economic Perspectives on Privatization', *Journal of Economic Perspectives,* Vol. 5, No. 2, pp.111-132.

Vind, K., (1991), 'Independent Preferences', *Journal of Mathematical Economics,* Vol. 20, No. 1, pp.119-126.

Appendix 1

Table 1 below illustrates the fact that in 1990, of the European countries analysed, the UK had on average the most expensive rail ticket prices. British Rail also received the lowest level of per capita subsidy (£12) and the second lowest amount of subsidy (£683 million). The UK also had the second highest level of $C0_2$ emissions (10.5 tonnes per capita) and British Rail provided the second lowest per capita level of rail journeys (13). Although this was better than the situation in Italy where the total level of subsidy and per capita level of subsidy is highest and rail travel is cheapest, but the number of rail journeys per capita is also the lowest, from a transport policy perspective privatization of British Rail passenger services could still be considered a failure if it does not lead to an increase in the average number of train journeys and rail travel in the UK.

Table 1. Rail transport : A comparison of the UK with some other countries.

	Belgium	France	Germany	Italy	Netherlands	UK
Per Capita No. of Rail Journeys	15	14	18	8	22	13
Cost of 60 mile standard single ticket - £	6.80	9.95	9.60	3.30	8.40	11.90
Per capita level of rail subsidy-£	80	58	60	107	31	12
Total rail subsidy -£ millions	788	3422	3960	6276	510	683
Environmental impact -$C0_2$ emissions tonnes per capita	8.7	7.1	11.7	6.9	9.8	10.5

Source: Railway Gazette 1991 and International Railways Association Publications 1991.

Notes

1. In theory it might be possible to evaluate the decision to privatize or not to privatize a particular public sector company or group of companies. This could be tested empirically with the use of econometric methods.

One way to do this may be to hypothesize that the decision to privatize is a discrete i.e. non-continuous (0 or 1) choice dependent variable which is determined by the coefficient values of a vector of explanatory variables. The parameter values of the coefficients might be considered to influence the decision to privatize or not to privatize. A model derived from the summation of these values might cover a variety of functional forms determined by a variety of probability distributions for the random disturbances conditioned by the characteristics of the chooser (government) leading to conditional random utility maximization logit or probit models of the decision to privatize.

2 In theory it is also possible to analyse the potential profitability and behaviour of franchises. For simplicity it could be assumed that as in all auctions; there is a minimum reserve price for the rail service route franchises. This minimum acceptable government reserve price for a route would be determined by the level of past revenue and profitability on a particular route. The relationship between the reserve price and operator franchise offer could be seen as a form of game; as in Kamien *et al.* (1992), Meirnadus and Waltz (1991), Vind (1991) and Kazuhiko (1991). This could be developed by using the number of observed passengers on routes; given some fare indicators, and frequency data, relative (cross-section of routes) and level of fixed and variable costs. As a result it might be possible to forecast the likely relative revenues and levels of profitability. It is accepted that at best the revenues/profitability calculated this way might only be shadow prices of true values. Nevertheless the relative differences in expected revenues derived from the above calibrations could enable a pricing structure for the franchises. To evaluate the extent to which a pricing mechanism can be used to reflect the potential risks/returns of operating particular rail franchises, a pricing mechanism can also be developed to evaluate the impact on, and differences in, potential operational risk, and liabilities of, potential franchise buyers of British Rail service and route franchises. Of particular interest would be an attempt to test the dynamics of the new rail operations by examining the extent to which the potential cost of services varies with the perceived riskiness of investment in particular BR franchise operations. This is interesting because although this might, to a limited extent, be consistent with contestable market theory (see Baumol 1982) it does not fit wholly with financial theory. This issue is also of importance because it may have significant structural

implications for the railway's long run service quality and efficiency in rail passenger services, and transport policy in general.

3 The government has introduced a system of shadow franchises to enable it to be able to get a track record of ex post rates of return. Accordingly there are shadow franchises in operation on the Gatwick express (London Victoria to Gatwick airport) route, which is acknowledged as one of the most profitable of BR passenger services. Three operators now serve this route. British Rail with a one way ticket price of £8.60 and BR South central and Thameslink with an identical one way ticket price of £7.30; for a slower service which stops at intermediate stations. The results of this experiment appear disappointing because the performance of the shadow franchises on the London Victoria to Gatwick route is providing evidence that; given the way the franchise agreement has been specified, it is going to be difficult to make adequate returns on the franchises. If franchise operators find it difficult to make adequate returns on the Gatwick express route, how will they perform on other routes ?

4 Ignarski (1993) notes that 'Those of us who insure carriers liability see a new market. In place of the huge BR monopoly there will be many smaller companies running their own freight operations - perhaps only a few trains a day over specific routes. BR, with it's enormous asset base and revenues running into billions has self-insured a large part of its risks, but this will not be appropriate for the new private sector operators....... It might be thought that the risk and liabilities arising out of railway operations are well known and easily quantifiable.........Yet the nature of the new style railway could significantly affect the liability position, and consequently insurance premium.'

5 This is likely, and there is evidence (Haskel and Szymanski, 1992) that in a bargaining model of the manager/workforce relation framework the level of industry employment is likely to fall when firms are privatized, markets liberalized or government objectives become more commercial.

6 Of course it is possible to argue this point from a different perspective. British Rail as a public sector service organization may not currently make as much profit as it might if it were to be transferred to the private sector, yet the true cost of consuming the services or products it produces may actually decrease consumer welfare by a greater extent. In other

words the lower level of profits of the public sector organization may not be price related, but may be a function of a lower level of efficiency. Given the service quality level, the financial price charged, even if it is nominally lower, may actually have a higher economic price. See Jenkins (1993) for more British Rail management of services and products.

7 It can be, and it is regularly argued that British Rail (BR) is operating in a competitive market due to the presence of coach operations, private motor cars and other transport modes. Yet the fact is that British Rail continues to be a monopoly supplier of rail transport. Competition purists would argue that it is in indirect competition with other forms of transport. However this overlooks the fact that because of subsidies on the majority of rail routes and services, the unit cost and therefore potential marginal price of rail transport on these routes is less than for other transport alternatives. This allows inefficient capacity in the passenger transport industry where the dominance of market supply by one producer distorts optimal passenger consumer choice and welfare. Furthermore, competitive advantage in land based travel increases for railways as origins and destinations increase.

8 It is assumed that firms in such an industry do not have profit levels which deviate substantially from the mean. The profits of the private transport sector are such that a slack exists. This slack can proxy a vector of variable costs which may, but are more likely not to be, directly related to output and may entail some form of managerial incentive to the workforce. However on entry and with its pricing policy the privatized franchisees supported by government subsidies will reduce this slack. So first the slack erodes followed by the profits. Exit of firms begins to take place as profits decline. The true level of consumer choice is reduced as transport firms exit. The transport firms that exit may have been fairly efficient but in the new competitive framework were unable to make adequate rates of return. In the short-run transport industry efficiency would increase. However in the long run transport industry structure output and market supply may then be left to operators which can best mimic the revenue maximizing marginal price strategy of the new rail franchise transport entrant. These may not be the most efficient firms. Since industry output is dominated by inefficient firms the overall efficiency of the industry will decline. For this argument to

hold more fully it is necessary to assume that the franchise operators do follow dissimilar market and corporate strategy and that they are capable of supplying greater output than other private sector competitors. It would then be possible to suggest that '....long run industry efficiency increases with privatisation if and only if the long run pre-privatization output of the public firm is lower than that of the private oligopolist.' De Fraja (1991). The marginal price may not cover fixed costs and in effect the newly privatized franchise railway firms will be running budget deficits. The current government intends to finance these deficits by providing subsidies. Yet other transport sector firms will suffer negative welfare effects as a result.

9 Sen (1987) page 34 has suggested that by relating the results of market equilibrium under perfect competition with Pareto optimality, under certain conditions such as the removal of externality i.e. the removal of inter-dependencies central to the market then every perfectly competitive equilibrium is Pareto optimal and with other restrictions such as the removal of large economies of scale) Pareto optimal social state is also a perfectly competitive equilibrium with respect to some set of prices (and for some initial distribution of people's endowments).

10 Button and Keeler (1993) note that ' One important issue in the working of transport markets is that of contestability. Evidence so far indicates strongly that actual competition is considerably more effective in reducing market power than is potential competition. But even those sceptical of the contestability of transport markets nevertheless find evidence that the market power of firms in these markets is no where strong enough to justify regulation.'

11 Of course it is possible to argue this point from a different perspective. British Rail as a public sector service supplier may not make as much net profit as it might if it were to be transferred to the private sector yet the true cost to the consumer of consuming the services or products which it produces may actually decrease consumer welfare by a greater extent. In other words the lower level of profits of the public sector firm may not be price related but may be a function of a lower level of efficiency. The quality of service level at the financial price charged even if it is nominally lower may actually have a higher economic price.

12 In this respect the government will be criticized no matter what decision

it takes.

13 A Transport 2000 report suggests that the option preferred by Network SouthEast was to raise the price of the all-zone London Travel card by 16.2 per cent, single fares by 12 per cent and season tickets by 7.9 per cent. For political reasons this was not acceptable.

14 This is like the general privatisation argument where it has been argued by some e.g. Vickers and Yarrow (1988) that the distinction between a highly regulated private company which has been transferred to the private sector and a public enterprise, i.e. one which is still publicly owned is in fact really a semantic difference. It is for this reason that the argument with regard to change or nominal change of ownership put forward by some e.g. Pirie (1990) is too simplistic. They have not fully explained what the social costs of market failure may be if and/or when private sector ownership is not socially optimal. Bearing in mind the politics of railway privatization it is also naive to argue, as free market theorists are prone to that the social costs are irrelevant since the market equilibrium in the distribution of ownership rights is the long run optima.

15 This may involve the underpricing of routes/services so that a larger number of franchise operators have a reasonable opportunity of participating in the bids, and the potential benefits of each franchise scheme may be evaluated. The highest financial bid may not be the best bid.

11 Improving management in Government? The creation of the executive agencies

Tom Clarke

Introduction

> All government work should have to pass five tests: 'Can it be abolished? Can it be privatized? Can it be contracted out? Can it be market tested? Can it be given agency status?' Stephen Dorrell, Financial Secretary to the Treasury, *Daily Telegraph,* 24 September 1993.

In 1988 Sir Robin Ibbs, who had replaced Lord Rayner as head of the Efficiency Unit presented a report to the Prime Minister, *Improving Management in Government: The Next Steps,* recommending that agencies be established to carry out the executive functions of government, within a policy and resources framework set by a department. The executive agencies would have their aims and targets outlined in framework agreements with the departments concerned. As William Waldegrave, Minister of Public Service and Science, explained in the December 1992 *Review* of the Next Step Agencies, the agency model involved taking an area of government work, 'the appointment of a chief executive with personal responsibility for success and the freedom to manage; setting of tough but realistic targets by Ministers; and effective monitoring of subsequent performance.' (1992:2)

Within four years the Next Steps agency programme swept through the civil service and by 1992 there were 76 Executive Agencies, with 30 Customs and Excise Executive Units and 34 Inland Revenue Executive Offices working on Next Steps lines. Between them they employed over

290,000 civil servants, over half the UK total civil service of 594,000, with a further 29 agencies planned employing 69,265 civil servants. (See Table 1) As Richard Mottram, the Next Steps Project Manger indicated, 'The scale of this transformation, and its continued momentum, is an indication that Agencies have become firmly rooted in the machinery of government.'

The agencies are one manifestation of the new forces for change which have acted as a catalyst in transforming much of public sector provision: the insistent interventions of impatient government politicians; new demands created by social change; transformed thinking about the nature of effective management; and heightened consumer awareness. These have combined with much tighter financial controls; close external scrutiny of spending and performance and renewed commitments to quality in public service delivery, to encourage a climate of improved performance. In recent years traditional public sector practices have been successfully challenged, and a change in orientation is taking place:

- From an emphasis on internal procedures to a concern for outcomes;
- From an emphasis on hierarchical decision-making to an approach stressing delegation and personal responsibility;
- From a focus on the quantity of service provided to one also concentrating on quality;
- From a culture that values stability and uniformity to one that cherishes innovation and diversity (Hambleton 1992:10).

Before there was in the British civil service what Metcalfe and Richards refer to as an impoverished conception of management: thinking of management as an executive function with a clear definition of objectives; management as an intra-organizational process concerned with internal routines and procedure; co-ordination and control achieved through well defined hierarchies; and that these broad principles would apply with minor adaptation to all organizations. 'These elements in combination impose severe restrictions on the scope of management. They limit the role of public managers to programmed implementation of predetermined policies. They disregard the problem of adapting policies and organisations to environmental change. If this is all management means, giving more weight to it is likely to cause confusion and frustration rather than lead to long term improvements in performance...Civil servants need a richer and more precise language for diagnosing complex management problems and developing workable solutions to them.' (1990:17,22) In the absence of a more creative and dynamic approach, the critics of the public sector are free to equate cutting expenditure with efficiency gains, assuming greater productivity is the only realizable management goal.

The new wave of management thinking in the public sector has an explicit emphasis on the management of change with the object of a metamorphosis in organization culture, improving the quality of service by moving the locus of managerial authority and budgetary responsibility from the policy centre closer to the point of delivery, getting closer to the public and attempting to shift the balance of power in favour of those who the organization is intended to serve. This emphasis on listening to the customer, and delegating as much decision-making as possible to the operational level, has achieved positive results (Thomson, 1992; Hambleton, 1992).

Different strategies for managing change

Strategies for achieving change in the public sector have been classified into two types: those driven by planning and central direction, and essentially managerialist in nature, and those driven by competition in markets (Hirschman 1979; Hood 1991). Richards and Rodriques have developed this dichotomy of strategies and applied it to the analysis of UK public service reform over the last fifteen years. The first strategy involves strengthening the capacity to plan by establishing closer control over the definition of purpose, and devolving implementation within a tight framework. This involves the establishment of strong corporate management, and the development of a devolved budgetary system which established a clear line of responsibility and accountability for performance. The second strategy entails the introduction of a framework of competition in markets to produce efficiency-seeking behaviour. This involved privatization into competitive markets; privatization in regulated markets, or competitive tendering for services (1993:34).

Government usually favoured the first strategy when it felt it possessed powerful enough levers of control. In the Civil Service the Financial Management Initiative (FMI) established clear lines of responsibility; understanding of costs, and a focus on results. The executive agencies developed the FMI concept further, with framework agreements giving the devolved management structure a quasi-contractual basis. Similarly the reforms in the health service, while they have often been framed in the language of the market, have tended to rest upon the strengthening of strategic management in the NHS. When government has pressed for the second strategy, the introduction of competition to achieve efficiency, often the changes achieved have been similar to those involved in the first strategy. In the case of privatization, only rarely has effective competition been introduced, though the impact of regulation, and the threat of competition has often been sufficient to force through a lowering of costs and improvement of performance. In the local authorities threatened by compulsory competitive tendering, the response has been to strengthen strategic management; clarify objectives; control unit costs; reduce overheads and change work practices (Walsh, 1991c).

The 1992 *Review* of the Next Step Agencies suggests that in many agencies there has been an energetic pursuit of performance improvements, with new objectives set each year. This improvement may often be in the context of a growing and unsatisfied demand, but at least the Agencies seem to be making better use of the resources they have in achieving results such as:

- The Social Security Benefits Agency ensuring benefits are delivered more promptly at lower unit costs;
- Regulatory Services such as the Vehicles Inspectorate carrying out their work with greater consideration for service users;
- Services like the Land Registry have been able to reduce their expenditure to match their work load; to speed up the service, and to develop systems to meet future land information needs.

With this kind of progress, the sudden government inclination away from the agency form, in the direction of market testing, which puts civil service work out to competitive tender - whereby important elements of work could conceivably end up being done in by the private sector, seems inexplicable on anything other than ideological grounds (Richard and Rodrigues, 1993:33). By the end of 1993 market testing had been applied to £700 million of civil service work, from a target of £1.5 billion. In 1994 a further £300 million of work would be market tested, involving the jobs of 35,000 civil servants. Around 10,000 civil service jobs would go as a result of the first year of market testing, most would be redeployed to other branches of the civil service, while some would be transferred to the companies which had won the contracts. However the failure to clarify the employment rights of staff whose jobs were contracted out, delayed market testing and provoked the hostility of the civil service unions (*Financial Times,* 5 November 1993).

Accountability, efficiency and ethos

The arrival of this army of executive agencies has occasioned many constitutional doubts and diagreements, which Government has preferred to ignore rather than confront. In the Prime Minister's statement to the House of Commons on 18 February 1988, approving the establishment of the agencies, she said, 'These agencies will generally be within the Civil Service, and their staff will continue to be civil servants,' referring to agencies as 'units clearly designated within Departments.' Given this decision no legislation was required for this measure, which accounts for the remarkable speed with which it was implemented, the ignorance of the general public that anything has happened, and the bemusement of agency staff concerning what exactly *is* happening to them. Sir Leo Pliatzky, a former Permanent Secretary, regards the continued relationship between the agency and the responsible department as critical:

> All this adds up to a major reform of the civil service. I have no doubt that the decision to keep agencies within government, and to abjure the creation of a host of new non-departmental bodies, was crucial to the success and acceptability of the initiative... There are crucial differences between quangos (non-departmental bodies) and the Next Steps agencies (which are departmental bodies); these have an important bearing on ministers' accountability. The point of devolving a function to a non-departmental body, as we have already observed, is to distance government from the performance of that function. To achieve this effect, a council or commission is set up, and powers and responsibilities are conferred upon it, normally by legislation though in some cases by Royal Charter or by appointing a board of directors under the Companies Acts. Responsibility for performing the function then lies with the Council or Commission...Ministers have no part to play in the day-to-day operations of, say, the Health and Safety Commission, or the Civil Aviation Authority. The government can of course have an important effect on the work of bodies such as the Arts Council and the Research Councils through the amount of public money made available, but responsibility for the way money is spent lies with the councils (1992:559).

Table 1: The next steps agencies at December 1992

Executive Agency	Staff	Budget/ Turnover	Ministerial Responsibility £M
Accounts Service Agency	90		Trade and Industry
ADAS	2 ,500		Agriculture
Building Research Establishment	720	37	Environment
Cadw(Welsh Historic Monuments)	258	15	Wales
Central Office of Information	628	151.6	Duchy of Lancaster
Central Science Laboratory	400	15.6	Agriculture
Central Statistical Office	1,250	40	Treasury
Central Veterinary Laboratory	600	20	Agriculture
Chemical and Biological Defence Establishment	600	28	Defence
Civil Service College	220	15.9	Duchy of Lancaster
Companies House	1,157	30.9	Trade and Industry
Compensation Agency	150	3.4	Northern Ireland
HM Customs and Excise (Executive Units)	24,500		Treasury
Defence Analytical Services Agency	150	6.5	Defence
Defence Operational Analysis Centre	180	9	Defence
Defence Postal and Courier Service	500	12	Defence
Defence Research Agency	11,267	410	Defence
Directorate Gen'l of Def Accts	2,130	43.7	Defence
Driver and Vehicle Licensing Agency	4,900	187	Transport
Driver and Vehicle Testing Agency	260	7.3	Transport
Driving Standards Agency	2,000	50	Transport

Executive Agency	**Staff**	**Budget/ Turnover**	**Ministerial Responsibility £M**
Duke of York's Royal Military School			Defence
DVOIT	490	26	Transport
Employment Service	46,000	804.5	Employment
Fire Service College	300	15	Home Office
Forensic Science Service			Home Office
Historic Royal Palaces	415	32	National Heritage
Historic Scotland	600	33	Scotland
HMSO	3,270	381	Duchy of Lancaster
Hydrographic Office	840	29	Defence
Inland Revenue (Executive Units)	67,200	1,640	Treasury
Insolvency Service	1,585	40.6	Trade and Industry
Intervention Board	1,000	53	Agriculture
Laboratory of the Government Chemist	350	14.5	Trade and Industry
Land Registry	9,400	208.3	Lord Chancellor
Medicines Control Agency	350	21	Health
Meteorological Office	2,500	122	Defence
Military Survey	1,200	60	Defence
National Physical Laboratory	800	55	Trade and Industry
National Weights & Measures Laboratory	48	2.4	Trade and Industry
Natural Resources Institute	430	27.5	Overseas Develop.
Naval Aircraft Repair Organization	1660	135.8	Defence
NEL	390	21	Trade and Industry
NHS Estates	130	10	Health
NHS Pensions	650	20	Health
Occupational Health Service	110	4.7	Duchy of Lancaster
Ordnance Survey	2,300	71	Environment

Executive Agency	Staff	Budget/ Turnover	Ministerial Responsibility £M
Ordnance Survey of Northern Ireland	200	6.9	Northern Ireland
Patent Office	1,069	47	Trade and Industry
Planning Inspectorate	600	26	Environment
Public Record Office	450	25	Lord Chancellor
Queen Elizabeth II Conference Centre	64		Environment
Queen Victoria School			Defence
Radiocommunications Agency	520	30	Trade and Industry
RAF's Support Command Maintenance Group	13,600	624	Defence
Rate Collection Agency (N.Ireland)	270	4.9	Northern Ireland
Recruitment and Assessment Services	200	12	Duchy of Lancaster
Registers of Scotland	1,360	30	Scotland
Royal Mint	1,000	83	Treasury
Scottish Agricultural Science Agency	155	4.8	Scotland
Scottish Fisheries Protection Agency	240	13	Scotland
Service Children's Schools (NWE)	2,200	70	Defence
Social Security Agency (N.Ireland)	5,500	121	Northern Ireland
Social Security Benefits Agency	62,000	1,700	Social Security
Social Security Contributions Agency	9,000	121.4	Social Security
Social Security Information Technology			Services Agency
Social Security Resettlement Agency	460	27	Social Security
Teachers' Pension Agency	300		Education
The Buying Agency	100	4	Environment
Training and Employment Agency (NI)	1,640	27	Northern Ireland
Transport Research Laboratory	600	38	Transport
UK Passport Agency	1,300	36.7	Home Office
Valuation Office	5,000	186.3	Treasury
Vehicle Certificate Agency	80	2.5	Transport

Executive Agency	Staff	Budget/ Turnover	Ministerial Responsibility £M
Vehicle Inspectorate	1,900	54	Transport
Veterinary Medicines Directorate	90	5.8	Agriculture
Warren Springs Laboratory	300	12.9	Trade and Industry
Wilton Park Conference Centre	29	0.4	Foreign Office

Source: HMSO, The Next Steps Agencies Review 1992, Cmnd 2111

This distinction between the agencies and the earlier quangos would be important for a government that had committed much of its earlier life to ruthlessly culling the existing quangos on the basis of a rather atavistic view of the free functioning of a market economy, as indicated by the hostility expressed in the Adam Smith Institute's amusingly entitled pamphlet, *Quango, Quango, Quango* :

> Ministers have discovered that the system can be used for shedding personal responsibility, rewarding friends, expanding the corporate state, diminishing the authority of Parliament, and enabling themselves to retain a measure of control over the interpretation of their own statutes. On its present scale, the vast and complex network of Quangos encourages an abuse of patronage and invites corruption. (Holland, undated)

In view of this ealier campaign against quangos, it is remarkable that the government was able to adopt in such an enthusiastic way the wholesale transformation of the civil service into executive agencies, though as Pliatzky drily points out, 'Theories of organisation do tend to go in and out of fashion' (1992:557).

However others have not been reassured by the government's insistence that a continuing close relationship will exist between departments and agencies. Vernon Bogdonor has insisted we are faced with a constitutional as well as a managerial revolution:

> The fundamental rationale behind the reforms in the public services has been that they will be delivered more effectively if government operates along business lines. But the analogy between government and business misleads as much as it enlightens. In particular, it prevents us from

grasping how our consititutional principles are threated by the reforms now in train. First, there is the obvious point that many of the services which are being delivered by government are a public responsibility precisely because it is not in the interests of any private business to deliver them. As Lord Rayner has put it, 'Government has to provide services which no sane business would undertake.'

But, more important perhaps from the constitutional point of view, it is highly doubtful whether there is any counterpart in the business world to those constitutional principles designed to ensure the accountability of ministers and the integrity and impartiality of civil servants. The principles I have in mind are ministerial responsibility, the unity of the civil service and the conventions governing what is proper behaviour on the part of civil servants. Each of these principles is...under threat from the ill-considered way in which the public service reforms have been carried out' (1993:10-11).

From the different point of view of the chief executives of the new agencies the relationship with their departments is not entirely satisfactory: they feel caught in a power game, reflecting the difficulty of dismembering a monolithic structure, and the centre's need to maintain public service values of fairness and equality, while the periphery wants freedom to apply local conditions and a more proactive approach. 'Chief executives find themselves blocked and second-guessed at every turn. The Agencies grow in order to discharge their own functions, but the centre does not shrink correspondingly' (John Willman, *Financial Times,* 8 February 1993; Mellon 1993: 30)'.

A way out of the present managerial and constitutional malaise, offered by Bogdonor, is for the relationship between ministers and officials to be made explicitly contractual, so that specific responsibilities are delegated to officials, Ministers then remain responsible only for the terms of the delegation. Secondly the direct accountability of the chief executives of the agencies to the relevant Select Commitee of the House of Commons would need to be formalized. Chief executives would appear not as other civil servants do, merely as the spokesperson for their ministers, though they would not be allowed to comment on matters of *policy,* only on operational matters (1993:14-5).

Preserving the unity of the civil service is a more intractable matter. If public service in the UK has always been characterized by institutional diversity and pluralism, there have nonetheless been certain unifying characteristics according to Sir Robin Butler, Head of the Civil Service, which have served as glue holding together disparate activities: 'impartiality, integrity, and objectivity...selection and promotion on merit..and accountability through ministers to Parliament' (Bogdonor, 1993:16). The danger is that as the agencies develop separate identities they will become unconnected elements in the public sector. As from April 1994 all agencies with a staff of over 2,000 will have responsibility for pay delegated to them. The agencies will negotiate with the civil service unions on matters of pay and conditions of service in place of the Treasury. With the freedom to recruit and pay staff at market rates, agencies will be able to compete for staff with the local and regional offices of Whitehall departments. The Treasury and Civil Service Select Committee insisted the route to the top of the civil service, 'should combine management within agencies together with experience of policy work.' However it appears inevitable that a two tier civil service will emerge with a small core with job security and career prospects, and a wide periphery with short-term appointments and a range of conditions of employment (Bogdonor, 1993:16).

The final constitutional principle is the undermining of the civil service ethos, with the erosion in particular of civil servants commitment to political neutrality. Anxieties concerning this abound, because, 'the reforms implemented by the government seek to bring the commercial ethic into the public service and minimize the deep-seated conflict between the public service ethic and the commercial ethic' (Bogdonor, 1993:20). The fact that many members of the public are unable to employ the commercial mode of accountability, by taking their business elsewhere, emphasizes the need to strengthen forms of public accountability through the development of a constitutional code, strengthening the role of parliament, and devolution and decentralization.

Conclusions

The transformation of the civil service caused by the creation of the executive agencies and related reforms, has posed many questions still left unanswered. There is a lingering sense that after fifteen years of one party government, the civil service has not only lost its capacity for political neutrality, but of dispassionate assessment of policy, simply providing whatever answer ministers require. There are not only profound political dilemmas involved in this collapse of the professional ethic of the civil service, but also serious implications for the efficiency of the public service. For example the swing of government opinion away from the agency solution towards market testing represented a dislocating force at a time when greater effectiveness may have been achieved by getting relationships between agencies and their departments right. An impression is given of a group of politicians impatient for immediate results, insensitive to the damage caused by their actions, and ignorant of the longer-term consquences for the integrity and performance of the public services:

> The timescale of organizational change does not fit well with the career imperatives of ministers and advisers. Quick wins are sometimes available, and reputations are often built on them. But the important and difficult changes in culture take time. Painstaking efforts to bring about cultural change should not be cast aside without fully counting the cost of doing so. Perhaps we need to invent an investment appraisal technique which calculates the opportunity cost of management time and energy spent on 'quick fix' solutions, so that we can compare the costs and benefits' (Richards and Rodrigues, 1993:37).

In the absence of any government inclination towards a more considered view of how to provide essential services, that can in practice only be provided ultimately by the public sector, the only thing civil servants can be sure of is that they are in for a bumpy ride.

References

Argyris, C. and Schon, A. (1974), *Organizational Learning,* Reading:Mass, Addison-Wesley.

Batley, R. and Stoker, G. (1991), *Local Government in Europe- Trends and Developments,* London, Macmillan.

Bellamy, C. and Taylor, J. 'Informatization and New Public Management: an alternative agenda for Public Administration,' *Public Policy and Administration,* Vol 7, No 3, pp. 29-41.

Bellone, C.J. and Goerl, G.F. (1992), 'Reconciling Public Entrepreneurship and Democracy,' *Public Administration Review,* March/April, Vol 52, No. 2, pp.130-4.

Bereton, D. 'From Scrutinies to Market Testing: the Work of the Efficiency Unit,' *Public Policy and Administration,* Vol. 7, No. 3, pp.71-79.

Bichard, M. (1991), Experience from the Benefits Agency,' *Managers, Citizens and Consumers,* London: Office for Public Management.

Bogdonor, V. (1993), 'Ministers, Civil Servants, and the Constitution: A Revolution in Whitehall?', *Institute of Advanced Legal Studies Bulletin,* Issue 15, October, pp.10-22.

Brodtrick, O. (1992), 'When Do Practitioners Implement Research Findings?' *Research and Practice: Shaping the Future of Public Management,* Conference Paper 1, London, Public Management Foundation.

Buckland, Y. and Joshua, H. (1992), 'Nottingham into the 1990s - Managing Change in a District Council,' *Public Money and Management,* July-September , pp. 21-25.

Butler, R. (1992), 'The New Public Management: the Contributions of Whitehall and Academia,' *Public Policy and Administration,* Vol. 7, No. 3, pp.4-14.

Caiden, G.E. (1991), *Administrative Reform Comes of Age,* Berlin, Walter de Gruyter.

Chandler, J.A. (1991), 'Public Administration and Private Management: Is There a Difference?' *Public Administration,* Vol. 69, No. 3, pp.385-91.

Clarke, T. (1990), 'Socialized Industry: Social Ownership or Shareholding Democracy?' in, S.Clegg, (ed.), *Organization Theory and Class Analysis,* Berlin, Walter de Gruyter.

Clarke, T. (1994), 'Reconstructing the Public Sector,' in, T.Clarke, ed., *International Privatization Strategies and Practices,* Berlin, Walter de Gruyter.

Cmnd 1599 (1992), *The Citizen's Charter: Raising the Standard,* Her Majesty's Stationery Office.

Common, R., Flynn, N. and Mellon, E. (1992), *Managing Public Services : Competition and Decentralization,* London, Butterworth-Heinemann.

Davies, K. and Hinton, P. 'Managing Quality in the Health Service,' *Public Money and Management,* Oxford, Blackwell, January-March, pp.51-54.

Deakin, N. and Wright, A. (1990), *Consuming Public Services,* London, Routledge.

Dopson, S. (1993), 'Are Agencies an Act of Faith?,' *Public Money and Management,* Oxford, Blackwell, April-June 1993.

Eccles, E. (1991), 'The Performance Measurement Manifesto,' *Harvard Business Review,* Jan-Feb.

Elcock, H. (1993), 'What Price Citizenship? Public Management and the Citizen's Charter,' *Waves of Change in the Public Sector,* Sheffield Business School, 5-6 April.

Epstein, P.D. (1992), 'Get Ready: The Time for Performance Measurement Is Finally Coming!' *Public Administration Review,* September/October Vol. 52, No. 5, pp. 513-519.

Farnham, D. and Horton, S. *Managing the New Public Services,* Basingstoke, Macmillan.

Farnham, D. and Horton, S. 'Human Resources Management in the New Public Sector: Leading or Following Private Employer Practice?', *Public Policy and Administration,* Vol. 7, No. 3, pp. 42-55.

Flynn, M. (1990), *Public Sector Management,* Brighton, Harvester-Wheatsheaf.

Fogden, M.E.G. (1993), 'Managing Change in the Employment Service,' *Public Money and Management,* Oxford, Blackwell, April-June, pp. 9-16.

Garratt, B. (1990), *Creating a Learning Organization,* Director Books, Simon and Schuster.

Geddes, M. (1991), 'Scenarios for the Future of Public Services in the Economy,' *Warwick Business School Research Papers,* No. 21, September.

Glynn, J. (1992), 'Auditing the Three E's: The Challenge of Effectiveness,' *Public Policy and Administration,* Vol. 7, No. 3, pp. 56-69.

Gordon, P. (1991), 'Experience From Sheffield City Council,' *Managers, Citizens and Consumers,* Conference Paper 6, London, Office for Public Management.

Goss, S. (1991), 'The Poverty of Consumerism,' *Managers, Citizens and Consumers,* Conference Paper 6, London, Office for Public Management.

Gyford, J. (1991), *Citizens, Consumers and Councils,* London, Macmillan.

Hadley, R. and Young, K. (1990), *Creating a Responsive Public Service,* London, Harvester/Wheatsheaf.

Hambleton, R., (1992), 'Decentralization and Democracy in UK Local Government,' *Public Money and Management,* July-September, pp.9-20.

Hancock, C. (1990), 'What Professionals Expect From Managers,' *Managers and Professionals,* Conference Paper 4, London, Office for Public Management.

Hanuch, H. (ed.) *Anatomy of Government Deficiencies,* Berlin, Springer Verlag, pp. 125-38.

Harden, G. (1992), *The Contracting State,* Buckingham, Open University Press.

Harman, R. (1993), 'Railway Privatization: Does it Bring new Opprtunities?,' *Public Money and Management,* Jan-March, pp. 19-25.

Hayes, R.H., Wheelwright, S.C., Clark, K.B. *Dynamic Manufacturing - Creating the Learning Organization,* New York, Free Press.

Heater, D. (1992), 'Civis Britannicus Sum,' *Parliamentary Affairs,* Vol. 45, No. 3, pp. 439-40.

Hedberg, B., Nystrom, P., Starbuck, W.H. (1976), 'Camping on Seesaws: Prescriptions for a Self-designing Organization,' *Administrative Science Quarterly,* 21, pp. 41-65.

Hedberg, B. (1981), 'How Organizations Learn and Unlearn', in, P.C.Nystrom and W.H.Starbuck.

Hirschman, A.O. (1979), *Exit, Voice and Loyalty,* Cambridge, Mass.,Harvard University Press.

HMSO, (1990), *Improving Management in Government - The Next Steps Agencies, Review 1990,* Cmnd 1261, London, HMSO.

HMSO, (1992), *The Next Steps Agencies Review,* Cmnd 2111, HMSO.

Hood, C. (1991), 'A Public Management for All Seasons?' *Public Administration,* Vol. 69, No. 1, pp.3-19.

Hunt, M. (1993), 'Accountability, Openness and the Citizen's Charter,' *Waves of Change in the Public Sector,* Sheffield Business School, 5-6 April.

Institute of Personnel Management & Incomes Data Services Public Sector Unit (1986), *Competitive Tendering in the Public Sector,* Woking, Unwin Brothers.

Jackson, P. and Palmer, B. (1989), *First Steps In Measuring Performance in the Public Sector,* London, Public Finance Foundation.

Jeding, L. (1992), 'Speeding the Winds of Change,' *Research and Practice: Shaping The Future of Public Management,* Conference Paper 1, London: Public Management Foundation.

Jones, R. (1993), 'The Citizen's Charter Programme,' *Waves of Change in the Public Sector,* Sheffield Business School, April.

King, D. and Pierre, J. (1991), *Challenges to Local Government,* London: Sage.

Lan, Z. and Rosenbloom, D. (1992), 'Public Administration in Transition?' *Public Administration Review,* Nov-Dec 1992 pp. 535-7.

Landau, M. (1973), 'On the Concept of the Self-Correcting Organization,' *Public Administration Review,* 33, pp.533-42.

Landau, M. and Stout, R. (1979), 'To Manage is Not to Control,' *Public Administration Review,* March/April 148-56.

Lawton, A. and McKevitt, D. (1993), 'Strategic Change in Local Government Management,' *Waves of Change in the Public Sector,* Sheffield Business School, 5-6 April.

Lawton, A. and Rose, A. (1991), *Organization and Management in the Public Sector,* London: Pitman.

Leavitt, H. (1983), 'Management and Management Education in the West,' *London Business School Journal,* VIII(I): pp. 18-23.

Le Grand, J. (1991), 'Regulation and Freedom in a Public Market,' *Managers, Citizens and Consumers,* Conference Paper 6, London: Office for Public Management.

Levine, C. (1984), 'Citizenship and Service Delivery: The Promise of Coproduction,' *Public Administration Review,* Vol. 44, pp.178-87.
Lewis, N. (1992), *Inner City Regeneration*, Open University Press.
Linblom, C.E. (1965), *The Intelligence of Democracy,* New York: Free Press.
Local Government Training Board (LGTB) (1985), *Good Management in Local Government: Successful Practice and Action,* Luton: LGTB.
Lorenz, C. (1992), 'Learning from Change,' *Managing Fundamental Change,* Conference Paper 7, London: Office for Public Management.
McDonald, O. (1992), *The Future of Whitehall,* London: Weidenfeld & Nicholson.
McGregor, E.B. (1984), 'The Great Paradox of Democratic Citizenship and Public Personnel Administration,' *Public Administration Review,* Vol. 44, pp. 126-132.
March, J.G., and Olsen, J.P. (1983), 'Organising Political Life: What Administrative Reorganization Tells Us About Government,' *American Political Science Review,* 77, 281096.
Margetts, H., and Willcocks, L. (1993), 'Information Technology in Public Administration: Disaster Faster?' *Public Money and Management,* Oxford: Blackwell, April - June, pp. 49-56.
Marsh, D. (1991), 'Privatization Under Mrs Thatcher: A Review of the Literature,' *Public Administration,* Royal Institute of Public Administration, Vol. 69, Winter, pp. 459-480.
Massey, A. (1992), 'Due Process and Rectitude: US and British Civil Service Reforms Contrasted,' *Public Money and Administration,* Vol. 7, No. 3, pp. 80-88.
Mather, G. (1991), 'Serving Your Right,' *Marxism Today,* May.
Mellon, E. (1993), 'Executive Agencies: Leading Change From the Outside-in,' *Public Money and Management,* Oxford-Blackwell, April-June, pp. 25-31.
Metcalfe, L. and Richards, S. (1990), *Improving Public Management,* London: Sage.
Metcalfe, L. (1981), 'Designing Precarious Partnerships,' in, Nystrom and Starbuck, 1981, Vol. 1.
Mintzberg, H. (1982), 'A Note on that Dirty Word 'Efficiency', *Interfaces,* 12, pp. 101-5.
Mulgan, G. (1991), 'Power to the Public, *Marxism Today,* May.
Murray, R. (1991), 'The State After Henry', *Marxism Today,* May.
Nystrom, P.C. and Starbuck, W.H. (1981), *Handbook of Organizational Design,* Vol. 1, *Adapting Organizations to Their Environments,* Oxford: Oxford University Press.

Office of Electricity Regulation (Offer) (1992), *Management Plan 1992-1996,* Offer.

Osborne, D. and Gaebler, T. (1992), *Reinventing Government,* Reading,Mass: Addison-Wesley.

Peacock, A. (1983), 'Public X-efficiency: Informational and Institutional Constraints,' in, Hanuch, H. (ed.) *Anatomy of Government Deficiencies,* Berlin: Springer Verlag, pp.125-38.

Pedler, M., Boydell T., and Burgoyne, J. (1991), *The Learning Company,* McGraw-Hill.

Pettigrew, A., Ferlie, E. and McKee, L. (1992), 'Shaping Strategic Change - The Case of the NHS in the 1980s,' *Public Money and Mangement,* Oxford: Blackwell, July-September, pp. 27-31.

Pinder, K. (1993), 'Service Level Agreements And the Internal Market in Local Government,' *Waves of Change in the Public Sector,* Sheffield Business School, 5-6 April.

Pliatzky, L. (1992), 'Public Management Quangos and Agencies,' *Public Administration,* Vol. 70, pp. 555-563.

Pollitt, C. (1990), *Managerialism and the Public Services,* Oxford: Blackwell.

PSI (1990), *Britain in 2010,* London: Policy Studies Institute.

Reed, M., and Anthony, P. (1993), 'Between and Ideological Rock and an Organizational Hard Place: NHS Management in the 1980s and 1990s,' in, T. Clarke and C. Pitelis, *The Political Economy of Privatization,* London:Routledge

Richards, S. (1992), *Who Defines the Public Good? The Consumer Paradigm in Public Managment,* London: Public Management Foundation.

Richards, S.. and Rodrigues, J. (1993), 'Strategies for Management in the Civil Service: Change of Direction,' *Public Money and Management,* Oxford: Blackwell, April-June, pp. 33-38.

Riley, K. (1993), 'The Abolition of the ILEA:Implications for the Restructuring of Local Government,' *Public Money and Management,* Oxford: Blackwell, April-June, pp. 57-60.

Roberts, G., and Scholes, K. (1933), 'Policy and Base Budget Reviews at Cheshire County Council,' *Waves of Change in the Public Sector,* Sheffield Business School, April 5-6th.

Ross, N. (1991), 'What Does the Public Want From Public Services?' *Managers, Citizens and Consumers,* Conference Paper 6, London: Office for Public Management.

Sanderson, I. (1993), *The Management of Quality in Local Government,* Longman.

Sanderson, I. (1993b), 'Evaluating Quality: Principles and Issues,' *Evaluation and Performance in Local Government,* Leeds Business School, February 1993.

Saxton Bampfylde International (1992), *Privatising People: Career Moves Between the Public and Private Sectors,* London: Saxton Bampfylde.

Senge, P.M. (1990), *The Fifth Discipline: The Art and Practice of the Learning Organization,* Doubleday/Currency.

Staw, B. (1977), 'The Experimenting Organization,' *Organizational Dynamics,* Summer pp. 2-18.

Stewart, J. (1986), *The New Management of Local Government,* London: George Allen & Unwin.

Stewart, J. and Clarke, M. (1987), 'The public service orientation: issues and dilemmas,' *Public Administration,* 65, pp. 161-177.

Stewart, J. (1988), *Understanding the Management of Local Government,* Harlow: Longmans.

Stewart, J. and Stoker, G. (1989), *The Future of Local Government,* London: Macmillan.

Stewart, J. (1990), 'Professionalism, Politics and Public Service,' *Managers and Professionals,* Conference Paper 4, London: Office for Public Management.

Stewart, J. and Walsh, K. (1992), 'Change in the Management of the Public Services,' *Public Administration,* Vol. 70, pp. 499-518.

Stoker, G. (1991), 'Introduction: Trends in European Local Government,' in R. Batley and G. Stoker (eds.), *Local Government in Europe,*: Macmillan.

Strand, T. (1984), 'Public Management, Conceptual Issues and Research Suggestions,' *Conference on Public Management in Europe,* The Hague, Netherlands.

Thomson, P. (1992), 'Public Sector Management in a Period of Radical Change: 1979-1992,' *Public Money and Management,* July-September 1992, pp. 33-41.

Thomson, W. (1992), 'A Perspective From Local Government,' *Research and Practice:Shaping the Future of Public Management,* London: Public Management Foundation.

Uttley, M. (1993), 'Contracting-Out and Market Testing in the UK Defence Sector: Theory, Evidence, and Issues,' *Public Money and Management,* Oxford: Blackwell, January-March, pp. 55-60.

Walsh, K. (1991a), 'Quality and Public Services,' *Public Administration,* Winter, pp. 503-514.

Walsh, K. (1991b), 'Citizens and Consumers: Marketing and Public Sector Management,' *Public Money and Management,* Summer, pp.9-16.

Walsh, K. (1991c), *Competitive Tendering in Local Government: Evaluation Report,* HMSO.

Weick, K.E. (1976), 'Educational Organizations as Loosely Coupled Systems,' *Administrative Science Quarterly,* 21, pp. 1-19.

Weil, S. (1992), 'Learning to Change,' *Managing Fundamental Change,* Conference Paper 7, London: Office for Public Management.

Wildavsky, A. (1972), 'The Self-Evaluating Organization,' *Public Administration Review,* September-October, pp. 509-520.

12 NHS plc?

Chris Potter

Introduction

The National Health Service (NHS) is considered by many to be the flagship of the British welfare state. Over the years it has frequently been described as the envy of the world. Mrs Thatcher apparently described it as a heffalump trap ready to catch unwary politicians who attempted to change it. Survey after survey has shown that the British public, whilst complaining about various aspects of the services provided, nevertheless is very protective about the free at the point of use comprehensive health service it represents.[1]

Comparisons with health systems around the world demonstrate that the NHS represents exceedingly good value for money.[2/3] The UK was almost bottom of the international league table of GDP expenditure on health throughout the period 1975-1987. Yet the range of services offered by the NHS is enormous, far wider, for example, than that offered by HMO's or insurance packages in USA. Even though the proportion of GDP spent on health in the UK is small in international terms, most of this expenditure is public expenditure, and represents a large proportion of government spending. The Department of Health receives only a little less funding than local Government, although both together do not equal the massive proportion of public expenditure on social security. These three big spenders together receive more public money than all other government spending combined (including the health expenditure of the Welsh Office, Scottish

Office and Northern Ireland Office).

Such a level of public expenditure naturally invites attention from Conservative politicians, and there is a continuing, underlying fear that despite public esteem and good value for money, the NHS is being 'privatized' by successive government reforms. This chapter will analyse some of the changes which have been introduced to the NHS over the past years, and will assess both the extent to which privatization has already occurred, and the extent to which the foundations may have been laid for moving to a more privatized system.

What is meant by privatization? Essentially, privatization means that the means of production are in private hands, and as a corollary, customers or clients need to pay a fee for access to the product or service on offer. Governments may decide that particular goods or services should not be in private ownership, and/or that payment should not be at the point of use but through general taxation. They have the option of nationalizing the means of production, or of introducing alternative funding methods. Talk of privatizing health services can therefore refer to changes in the ownership of the means of production or changes in the means of paying for care, with a return to full or partial fee paying. Besides this more narrow definition of privatization is the idea that some aspects of the NHS, perhaps hotel services, could attract fee payments; or that a two tier system might be introduced with 'amenity beds' (for which patients pay a fee); or that more private agencies would provide aspects of care (with or without a fee at point of use).

In 1948 most of the hospitals in England and Wales came under public ownership.[4] At that time most were organized into hospital management committees (HMCs) whose members were drawn from the medical profession and the local community. Boards of Governors controlled teaching hospitals, and these had direct access to the Minister of Health. The HMCs were monitored and supervized by regional hospital boards (RHAs), again made up of community leaders and professional (medical) representatives. At the same time, fees for service were largely abolished. Although health services under the NHS could not be said to be provided free, in that taxes had to be paid, they were nevertheless free at the point of use.

As is now widely appreciated, the general belief in the period between the NHS Act being published and its implementation (1946-1948) was that illness and disease could be largely eradicated by the introduction of the NHS, and by parallel developments in housing, education and nutrition.[5] The NHS would pay for itself by increases in production as the British workforce was kept healthier, and had less time off work. Almost immediately, however, it became clear that there would be an accumulating agenda of demand. Demand for health care rose enormously. It became obvious that there had been a genuine hidden demand for health services, as well as a new feeling that as services were free patients should claim all they could under the NHS. (Beveridge had recommended charges for dentures and spectacles to control demand, and 'hotel charges' for hospital patients.[6])

Although it is widely assumed that this was a Labour Party inspired act to de-privatize the health care industry, historians and policy analysts take a different view. The NHS was built on the Beveridge Report (Beveridge was a Liberal peer commissioned by a coalition government with a Conservative Prime Minister), and there was widespread support for reform. Walters, for example, concludes that the Labour Party and trades unions had only sporadically pursued a national health service, that the middle classes were previously the most deprived group as far as health care was concerned, and that the NHS legislation was an attempt to solve the health care sector's organizational and fiscal problems, rather than being idealogically inspired.[7]

In the opening words of the 1946 Act the Secretary of State is made responsible for providing a 'comprehensive' health package. In this regard the health service is unlike almost any other welfare service provided. There are no restrictions on the word comprehensive. In the Act it was defined as meaning both available to the whole population, and covering 'all necessary forms of health service'. As Thwaites has noted[8], the 1973 and 1977 Act qualified this latter obligation somewhat but there was still no clear definition of illness, health or the care to be provided. If someone somewhere can make a claim that a person's health is being adversely affected, and that a treatment or intervention is available to avoid this situation, it can be included under the rubric. The NHS is filled with imaginative professionals who are keen to develop their own careers and develop new specialties and treatments. There are many vocal pressure groups who will argue that their particular conditions ought to be treated by the NHS, and their claims will be supported by opposition politicians and the media. If the NHS cannot or will not deliver there will be well publicized cases treated abroad, possibly following a public appeal. Technological advances push back the frontiers of what can be offered to potential patients. Under these pressures there has been a steady, inexorable growth in the range of services the NHS is supposed to provide. In perhaps every other publicly provided service there is a much clearer understanding of the agenda that the service is supposed to address. It is fairly clear what schools are supposed to be providing for whom. Even though there is ongoing acrimony about curricula, and some debate about the power of schools to reject pupils no-one argues that a middle-aged person should be given access to French lessons, or pensioners should be allowed to study for GCSE exams alongside teenagers. It would be absurd. Analogous situations for the NHS are featured on TV programmes as ethical dilemmas. The police and the army are called on to provide a wide range of services, but nevertheless there is less sense that the public has a right to expect such services to meet any need they care to present. With the health service, not only direct technical medical services are expected to be provided free, but so also is transport to and from the hospital (the ambulance service), a wide range of education and support services, hotel services, and even car parking at hospital and clinic premises. There is considerable talk of 'under funding' of the NHS, and by proportion of GDP consumed it is clearly less well resourced than other countries. (One reason for this is the relative low payment of NHS workers. The average salary of a UK doctor in 1991 is reported by the World Bank to have been US $40,544, compared to $56,437 in Sweden, and $132,300 in USA. Both Sweden and USA have more doctors per head of population than UK). However, funding can rationally only be defined as 'over' or 'under', against a known agenda of activity. In the situation described here, one canot say the NHS is either under funded or over funded. Yet politicians will be very unwilling to risk unpopularity by defining the boundaries of care, and the so called 'Oregon experiment' shows how difficult it is to take an entirely logical position on health care agendas. In the author's view the Working for Patients reforms (described below) are an attempt by government to side step the need for boundaries to be set centrally, by passing the problem to 'purchasers' who will define local needs, and through contracts and service agreements put the boundaries around what is considered 'NHS treatment' and what is not.

Payment for services

Because of the increasing demand for health services the first prescription charges were introduced in 1951 by the Labour Government. The NHS in its original form provided for charging for repairs or replacement to dentures or spectacles if due to carelessness. The new charges were to cover part of the cost of all dentures and spectacles, but exempting certain groups. When the Conservatves returned to power in 1952 they imposed charges on prescriptions, surgical appliances, dental treatment and day nursery care. By 1956 the Guillebaud Committee openly acknowledged that the pre-1948 expectations of a NHS whose success would reduce demand on it was an illusion. Although there were a variety of views on the effects of charging, there was unlikely to be any return to the view that free services were self-limiting.[9]

Charges have been increased, changed and expanded over the years. They now include sight testing charges, and charges related to road traffic accidents. Every time prescription charge prices are increased there is a considerable political hue and cry, but the reality is that of all prescriptions processed only 10 per cent attract charges. (Information supplied by the Welsh Price Prescription Office). Currently, exemptions to charges include drugs, appliances and elastic hosiery supplied to children under sixteen or students under nineteen in full time education; men aged sixty-five or over and women aged sixty or over. Exemption certificates are issued to expectant mothers, women who have borne a child in the last twelve months and people suffering from physical disabilities etc. DSS exemption certificates are issued to war service pensioners (for prescriptions related to their accepted disablement); to people receiving income support or family credit; and anyone sixteen or over (except students in full time education under nineteen) whose income is not above income support level. Some relief from payment is also available to people requiring more than fourteen items a year by purchasing prepayment certificates (in effect 'season tickets'). In terms of prescription charges it is not clear that the NHS is any more 'privatized' now that it was in the mid 1950s or during the 1960s. Charges have been levied throughout this period, and allowing for inflation and real levels of earning, it is difficult to make a case that people are having to pay significantly more for the health service at the point of use than they were during that period. However, there has been an increase in charges for dental and opthalmic services, which has led to a fall in demand for those services. This augurs badly for increasing charges in other aspects of NHS provision, if the health of the population is not to suffer. In 1989 the Consumers Association identified that one in three people had reduced the frequency of their visits to the dentist because of charges, and one in five reported they were not having check ups. The cost of all adult check ups and treatment currently is £880m per annum, and NHS dental charges raise £380m[10], but in terms of total NHS spending it can be argued that it is insignificant.

Table 1 shows the Welsh Office's Receipts and Payments Return, 1991/92. It will be seen that although £22,103,284 income is shown, £18,374,077 of this comes from staff medicals and accommodation, and revenue from shops.

Privatization of the means of production

Setting to one side for the time being the question of the strictly private sector i.e. BUPA and other privately owned providers of health care whether for profit or charitable, to what extent have the means of production of health care been privatized by the recent reforms? What the Conservative Government has done with its 'Working for Patients' reforms is to make a distinction between the purchase or commissioning of health services, and their provision. There is a recognition that a health authority does not necessarily have to define the need, provide the health care, and provide all of the sub-services

Table 1: Receipts and payments return - Wales 1991/1992

HEALTH SERVICE REVENUE INCOME RECEIPTS (APPROPRIATIONS IN AID)	
From patients - supply of drugs and supply and repair of appliances: for appliances more expensive than prescribed	13,666.56
for repair and replacement of appliances necessitated by lack of car	1,125.72
for dental and optical appliances	8,719.60
for prescriptions dispensed by hospitals etc. (including wigs, fabric supports)	338,755.04
for prescriptions on form FP (10) HP	49,638.06
From patients - accommodation single rooms or small wards (Section 63 NHS Act 1977)	132,337.65
Private in-patients (Section 65)	1,517,729.91
Private non-resident patients (Section 66)	492,983.59
Overseas visitors (Section 121)	190,824.99

C/F	2,745,780.90
Accomodation and services provided under Section 58 of the NHS Act 1977	30,006.75
Under the Road Traffic Act 1972	508,186.57
Blood Handling Charges - under Section 25 of the NHS Act 1977	11,530.20
Registration fees for Nursing Homes - under the Registered Homes Act 1984	273,713.91
Miscellaneous:	
Rents (Land and Premises)	114,606.49
Sales of inventory items and equipment	42,537.26
Maintenance charges, working patients	2,844.82
Other: Meals, Lodging charges, Shops & Canteens	18,374,077.85
TOTAL HEALTH SERVICE REVENUE INCOME RECEIPTS (APPROPRIATIONS IN AID)	**22,103,284.97**

through directly managed labour, to ensure that their patients receive a high quality health care service. Indeed, in so far as health authorities try to set health policy, be first class providers of technical care, provide transport services, provide hotel services, and so on, there was a widespread belief that they had become too unwieldy. At a time when industry was being encouraged to 'stick to the knitting', to streamline itself and divest activities in which 'value added' was not clear, the District and Regional Health Authorities were seen as large enterprises with many thousands of staff and multi-million pound budgets trying to do too much. They were bureaucracies brought down by their own size and by the nature of national agreements and policies such as the Whitley Council rules and regulations on terms and conditions of service for staff. The recent reforms have attempted to split responsibility for providing health care from the responsibility for deciding what health care is required in any area. In order to encourage this split, hospitals and community services have been encouraged to separate themselves managerially from health authorities to become so called Trusts (an ironic name, as they have failed to ensure that they enjoy public trust). As such, these Trusts are still in public ownership. There is currently no question of private ownership, although the managers of NHS facilities are now responsible for ensuring that they take cognizance that they are the guardians of important publicly owned assets through the mechanism of 'capital charges'. In other words, Trusts will have to make payments to the Secretary of State based on the value of the assets they take over, plus having to pay commercial interest rates when raizing new capital.

There is an ongoing argument that the health service has in fact been a middle class institution, run by the middle classes for the middle classes. Rather than being a health service, it is accused of having been a disease oriented service, with the bulk of its services geared towards the ailments that bother the professional classes, and services which are of intrinsic interest to those who provide them. For the great majority of patients, who suffer hernias, varicose veins, prolapses, and other frequent complaints, there have been increasing waits, and waiting lists have become a major political football. To tackle this, the reforms have attempted to introduce a degree of competition between providers of health care, the so called internal market. This has been attempted in two ways. Firstly, rather than leaving providers to offer a range of services which to a large extent their professional members chose to offer (waiting lists are merely a reflection of the services which the professionals do not want to provide) providers must now respond to service agreements or contracts set by the purchasers. These purchasers are the old District Health Authorities transformed into commissioning bodies responsible for identifying the health needs of their population, or fund holding GPs (see below). The fact that by and large the new purchasing authorities had little idea how to go about determining what services were required, is perhaps an indication of how necessary it was to introduce reforms and a sad indictment of the way the health service developed over the first forty years of its life.

The second way in which competition was supposed to act was in making more explicit the performance criteria of providers by introducing a mechanism whereby their cost and quality could be directly compared, money would follow the patient, and less effective units would either have to improve their services, or 'go out of business'.

This last expression indicates the extent to which the language of commerce has been introduced into the NHS, and this perhaps contributes to the view that privatization is somehow taking place. GPs wishing to become fund holders, Trusts putting in their applications, and other units of service, are all having to produce 'business plans'. There has been much talk about 'contracting' the services between different parts of the NHS. There is talk about competition, and SWOT analyses have become commonplace. But the reality is that there is still comparatively little competition, because of the pattern of existing services and the limited opportunity for purchasers to shift patterns of demand, at least in the early years of the reforms. Furthermore, there are so many rules and regulations about the way prices can be set (managers have little opportunity to cross-subsidize, or to package services in a creative way) that 'business plans' end up looking very different than those from the commercial sector. Even early talk about 'contracts' was modified so that 'service agreement' replaced 'contract'.

The health care 'market' is also very unusual. It is an imperfect market in that clients do not have ready access to information which will enable them to make choices. 'Middle men' i.e. GPs determine access to services, and there is very limited opportunity for providers to enter the market because of cost of investment and central control. Providers are also prevented from adopting commercial strategies such as keeping patients in hospital for longer, which would make commercial sense because there are less costs generated for laboratory and other care during later stages of an in-patient episode. In practice,providers are under pressure to reduce length of stay and increase the throughput of patients. Because this costs them more, they fall into the so-called 'efficiency trap', i.e. the more efficient they are, the more patients they see, the sooner their budgets run out.

Consumerism

Although there has been little or no privatization of means of production, or increase in fee for service, the NHS has been encouraged to act as though it was a (non-monopolistic) private organization, offering greater consumer choice and improving the quality of services. Ironically, the reforms have reduced the number of lay members on management boards (and the 'non-executive' directors are drawn from a narrower range of the public than ever before, with emphasis given to business experience). They have also reduced the choice for patients. Until the reforms, patients were able to access specialist care wherever their GP was prepared to refer them. With the introduction of ECRs (extra contractual referrals) these options are severely curtailed and patients are faced to a greater extent than before with a 'take it or leave it' approach. Particularly if a patient's GP is a fund holder, he/she may find themselves limited by the range of contracts that the fund holder has established, or the fund holder's willingness to refer for care given the cost of that care. This smacks more of an old fashioned nationalized industry than a truly privatized one.

It can be argued that money has not followed the patient because money has not been put into the system. Indeed, so called efficiency savings have reduced available monies year by year.[11] Thus, an efficient provider of services can meet a number of objective performance targets, only to be penalized, and facilities stand idle because there is more capacity than the purchasers are willing to buy. Yet because of the political climate within which health operates, it is not possible to sell new forms of service using those facilities - especially if waiting lists remain long. Elderly care units stand idle in the summer or at weekends, when relatives might be willing to pay for respite care - but this would be politically sensitive. Operating departments are used only at certain hours, but, because of purchasers being reluctant to significantly change patterns of care, more work does not attract more money, they cannot be manned, and waiting lists grow. These are characteristics of centralist bureaucracy not private organizations.

A further attempt to introduce 'commercial sector' discipline to the NHS has been central sponsorship of quality initiatives such as the Kings Fund Audit and various TQM drives, and the Patients Charter Initiative. Unlike the commercial sector which has been encouraged by TQM/CQI in particular to become more sensitive to consumer wants and to high quality outcomes in terms of interpersonal relations, the NHS still tends to emphasize adherence to professionally determined processes and standards and to play down outcome results.[12] To some extent this is inevitable, but the effects of consumerism and raizing expectations will need to be increasingly taken into account if patients and potential patients are not to change from support to criticism of the NHS. Improving service in the commercial sector will be the biggest stimulus for more competition and more privatization of the NHS, unless it can add demonstrable service to value for money.

The role of the private sector

There has always been a private sector operating within the UK, but until recently it operated quite outside the NHS, and indeed in competition with it. Stimulated by pay freezes in the 1970s and the search for recruitment 'perks' prior to the current recession, there has been steady growth of private health insurance, although much lower than Conservative politicians and industry predictions ancitipated.[13] The private hospital picture has changed rapidly since the early 1970s when they were mostly small hospitals owned by charities or religious orders, to chains of hospitals owned by private companies. These latter have been quite volatile, with US companies entering the market in the mid 1980s (evidently they saw bed occupancy figures of around 50 per cent as good, based on USA experience, whereas in UK they were thought of as poor performers) and selling out in the late 1980s. The two biggest changes have been firstly, in the nursing home market where Higgins reports a fourfold and two and a half fold increase in private residential care homes and private nursing home beds respectively; and secondly, in the potential for NHS: private provider collaboration. By separating out the commissioning of services from provision of services, the way has been opened for commissioners to make much wider use of private providers of care. This had occurred on a small scale in the past. For example, some hospitals used commercial providers of renal dialysis, either because it was cheaper to buy in the service or to avoid the capital costs of building new units etc. Mobile cardiac catheterization facilities are available from private suppliers, and in Morriston Hospital, Swansea, for example, the new cardiac services must be tendered for by outside private interests, as well as by the in-house team. NHS trusts also have increased their capacity to provide private facilities (which legislation allows them to do so long as NHS contracts are not jeopardized), and have squeezed the private sector. Whether in NHS or totally private facilities, 25 per cent of all elective surgery is now carried out privately, so the public/private distinction is becoming more blurred. It can be argued that some services have been privatized, in that waiting lists have forced patients to look to the private sector, e.g. in 1985 a quarter of all hip replacements, cholecystectomies and hysterectomies were carried out privately. However, it should be noted that a significant proportion of these were performed on foreign patients, and that there is a strong belief within the industry that it is surgeon behaviour not government policy that nudges patients into the private arena.

Ministers have encouraged health authorities and trusts to look to private developers to raise capital for new building. There is, therefore, privatization of the capital asset base. Similarly to the extent that we define privatization as labour not being employed within the public sector, then there is an argument that privatization is increasing in the NHS as more support services are contracted out to private companies. Sometimes this is a deliberate attempt to provide services more cheaply, because centrally negotiated Whitley Council terms and conditions of service may be higher than the market rate in some parts of the country, or it may be that there are restrictions which mean that if the NHS provides the service directly, it must carry more highly paid supervisors and trained staff than would the private sector. In this respect we will certainly see an increasing level of privatization, although it will not necessarily affect payment at the point of use. Already, we see a wide range of services being bought in, e.g. hotel services, transport and security services, and even commercial management services for some activities, as well as private financial consultancy. It is likely that the private sector will offer a wider and wider range of medical and technical services which the NHS may feel it appropriate to buy in.

Milne[14] points out accurately that there is much confusion about competitive tendering and privatization, and highlights the preponderance of contracts that have been won by internal bids, i.e. NHS staff themselves bidding. Commercial involvement has been less rapid, therefore, than is often supposed. Where radical new approaches have been proposed, as in Reading, where a whole variety of administrative and support services were to be delivered by a commercial contractor, the health service has been reluctant to implement. On the whole there has been considerable disappointment with the performance of third party contractors, both qualitatively and in their financial performance. One problem has been that because of in-house tendering and because financial savings have been emphasized over quality, margins from competitive tendering have been very low. Few companies have therefore been tempted into the market, or have stayed in it, so it has proved difficult to enforce compliance to contract standards - there are no competitors to turn to. This contrasts markedly with USA.[15] Similarly, NHS clients are inconsistent, e.g. Guys Hospital announced major ancilliary staff cuts despite having a contract with Service Master to manage hotel services with agreed numbers of staff.

Because of pressure on hospital sites, there will be further pressure to disengage support services from the strictly clinical and professional services and to move them to lower rent peripheral locations. Once this happens, it becomes conceptually easier to imagine these services being provided by third party commercial providers. In this respect it is therefore quite possible that we will see an increasing range of support services, and technical services such as pathology, provided by private sources, although the patient will still receive services free at the point of use. What we may see in the future is the introduction of the 'Hospi Mall' rather than the 'hospital'. In other words, as in a shopping mall, an owner of the capital assets could tender for, lets say, ophthalmology or paediatrics services, allowing the successful bidder to use the facilities available. The hospimall owner could provide central services, including nurses or allowing the contractors to provide their own. The quality would be controlled through contracts.

Not only do we have to differentiate between privatization of the means of production in health care and whether or not the public pays, but in the latter category we ought to differentiate between the strictly health component of services received from the NHS, and associated peripheral services. In some instances it seems reasonable that the public should expect to pay for what may be convenience aspects of the service. For example, it is not clear why patients (or staff) should expect to be able to park their cars on NHS land, yet attempts to raise such charges are described as 'privatization', and it is implied that the public is receiving a lower quality of service. In many respects, one might anticipate that better services would be provided if charges were levied. If it meant that hard pressed hospitals could provide better car parking, security etc. if they levied a charge, then patients would receive better services not worse. Furthermore, there would be additional monies available for the provision of direct medical care, again to the benefit of the community.

Conclusion

There has clearly been significant privatization of the nursing home sector, but not of the hospital and community service sectors. GPs, private practitioners working within the NHS, are in charge of an increasing proportion of the NHS elective surgery budget, but as yet still favour the use of NHS hospital services. Ownership of the latter is still in the public sector, and most professional staff are still employed by the NHS. Therefore, NHS plc is not with us yet.

Overall it seems that the government reforms may have paved the way for increasing privatization of health services by more accurately identifying what services are provided and what they cost, and thereby enabling different strands of what constitutes the NHS to be teased apart. The reforms have shifted discussion away from the Secretary of State's liability to provide a comprehensive health service to the need for commissioners or purchasers to define a package of services which they can afford from the budgets given to them. Providers are expected to respond to those service agreements rather than providing that range of services which they felt were good for the public, and which frequently were no more than an expression of professionals' interests.

It can be argued that before the reforms the NHS was not owned by the public, but was owned by the professionals who work within the service. It was the various medical and non-medical professions who provide services, who were able to define to a large extent the shape and feel of the NHS. Through their regulatory and statutory powers they could define who provided what services, and often how, when and where. The local pattern of services often owed little to rational analysis of clients' needs, and a great deal the attitudes of local professionals. In some respects the recent reforms have taken this ownership away from the professionals, who were only loosely monitored by politicians and their agents (the managers and health authority members), but it is not yet clear where the new ownership lies. What is clear is that care continues to be offered free at the point of service in most cases, and that politicians in the short term are unlikely to change this approach.

Health providing agencies are being forced to become more responsive to the needs of their client groups, and there is much more emphasis on quality and customer awareness than before. In this respect they are taking on some of the attributes of privatized organizations, without being privatized.

It must be assumed that on ideological grounds a Conservative government would want to see more privatization both in terms of personal responsibility for at least partial fee payment, and in private means of production. Even if there is little actual privatization evident in the NHS at present, the reforms have certainly cracked open the NHS monolith which will make such changes easier to bring about.

Footnotes

1 For a review of public opinion on the NHS see Judith Allsop's survey, *The voice of the user in health care*, in E. Beck, *et al*., 'In the Best of Health', London: Chapman and Hall, 1992.

2 For detailed country by country expenditure information see *Health Care Systems in Transition: The Search for Efficiency*, OECD, Paris, 1990, and *World Development Report, 1993: Investing in Health*, The World Bank/OUP, Washington DC, 1993.

3 Potter, C. and Porter, J. (1989), 'Five myths of Socialised Medicine', *Journal of Health Policy, Law & Politics*, Summer 1989.

4 There are many descriptions of the nationalization of the NHS. Still very readable is Harry Eckstein's *The English Health Service: Its origins, structure and achievements*, Harvard University Press, 1964.

See also *The Reorganised NHS*, Levitt, Ruth and Wall, Andrew (1984) Croom Helm, and R.G.S. Brown (1978) *The Changing NHS*, Routledge and Kegan Paul. For detailed information about the situation prior to 1948 see Brian Abel-Smith, (1964), *The Hospitals 1800-1948*, A study in Social Administration in England and Wales (1964), Heinemann.

5 According to John Eyler, a historian at the University of Minnesota, Minneapolis, specializing in the establishment of the NHS, the Labour Party's leaders believed that attention to housing, education and employment would automatically resolve health problems, and it was not until 1930 that the Socialist Medical Association persuaded them this was simplistic. Also in 1930 the BMA itself made proposals to reform health care provision, republishing them in 1938 as '*A Good Medical Service for the Nation*'. The 1946 NHS White Paper was the Ministry of Health's bringing together of the Medical Planning Commission's proposals and those of the Beveridge Report. Reform was seen as an economy measure not a political one.

6 Beveridge, Sir W. (1942), Report on Social Insurance & Allied Services, Cmnd 6404, London, HMSO.

7 Walters, Vivienne (1980), *Class Inequality and Health Care*, Croom Helm. See also *Planners, Politics & Health Services*, Partson, Greg (1980), Croom Helm.

8 *The National Health Service Act*, HMSO, 1946. An excellent analysis of the problems engendered by the obligation on the Minister of Health to promote a *comprehensive* health service is provided in *The NHS: The end of the Rainbow*, Bryan Thwaites, Health Care Management.

9 A very detailed account of the financing debate surrounding the NHS in its early years is provided by the BMA's report *Health Service Financing*, (1967), Jones, I.M., *et al*.

10 Figures from H. Bayley, MP, 'Bridge over troubled water', *Health Services Journal*, 24 June, 1993.

11 For more detailed analysis see 'Administrative and financial

management of Health Care Services', John Perrin, in E. Beck *et al.*, *ibid.*

12 Potter, C. and Morgan, P. (1993), 'Professional Cultures and Paradigms of Quality in Health care'. Paper presented at University of Stirling School of Management Conference on Professions and Management in Britain. In press.

13 For a recent analysis see Joan Higgins, *Private Sector Health Care*, in E. Beck *et al., ibid.*

14 Milne, Robin, 'Competitive tendering of Support Services' in E. Beck *et al., ibid.*

15 For a discussion of US experience see Potter (1985), 'When do American health care administrators use contractors?' *Hospital and Health Services Review*, Vol. 81, No. 2, March.

Section IV

Privatization's Effects on Consumers and Employees

13 Employees and the privatization of the water industry in England and Wales

Colin Harris

Introduction

We saw in Chapter 14 that privatization is explicitly intended to shift power from producers to consumers. Its proponents also maintain that it can bring advantages for employees as well. In his 1983 speech, John Moore assured his audience that privatization would result in 'better pay, conditions and employment opportunities for the employees' (1983, p.2). Furthermore, each major privatization has encouraged workers to buy shares in their company, and most have set aside a small number of free shares for employees with the result that over ninety per cent of employees in the majority of these companies own shares in them. The Government has argued that as employees accumulate shares in their company the industrial relations' climate will improve because workers will increasingly identify with the interests of the company.

This chapter examines the effect on employees of the privatization of the water industry in England and Wales in 1989. It is based upon a survey of employees in two privatized Regional Water Authorities; Southern and North-West Water. Three months before the authorities were privatized 177 employees in these two Regional Water Authorities were interviewed. These employees were contacted again eighteen months after the privatization had taken place and 107 were successfully reinterviewed. These interviews were supplemented by a small 'control group' of sixty-five water employees who had remained in the public sector and who completed short questionnaires at both phases of the project. Forty successful repeat cases were obtained.

From this survey data four main issues are considered. These are: what employees felt about the general principle of privatization, how they expected privatization to effect their work, what effect privatization has had on employees' working lives and whether now owning a small stake in their company actually means very much to the employees concerned. More detailed consideration of this research can be found in Saunders and Harris (1994).

Employeee attitudes to privatization

Privatization of the basic utilities never enjoyed wide public support. It was also unpopular with our employee sample. Prior to their company being privatized over two-thirds of our employee sample agreed with the general principle that essential services should be supplied by the Government rather than private companies. After eighteen months of working in the private sector their opinions had changed very little - around 60 per cent still agreed with this principle. Managers were the only group of employees with any real faith in private sector provision, for no managers, either prior to water privatization or after eighteen months in the private sector, strongly disagreed with the principle of private sector provision of essential services.

Our sample was similarly opposed to the privatization of the water industry. Whilst they were happy to accept the free shares offered to them and to participate in the other company share offers and schemes, water employees told us that they did not approve of the privatization of water. Before privatization half of our sample told us that they disapproved of the privatization of water and around a quarter told us that they approved. Eighteen months after privatization approval rates had risen to 44 per cent but this was due almost entirely to a turnaround in the attitude of managers, none of whom now disapproved of the privatization.

Opposition to water privatization has remained most deeply felt amongst manual and clerical employees, around one half of whom would be prepared to tolerate the further upheaval of returning the water industry back to the public sector. In contrast, no managers approved of such a move.

It is possible that the employees' hostility to the privatization of water reflects the deep conservatism of the British public such that a majority of people will say that they disapprove of virtually any major proposed change. This would be particularly acute for those who, like our employee sample, are directly affected by the change. However, our data lends stronger support to a different interpretation. The antipathy of our employee sample towards water privatization is grounded in a commitment, by all employees in our sample except managers, to a set of values committed to state provision. They have a strong commitment to public sector provision, feel that it is wrong for an essential service to be placed in the private sector (mentioned by 57 per cent of those who opposed the sale in 1989 and 64 per cent in 1991), and furthermore, that it was morally wrong to do so. They are also deeply worried that the private sector is far more concerned with increasing profits and looking after shareholders than providing a good service to the public. It is only managers who believe the private sector to be the best method of delivering an essential service.

The argument, put by Whitfield, that the Conservative Government have created an ideology 'lowering people's expectations about what the state should provide in an attempt to reduce the demand for public services' (1983 p.24) does not hold true for our sample of employees. They continue to endorse Gordon's claim that there is in Britain a 'public perception that water is a common need which no special interest should be allowed to exploit for private gain' (1989, p.141). Experience of the private sector has done little to deflect employees from the beliefs they held whilst working in the public sector. How then did they anticipate privatization would affect their working lives?

Employees' expectations of privatization

The overall impression from interviews with employees before water privatization was of a fairly contented workforce. For example, all managers and over three-quarters of the rest of our sample expressed satisfaction with their earnings. Nearly all management and lower manager/supervisor grades expressed satisfaction with the scope for showing personal initiative and responsibility in their job. Even two-thirds of our sample of manual and clerical workers who typically exert less control over work than management, told us that they were satisfied with this aspect . Around half of clerical and manager/supervisor grades and all but one manager was satisfied with the promotion prospects that the company offered. Manual workers, however, reflected the traditional view that manual work is least career orientated and, as such, tends to offer limited opportunities for advancement. Only one-third of manuals were satisfied with their prospects for promotion and advancement. Around 85 per cent of our sample told us that they were either satisfied or very satisfied with the security that their job offered whilst still in the public sector.

Various writers have suggested that the main source of employees' concerns when organizational change occurs is uncertainty about their future role in the organization (for example Schweiger and Ivancevitch, 1985). Nelson and Cooper found that employees facing the prospect of privatization 'were troubled by "factors intrinsic in their jobs" (in other words what would happen to their pay, hours of work, the design of their job), as well as "career and achievement issues", such as threat of redundancy, absence of career advancement, lack of opportunities etc.' (1993 p.18). Each privatization has been met with a mixture of positive and negative predictions from the media, this too can only have served to fuel employees insecurities. The trade unions were particularly negative. They claimed that jobs tended to be 'slashed both in preparation for privatization and as a result of it' (WIUC, 1985, p.24). Also Roy Watts, the chairman of Thames Water, was characteristically blunt about his expectations of managers in the newly privatized water companies: 'Pace will have to be quicker. Right decisions will have to be made at the right time on the right subject. Executives will have to learn to live without comfort, second guessing....executives judged on action not promise, rewarded accordingly....executives will have to learn to act more and write less. More action, fewer word processors' (1987).

Our sample had some fears about what the future might bring. They saw loss of job security as the greatest threat of privatization. When asked to look at the outcomes of privatization, around half of clerical and lower management/supervisor grades thought that their jobs would become less secure and around 40 per cent mentioned job security as a disadvantage of privatization. We might have expected managers to have been more worried than other employees about job security, for, as Watt's strong words above indicated, life was to be more difficult for management and, by implication, some would not be up to the task. It turns out that managers were the least worried about the security of their job; around two-thirds of managers thought that job security would either improve or stay the same as in the private sector.

Freeing management to manage was one the 'first and foremost' of the Government's objectives for privatization (Walters 1989, p.250). It was envisaged that management in the public sector, which had constantly had to mould their decisions to the whims of their political masters, would be freed by privatization to get on with the job. Watts believed that privatization gives greater managerial freedom, freeing managers 'from the shackles of restrictive statutes and government departmental and treasury supervision controls' (1988). Similarly John Moore, claimed privatization would 'set managers free to manage' (1983, p.11).

Managers in our sample thought too that they would be freer to carry out decisions after privatization. Over three-quarters told us that scope for showing personal initiative and responsibility would improve in the private sector and over one half cited 'job enrichment' as an advantage of privatization. They told us : 'Old practices will be questioned, management will be allowed to think', and that: (privatization) will open up boundaries - at the moment we are governed by central government, privatization will enable us to diversify, which will open up new staff opportunities'.

However, manual workers were not so optimistic. None of the manual workers in our sample anticipated any improvement in their autonomy upon privatization. Around half thought that it would stay the same and the rest were split between not knowing how things would turn out and fearing they would become less autonomous. It is likely that these fears were caused by the recent restructuring of the water industry. Since 1970 there has been cost cutting in the industry and from 1979 Government has imposed strict financial controls, as well as continuing to cut budgets. O'Connel Davidson (1989) has argued that in response to tighter financial controls managers have attempted to control work pace and produce greater productivity. This has resulted in the loss of control and freedom previously enjoyed by some manual grades in the industry.

Besides the very real fear of many of our sample about the effect that privatization might have on job security, expectations for the future were not all pessimistic. For example, three-quarters of managers and around half of the rest of the grades thought that earnings would improve after privatization. Although manual grades were unhappy with their prospects for promotion in 1989, only one manual worker expected further deterioration in the private sector, with over two-thirds telling us that this aspect of their job would stay the same. Over one-half of clerical and lower manager/supervisors thought that privatization would have no effect on promotion prospects, with a third telling us that they would actually improve. Managers were the most bullish about promotion prospects, with two-thirds telling us these would actually improve after privatization.

Overall, employees adopted a fairly pragmatic approach to privatization with some seeing it as an opportunity to enhance rather than detract from various aspects of their working lives. The one outstanding worry expressed by our sample was that privatization would make their jobs less secure. So how has privatization affected employees' working lives?

The effects of privatization on employees' working lives

The water trade unions had claimed that privatization would destroy jobs and that their members' pay would also suffer. In general, these fears have not materialized.

Much of the unions' argument that privatization destroys jobs was based on the experience of the BT where, by 1994, it is expected that seventy thousand jobs will have been lost since privatization. Clearly, many of these job losses were a result of the rapid pace of technological change and competition in the telecommunications industry and would have happened whether or not BT had been privatized (see Hallett, 1990). However, BT's transfer into the private sector undoubtedly made the shedding of staff politically easier.

The water industry has also seen employment decline since the mid-seventies when it was removed from local government and set up as the ten Regional Water Authorities. There have also been some job losses in the industry in the run-up to privatization as the Government attempted to raise productivity prior to the sale. As Letwin (1988) observes, the major shake-out of staff tends to occur before rather than after privatization so as to make them more attractive to investors. However, in the case of the water industry, the decline in employment has been longterm; much of it occurred before privatization had even been considered. As NALGO figures show, 20 per cent of the total jobs in the industry were lost between 1979 and 1989.

Indeed, contrary to union fears, employment in the industry actually increased after privatization, so that by 1992, the total numbers employed by the ten water plcs were back at around fifty thousand which is where it had stood before six thousand jobs were transferred to the National Rivers Authority in 1989. This increase was largely a function of the expansion of the new plcs into a range of subsidiary activities rather than of any growth of employment in the 'core' water and sewage businesses. Some employees have, however, been transferred from the 'core' business to the enterprise companies resulting in a significant decrease in the numbers employed in the 'core' businesses of water services. At the end of 1992 there were signs that some redundancies were going to be made in the 'enterprise' companies of the new plcs. Subsequent events have shown the trade unions' fears to be justified. For recently there have been substantial redundancies announced in the water industry. The most recent of which, in response to the Director General of OFWAT (Ian Byatt) announcement of price controls for the industry in July 1994, has been Welsh Water's announcement that 410 jobs are to be lost over the next three year period.

Although the problem of 'overmanning' in the water industry was tackled during the1970s and 1980s, the scope for further productivity gains through new technology has been limited. It would have been expected that the concern of OFWAT to monitor the standard of service offered by the privatized companies would further restrict scope for shedding labour in any significant numbers. However, Byatt's clear statement that profits and dividends (which have risen sharply in the industry since privatization) would have to be paid for in increased efficiency rather than higher water bills, has given rise to predictions that the ten privatized water companies would shed around 6,700 jobs within the next six years (Guardian, 16/8/94).

At the post-privatization interviews, employees outside of management told us that they still felt insecure about their jobs. Forty-two per cent, 49 per cent and 40 per cent respectively of manual, clerical and lower management supervisory grades told us that job security had got worse, yet all but one of the managers in our sample told us that their jobs felt at least as secure as they had prior to privatization. Nelson and Cooper (1993) provide some explanation for this. They have found that those in positions of less control are likely to suffer the most negative effects of major organizational change, this being particularly acute when the change is one outside their control and, when the implications and consequences of the change are less clear as in the case of privatizations (p.17). Although these claims are supported by our study it is likely that employees were not reacting purely to organizational change but had a sense that the change of emphasis from 'service' in the public sector to 'profit' in the private sector would threaten their jobs. Subsequent events have shown their fears to be justified.

All but one of the managers in our sample told us that their job felt at least as secure as it had prior to privatization yet, 42 per cent, 49 per cent and 40 per cent respectively of manual, clerical and lower management supervisory grades told us that job security had got worse.

Employees' continued perception of insecurity is a worry. For a workforce which prior to privatization was fairly contented and, although sceptical about privatization, was willing to grasp it as a positive opportunity now seems to be suffering from low morale through fears engendered by worries about job security. With over half of manual and clerical workers now telling us that communication between workers and managers had deteriorated since privatization, fears about job security are likely to be exacerbated.

Overall there is not much evidence to suggest that employees' pay has suffered since privatization. There is, however, evidence to suggest that the move into the private sector has resulted in higher rather than lower pay settlements as the water plcs have been freed from external financing limits and public sector pay restraints. It is possible to make a direct comparison between pay increases won by those employed in the private water plcs and those who in 1989 transferred to the NRA and who have therefore remained in the public sector. Figures from NALGO and NUPE for 1990, the year following privatization, indicate that employees in the privatized water companies did slightly better than those in the NRA (9.68 per cent compared to 9.25 per cent). By 1991 the differential was more marked with the water companies receiving an 8.63 per cent pay increase compared with 6.5 per cent for those employed by the NRA. It would seem therefore quite reasonable to deduce that the average pay rates of employees in the privatized water companies are almost certainly higher than would have been the case if the industry had remained in the private sector.

Besides being able to secure higher wage settlements than their public sector colleagues, NALGO and NUPE figures show that the 1991 wage settlements in the private water companies were above the RPI and in line with average earnings (NALGO and NUPE 1991) . Generally, our sample of employees did not see earnings as having deteriorated, only 5 per cent of clerical, 9 per cent of lower management /supervisor and 11 per cent of managers told us that their earnings had got worse since privatization, with around three-quarters of clerical and lower manager/supervisory grades saying that earnings had stayed the same. The two exceptions were manual workers and managers. One-third of manuals now thought their earnings had got worse since privatization. There is a simple explanation for this. The push for cost-cutting in the water plcs has resulted in a dramatic decrease in emergency call-outs and weekend work. As this work was almost exclusively carried out by manual grades their potential earnings have been reduced. In contrast, over three-quarters of managers in our sample told us that their earnings had improved This is almost certainly due to the introduction of personal performance-related contracts for managers. These have allowed managers to negotiate pay outside of any national agreements and, as John Moore claimed, made 'it possible to link pay to success and provide appropriate rewards' (1983 p.12).

With the exception of manual workers' overtime, there is no evidence to support the unions' warning that their members' pay would suffer as a result of privatization. Like employees in other privatized industries, employees in the water industry were offered free shares; the opportunity to purchase discounted shares and to participate in a SAYE scheme. Taking all this into account it is hard to see how employees can be said to have lost out financially as a result of the move to the private sector.

Manual employees' fears that their jobs may become less autonomous after privatization appear unfounded. For half the manual employees in our sample now say that they have more scope for showing personal initiative and responsibility in their work with a further third feeling that nothing has changed. Clerical and lower management/supervisory grades expressed similar sentiments. O'Connel Davidson and her co-authors (1991) found that managers were the most likely employees to have experienced increased autonomy since privatization. Our results also support the claim that the move to the private sector would leave managers freer to manage, for managers now tell us that they have been afforded an autonomy previously unavailable to them in the private sector.

As the new water companies have diversified into non-regulated 'profit centres' to compete as profit-making commercial ventures, managers are now likely to find themselves in control of budgets and responsible for profitability. One manager told us that where he previously 'just had to get the job done', he was now responsible for the successful operation of controlling the budget and the profitability of his 'profit centre'. He told us:

> It's all down to me now, if anything goes wrong it's my responsibility, if it goes well and we make a profit I get a pat on the back...not literally but I'm on performance-related pay so it shows in my wage packet.

We also see in Chapter 14 (Thomason) that management have been successful in changing their relationship with the trade unions. There is now increasing use of non-unionized labour which has allowed management greater control over staffing levels. Staff can now be taken on and laid off as workloads or budget restrictions dictate. As one manager told us:

> Privatization has given managers freedom to recruit essential labour, for example, private companies, subcontractors, and we are able to finance moves of essential personnel from other regions.

As privatization ideologues predicted, managers have felt empowered by privatization. They feel that their jobs have been enriched, that they are more autonomous and, that they are freer to use their initiative in decision making.

If John Moore's claim that privatization would leave managers freer to manage has proven correct, his claim that it would create better employment opportunities for employees has not. Only 8 per cent of manual, 16 per cent of lower manager/supervisor and 21 per cent of both clerical and management grades saw any improvement in promotion prospects after eighteen months in the private sector. Fifty eight per cent of manual workers and around a quarter of clerical and lower management/supervisors actually thought they had deteriorated. Our sample was most likely see no change (mentioned by 56 per cent of clerical and lower manager/supervisors and 78 per cent of management grades).

Lastly we looked at one of the common features of privatization - employee share ownership. What does this mean to employees?

Employee share ownerhip and privatization

Employees were offered four opportunities to buy shares in the privatized companies. Each employee was entitled to £140 worth of free shares plus another £2 worth of shares for every year of service. In addition, two free shares were offered for every share purchased up to a maximum of £200. This entitled employees to a maximum of £400 worth of free shares for an outlay of £200, although these shares could not be sold immediately. Furthermore, a 10 per cent discount was offered on share purchases up to £2350 with priority over applications from the general public on up to £14,350 worth of shares (discounted and priority purchases could be sold immediately). Finally, employees could join a SAYE scheme entitling employees with at least one year's service to buy ordinary shares on preferential terms. Those joining this scheme are required to take out a SAYE contract to save a specific amount each month for a minimum period of five years. At the end of this period the employee can either take the cash accumulated in savings plus a form of cash free bonus or use the savings to buy company shares at a unit price agreed at the start of the SAYE contract. Two schemes were offered: one at the time of the privatization and one a year later. At present these have been offered on a yearly basis.

Ninety-six per cent of employees in our samples at Southern and North-West accepted the offer of free shares. All those declining the offer did so because they disagreed in principle. Seventy-nine per cent of the sample purchased some matching shares, and 30 per cent bought shares in the discounted general offer. Forty-five per cent had joined one of the company SAYE share schemes at the time of our reinterviews. The higher the grade of employee, the greater the enthusiasm displayed for share purchase. The matching share offer was taken up by 58 per cent of manual grades compared with 80 per cent clerical, 88 per cent lower management/supervisory and 90 per cent management. Similarly, discounted shares were purchased by only 13 per cent of clerical and 17 per cent of manual grades but 67 per cent of management and the longer financial commitment of the SAYE scheme attracted 41 per cent manual and 42 per cent clerical grades but 79 per cent of lower managers and supervisors and

90 per cent of the higher level managers.

The Government has claimed that employees who now own a stake in their company will start to identify with the interests of company management as they will recognize their personal prosperity increasing with the profitability of the company. Thus in time, 'labour' and 'capital' should come closer together as horizontal class-based identification gives way to vertical identification. Eventually workers' interests as shareholders should compliment their interests as wage earners.

Implicit in this culture change is a shift in employees' attitude towards their trade union. As early as 1978 in a unpublished report on the nationalized industries, the Conservative Party emphasized the need to do something to reduce the power of the trade unions. One avenue by which it was thought privatization might do this was to realign workers' identification, through the vehicle of employee share ownership. It was envisaged that by breaking down the old distinctions between workers and owners, employee share ownership would cause workers to abandon their traditional horizontal allegiance with the trade unions and cause them to identify vertically with the company and management.

As John Moore explains:

> Employees who are also owners see immediately the absolute identity of interest between themselves and the success of the companies for which they work, and they take steps to ensure that success (Moore, 1986, p.5).

The unions, however, were scathing of such claims:

> The Government's claims that privatization gives employees a 'stake' in the organisation they work for. This touching regard for the well being of staff would be praiseworthy if it were sincere. The reality is rather different however (WIUC 1985, p.24).

While acknowledging that employees stood to benefit from a few hundred pounds worth of free shares, the unions argued that the amount was too small a stake in their company to influence decision making in any way and thus cause them to relate more to the company. Using BT as an example, the unions had argued that 'even including all the shares given free to staff, the total stake held by employees in the company is less than 2 per cent, far too small to make the slightest impact on company policy' (WIUC 1985, pp.24-25). The unions were confident that ownership of a few shares would do little to transform workplace behaviour and allegencies. In fact, the unions were generally indifferent to the question of employee share ownership. In interviews with water union officials both before and after the privatization of water we attempted in vain to discover any 'official ' union policy on the issue. The TUC now supports employee share ownership and its General Secretary claims to be 'a convert to wider share ownership' (*Independent* 5/7/90), but this support comes with warnings to employees who have small amounts to invest to be wary of tying up this capital in their employees, for this makes employees very vulnerable in the event of bankruptcy (see CBI 1990).

Some union officials, however, accepted that their members would and should take the opportunity to accept free shares. As one member of the GMB National Executive told us, 'You would take them, wouldn't you? Well so would I and that's what I am telling members who ask me. After all it's something for nothing'. However , others were less accommodating. For example, the NALGO branch at North West Water took a strongly oppositional line by launching its own 'Don't buy' campaign, but as figures for the uptake of shares among North West employees show , very few employees paid any heed to this advice.

Other studies have also found a marked indifference of the unions towards the question of employee share ownership. Badden and his colleagues found among union officials 'neutrality at best, a bored hostility at worst, but even then not taking on a high profile so as to make the operation of any such scheme difficult for management' (1989, p.248). Likewise, Poole found, among trade union activists, 'lukewarm or passive acceptance' and, among their leaders, 'no coherent overall position' (Poole & Jenkins, 1990). Thomas (1986) in interviews with union officials found that they all believed that employee shareholding would have little impact on industrial relations and was not therefore of any great relevence to the trade unions.

This indifference is highlighted by the unions representing workers in the electricity industry, who, during the run up to electricity privatization were actively negotiating with the Government for more shares to be given to their members (Chapman 1990).

The attitude of the trade unions towards share ownership may seem surprising for as Poole and Jenkins claim 'So far as industrial relations are concerned, no issue is more fundamental than the potential impact of employee financial participation on trade unions' (1990 p.11). Politicians certainly believe that employee share ownership can undermine trade union solidarity and reduce labour militancy and some studies have demonstrated that management also feel this to be true. Badden and his co-authors (1989) in their study of several companies found that one-fifth saw employee share ownership as part of a strategy for weakening the hold of unions over the workforce. Although they suggest that companies who attempt to introduce anti-strike penalties into their profit sharing arrangements run the risk of increasing collective solidarity amongst the workforce. However, other research on this issue has been inconclusive. Estrin and Wilson (1986) found that share ownership does seem to reduce industrial conflict, whereas Meade (1986) suggests that it might actually increase it. Poole and Jenkins (1990) suggest that employee share ownership schemes may produce a modest reduction in industrial disputes, but they describe the relationship between strikes and employee share ownership as complex.

Looking at other privatized companies there is scant evidence to suggest that employee share owners will refrain from industrial action because they are now part owners of the company. BT provides a good example. Soon after it was privatized management attempted to peg back a pay rise to just 5 per cent and to impose flexible working practices. The fact that over 90 per cent of BT's workforce had been made shareholders when the company was privatized did not prevent them from striking against the proposed changes and for a better pay deal. One BT employee when asked about the incongruity of an employee shareholder on picket duty argued that being a shareholder 'made no difference at all. It's just another kind of bonus' (quoted in Badden *et al.* 1989, p.51). Chapman (1990) notes that striking employee shareholders were later 'punished' by the company who refused to pay them profit sharing dividends on the grounds that they had shown total disregard for the company's profitability.

Turning to the water industry, Ogden (1993) believes that there is some tradition of militancy among the manual water unions which was demonstrated in 1983 by the one month strike over pay which ended by breaking the public sector pay targets set by the Government that year.

Our survey supports the view that manual workers are more militant than their white collar colleagues although the number of manual workers interviewed is too small to draw firm conclusions.We asked our sample of employees whether they would feel obliged to strike if asked to do so by their union, even if they did not agree with the union on the issue. Table 1 reveals that prior to privatization manual workers were the group most likely to follow a call to strike and that manual and clerical employees were more likely to strike than their supervisor, lower management and management colleagues. Moreover, what the table does confirm, is that taken as a whole the workforce is not strongly committed to the principle of collective action, for prior to privatization only 28 per cent said they would feel obliged to follow a union strike call. Eighteen months after privatization this proportion had reduced to just 19 per cent.

Table 1: Employee commitment to obeying a strike call from their union

	All Employees				Employees in SAYE Scheme		Employees not in SAYE Scheme		Control Group			
	1989		1991		(1991)		(1991)		1989		1991	
	Yes	No	Yes	No	Yes	No	Yes	No	Yes	No	Yes	No
Manual	58	42	25	75	29	71	0	100	50	21	71	14
Clerical	39	56	39	59	36	61	50	50	39	46	15	69
LMS	16	81	12	86	8	92	25	75	63	13	50	25
Managers	0	100	0	100	0	100	0	100	40	40	40	60

N=107 (control group N=40). Figures given as percentages

Looking at our control group of water employees in Scotland who have remained in the public sector we find that, while clerical, lower management/supervisory and management grades are less likely to strike now than in 1989, the manual workers are more likely to heed a strike call. This difference between the two samples would appear to indicate that privatization has some impact on work culture. The traditionally more militant section of the workforce - the manual workers - are now slightly less militant. However, the size of our samples means such a claim should be treated with caution as a chi-square test of statistical significance cannot be applied.

If the argument that employee share ownership encourages workers to identify more with management than their traditional representatives - the trade unions - were correct (the so-called unitarist thesis), we would expect some differences in attitude between those participating in the company SAYE scheme and non-participating employees. Table 1 also shows the differences in answers to employee attitudes to strike action between participating and non-participating employees. There is no evidence that the unitarist thesis is correct. The same thesis was examined in Table 2 where the relation between the extent of share ownership and inclination to obey a strike call is examined.

Table 2: Commitment to abide by a union strike call and level of share ownership

	YES	NO	DON'T KNOW
Passive	33(4)	58(7)	8(1)
Active	20(9)	78(36)	2(1)
Superactive	14(4)	86(24)	0
Hyperactive	33(3)	67(6)	0

Figures show per cent of employees at that level with actual numbers in ()
N=95
Note: these categories are the same as those used by Nichols and O'Connel-Davidson (1992).

Passive: employees who only accepted the free shares offered to them by the company at privatization
Active: employees who accepted the free shares offered to them and went on to buy further shares through either the matching or discount share offers or through the company SAYE scheme
Superactive: employee share owners who have the same relation to ownership as 'actives' but have also bought shares in other privatization issues and/or bought shares in other privatization stocks.
Hyperactives: a subgroup of 'superactives'who have bought shares in both in other privatization issues and own other non-privatized stocks.

Once more, there appears to be no significant relationship between share ownership and union militancy drawing us to support the conclusions of Ramsey *et al.* (1990) that employee share ownership schemes are unlikely to significantly undermine workplace trade union solidarity. The indifferent attitude of the trade unions to the prospect of their members becoming employee share owners appears to be vindicated by our study. However, we see in Chapter 14 (Thomason) that privatization has resulted in other developments more worthy of their attention.

If share ownership has not undermined trade union solidarity, has it promoted closer relationships between the company and employees and managers and workers? The White Paper for the privatization of the Water Industry claims that 'employees will benefit from.... closer identification with their businesses' (Cmnd 9734, 1986: para 7). Likewise, Lord Belstead (1987), (then Minister of State at the Department of the Environment) was so confident of the transforming qualities of share ownership that at the *Economist* conference on Water privatization, he declared 'the importance of a direct stake in the firm one works for, and the identification of one's own interest with that of the firm, hardly needs to be stated'. Similarly, John Moore believes 'it will break down the illusory barriers between "them" and "us", between employers and employees, between management and workers, that have been the bane of British society and have undermined British economic life' (1986, p.5).

There is some academic evidence to support these claims. Fogarty and White (1988) using four companies as case studies found that around half the employees questioned admitted that share schemes had made them feel like a partner in the company. However, less than 30 per cent felt that the schemes had caused any reduction in 'us and them' attitudes in the company. Bell and Hansen (1984) in their study of twelve companies report that around half the employees questioned agreed that share ownership increased their loyalty to the company and over two-thirds felt it made them feel more positive about the company.

However other studies have not found such positive evidence. Badden and his co-authors (1989) found that participation in share ownership 'is not significantly associated with a set of values which produce a rosy view of the company and its management' (pp.258-9). Nichols and O'Connel-Davidson (1992) in their study of two privatized utilities discovered that employees owning shares in their company were less likely to believe in the transformative effect of share ownership than non-owners. They found that 70 per cent of non-owners, compared with 85 per cent of those owning shares in their company, rejected the idea that share ownership breaks down the 'us and them' feelings between management and workers. Similarly, Poole and Jenkins (1990) in a case study of twenty-two firms found no evidence that share ownership caused employees to identify with their company.

Our results show that just giving employees free shares is no guarantee of making them feel more a part of the company. Prior to privatization over half our sample expected that owning shares and participating in share schemes would make them feel like partners and identify more with the company (67 per cent manual, 39 per cent clerical, 45 per cent lower management/supervisor, 68 per cent management) with 32 per cent saying that it would make no difference.

Eighteen months later only 38 per cent of our sample thought that share ownership had made them identify more with the company and 45 per cent said it had made no difference. Manual workers (the group least involved in SAYE schemes and further share ownership) showed the most marked turnaround, with only a third now feeling that the experience of share ownership has encouraged company identity. If we look at those employees in our sample who have opted to make a continuing commitment to further share ownership through a SAYE scheme, then we find that these employees are more likely to believe that increased identification is brought about by owning shares in their company. Over a half per cent of those participating in the SAYE scheme believe this to be so compared with 20 per cent of non-participators.

We also find that the more actively an employee is involved in share ownership the more likely that employee is to feel positive about the company. Around 20 per cent of 'passive' compared with 70 per cent of 'hyperactive' shareowners said that share ownership makes them identify positively with the company. Although we must bear in mind that management, who are mostly pro-privatization and most likely to feel positive about the company anyway are over-represented in this group.

There is no evidence from our study to support the claim that share ownership significantly breaks down any 'them and us' feelings between management and workers. In fact our evidence demonstrates the contrary. Prior to privatization there was a strongly held view across all grades that employees and managers worked like a team. Fifty-eight per cent of manual, 74 per cent clerical, 74 per cent lower manager/supervisor and 78 per cent management grades expressed this view. Privatization has, if anything, undermined this view amongst the lower grades with only 41 per cent of manual and 51 per cent of clerical grades now expressing this view. Fifty-eight per cent of manual grades and 49 per cent of clerical grades now feel that employees and managers do not work like a team.

Participating in share-schemes has also had little impact upon employee attitudes towards management. In fact, our results have a slight tendency to contradict a unitarist thesis. Manual workers participating in the share scheme are now less likely to express a unitarist view than their non-participating counterparts. Other levels of employee show no differences between participating and non-participating members.

Furthermore, increasing commitment to share ownership also has little effect on attitudes to employee-management relations. Although those most involved in share ownership - the 'hyperactives'- are slightly more likely to see workers and managers as a team (78 per cent) than 'actives' (70 per cent). This is not compelling evidence for the unifying powers of employee share-ownership.

Looking at our control group of water employees in Scotland there is no significant change between employees' attitudes on this issue between 1989 and 1991. This would appear to indicate that employee share ownership has some impact on work culture, but not in the manner claimed by its proponents. Its introduction into the new water plcs has, according to our findings, caused employees to feel that managers and workers now work less like a team. Again we must stress that the size of our samples means such a claim should be treated with caution as a chi-square test of statistical significance cannot be applied.

Lastly, we attempted to further guage employee identification with the company by looking at three areas of activity. We asked employees whether they followed the movements of their share price, whether they attended the company AGM and, whether they read the annual report. Weak gauges of participation these may be, but they are perhaps the basic minimal criterion of active share ownership and participation. Thirty-seven per cent of employees participating in the SAYE scheme compared with 17 per cent of non-joiners claimed to have attended the AGM and 20 per cent of joiners compared with 9 per cent of non-joiners claimed to have voted by proxy by returning the voting slip sent to them.The annual report (which is mailed to every shareholder) was read by 89 per cent of joiners compared with 67 per cent of non-joiners. Only three joiners and one non-joiner have approached the company with a shareholder query. Eighty-eight per cent of joiners compared with 50 per cent of non-joiners claim to regularly check the company shareprice and, only 24 per cent of non-joiners claimed to know the current share price of their company compared with 71 per cent of joiners. However, around half of these estimations were over 30 per cent wide of the mark. These findings were surprising considering that our case study companies appeared to have a policy of displaying the current share price (and often the place of the company in the WPLC's basket of shares) on screens and noticeboards in prominent positions throughout company buildings.

These findings endorse the view that employees participating in share ownership schemes show more interest in the company and its activities than non-participants, but not significantly so. However, the low figures for attendance at the Annual General Meetings and the low numbers of employees voting by proxy, combined with employees feeling unable to approach the company with a shareholder query, indicate that employees do not feel that they have a voice in the running of the company.

Our results show that the introduction of employee share ownership schemes has done very little to enhance employees identification with the company and that the trade unions were probably correct in their prediction that a small financial interest in a company would not be enough to encourage workers to actively participate in the running of the company. That one of our case study companies actively discouraged employees from attending the company AGM does beg the question of whether employee participation would be welcomed anyway.

Conclusion

The belief of the trade unions that privatization would result in job losses and reductions in pay was not justified in the case of water. However, other privatizations have resulted in large-scale redundancies both prior to and after the sell-off. In contrast, the total number of jobs in the water industry has actually risen since privatization as the new water companies have diversified their operations. Pay rates have also risen faster in the newly privatized water companies than in the section which remained in the public sector - the NRA.

Privatization appears to have achieved one of its main aims - to generally enhance managerial autonomy. Unfortunately this may have been done at the expense of the other main claim - the hope of changing the workplace culture. It seems there is a danger in introducing radical change to a workforce who, in general, already have fairly positive attitudes towards the company. Prior to privatization employees in our sample were fairly contented and happy with their company and they had a consensual public sector service ethic.The privatization has shaken this up, but not necessarily in the way the Government had intended. Outside of management grades the workforce is now more concerned about job security than about seizing the new opportunities that privatization may offer.

Trade unions' assertions that employees would own too little in the way of shares to influence their behaviour have been vindicated by our study, for the introduction of ownership through share offers and share schemes also appears to have had little noticeable impact on employee attitudes and allegiancies.

Government hopes that the introduction of share ownership would decrease union militancy and break down 'them and us' attitudes are unfounded. Share ownership appears to have no impact on employees' propensity to take strike action, nor does it cause employees to hold a more rosy view of management. Although in the case of water there was probably very little scope for improving workplace relations anyway. Such schemes may, as has been found in other studies, be 'preaching to the converted' (see for example, Dunn, Richardson and Dew, 1991).

It is possible that the introduction of share ownership schemes may have had the opposite effect to what was intended. Ownership of shares and participation in the schemes is skewed very much towards the better-off workers in the WPLCs, especially amongst middle and top managers. As more share offers are made it is likely to be these employees who participate further, leaving those unable to afford further commitment with their few hundred pounds worth of free shares as their only stake in the company. We could envisage a situation in the future when the 'them and us' attitude is further entrenched through divisions between those more seriously involved in share ownership and the rest.

Acknowledgements

This paper is based upon data derived from a research project funded by the Economic and Social Research Council entitled 'Privatization and Popular Capitalism'. The research was carried out jointly with Peter Saunders at the University of Sussex.

References

Badden, L., Hunter, L., Hyman, J., Leopold, J., Ramsay, H. (1989), *Peoples Capitalism? A critical Analysis of Profit Sharing and Share ownership.* London: Routledge.

Bell, D. and Hanson, C. (1984), *Profit Sharing & Profitability*. London. Kogan Page.

Belstead, Lord (1987), Presentation at Economist Conference, 'The Privatization of The Water Industry', Marriot Hotel, London 18/9/87.

Chapman, C. (1990), *Selling the Family Silver, has privatization worked?* London: Hutchinson.

Dunn,S., Richardson, R. and Dewe, P. (1991), *The Impact of Employee Share Ownership on Worker Attitude, a Longitudinal Case Study*, Centre for Economic Performance, London School of Economics.

Estrin, S. and Wilson, N. (1986), *The Micro Economic Effects of Profit Sharing: The British Experience*. Centre for Labour Economics, Discussion Paper No 247. London School of Economics.

Fogarty, M. and White, M. (1988), *Share Schemes - As Workers See Them*, London, Policy Studies Institute.

Gordon, S. (1989), *Down the Drain: Water, Pollution and Privatization. London:* MacDonald & Co.

Hallett, R. (1990) , 'Privatization & the Restructuring of a Public Utility: A case study of British Telecom's corporate strategy & structure' in Jenkins, G. & Poole, M. *New Forms of Ownership*. London. Routledge.

Letwin, O. (1988), '*Privatising the World*'. Cassell.

Meade, J.E. (1986), *Different Forms of Share Economy*. London: Public Policy Centre

Moore, J. (1983), *Why Privatise*?, London, Conservative Political Centre.

Moore, J. (1986), *The Value of Ownership*, London Conservative Political Centre.

NALGO & NUPE (1991), *The Water Companies: Information & Data for NALGO & NUPE Local Negotiators*. December 1991.

Nelson, A. and Cooper, C. (1993), *The Impact of Privatization on Employee Job Satisfaction and Well Being*. Manchester. UMIST.

Nichols, T. and O'Connel Davidson, J. (1992), 'Employee Shareholders in Two Privatized Utilities', *International Relations Journal*. Volume 23: No 2. Summer 1992.

O'Connel Davidson, J. (September 1989), *Subcontract Employment in the Water Industry*. Paper given at Cardiff Business School.

O'Connel Davidson, J., Nichols, T. and Sun, W. (1991), *Privatization & Change: Employee Attitudes to Privatisied Utitlities*. University of Leicester.

Ogden, S. (1993), 'Decline and Fall: National Bargaining in British Water. Oxford', *Industrial Relations Journal* Volume 24, No 1, March 1993.

Poole, M. and Jenkins, G. (1990), *The Impact of Economic Democracy*. London: Routledge.

Ramsay, H., Hyman, J., Baddon, L., Hunter, L., and Leopold, J. (1990), 'Options for Workers: Owner or Employee?', in M. Poole and G. Jenkins (eds.), *New Forms of Ownership*, Routledge.

Saunders, P. and Harris, C. (1994), *Privatization and Popular Capitalism*. Open University Press.

Schweiger, D.L. and Ivancevitch, J.M. (1985), 'Human Resources: the Forgotten Factor in Mergers and Acquisitions.' *Personnel Administrator*, 30 (11), 47-61.

Thomas, D. (1984), 'Privatization and the Unions'. *New Society*, 21 June 1984.

Walters, A., (1989), 'Comment on Vickers and Yarrow' in P. MacAvoy, W. Stanbury, G., Yarrow and R. Zeekhauser (eds.), *Privatization and State Owned Enterprises*, Boston, Klawer Publishers.

Water Industry Unions Committee (1985), *Public Ownership: A Watertight Case*, London, GMBATU, MATSA, NALGO, NUPE, TGWU, TWSA and UCATT.

Water Industry Union Committee (1985), *Public Ownership: A Watertight Case.*

Watts, R. (1987), Presentation at the Economist Conference, *The Privatization of the Water Industry*, Marriot Hotel, London 18/9/87.

Whitfield, D. (1983), *Making it Public: Evidence and Action Against Privatization*. London: Pluto Press.

14 Privatization and the employment relationship

George Thomason

Introduction

During the 1980s, a significant shift in the structure of employment relationships occurred in private industry and both its causes (Freeman and Pelletier, 1990; Green, 1992; Roots, 1990), and its consequence (Millward and Stevens, 1986; NEDO, 1986; Daniel, 1987; Beaumont and Harris, 1991; Gallie and White, 1993) have now been widely recorded. Changes in this relationship in the public sector (defined as including the traditional national and local government services, the organs of the Welfare State and the nationalized industries) have occurred more slowly. But the government's underlying intention has been to inject private enterprise values and methods into the public sector policies, in the belief that this will yield significant efficiency gains.

By the end of the 1990s, it was possible to identify three main strands which the government had hesitantly and iteratively woven into its programme of privatization for the public sector:

(a) the sale of public assets to private buyers, usually on favourable terms, as in outright privatization, in order to expose all activities to commercial competition;
(b) the division of previously monolithic services into separate purchaser and provider units and the creation of quasi-markets in which local unit

managements compete for the public funds available, thus effectively privatizing management but retaining assets in public ownership;
(c) the compulsion of public sector organizations to test the market for some or all of their non-core support services by inviting private tenders in competition with direct labour, implying a partial privatization of activities within public sector organizations.

A fourth strand, cash-limiting (which had been woven in earlier with the aim of restricting the cash available to a service from public sources), coupled with the levy of charges on recipients (cf. Heald, 1983) may be regarded as overtaken by and now subsumed in the development of internal markets.

This paper examines the ways in which these strategies have changed the approach to delivering public services in order to reduce costs or produce efficiency gains and to destabilize the traditional industrial relations structure which appeared impervious to the market influences that led to changes in the private sector. It is argued that, where outright privatization has had some success in creating a 'new realism' amongst former public sector workers, it may be questioned whether the other two strategies are capable of developing a sufficiently strong commercial orientation to those remaining within the sector.

Government Objectives

The strategies identified above were intended by government to contribute to the realization of three objectives.

(a) The most immediate economic objective was to reduce expenditure on public services to a level below 40 per cent of the Gross Domestic Product (GDP). Outright privatization and the early form of cash-limiting were most directly related to this.
(b) To this was added the objective of increasing the value obtained for the money spent on any Service remaining in public ownership. This was often grafted onto the first, not always felicitously, to give it greater respectability.
(c) The further purpose of reducing the power of the public sector trade unions to resist the attempts to realize its economic objectives was rarely far from the top of the Government's list of priorities (Bishop and Kay, 1989).

They also reflected the Government's belief that private enterprise, operating within competitive markets, provided the best model on which to base strategies. Therefore, where it was considered that a public sector operation could be converted into a viable private company (even if viability might require the assets to be underpriced), the public assets were sold, usually on favourable terms, either privately or to the public ('outright privatization'). Offering parts of other services for private tender - Compulsory, Competitive, Tendering (CCT) reflected this same faith in private enterprise.

These options were not open in respect of large parts of the sector, and an alternative was sought and eventually found in the concept of the 'internal market'. This concept was adapted to fit the circumstance of many State, local government, health and education services, but not until late in the decade. Where the outright and partial privatization strategies were developed in the 1980s, internal markets belong more clearly to the 1990s. They have therefore had less time in which to prove themselves as amounting to a viable strategy, although some actions which prepared the way - such as involving business leaders in governance of public sector organizations - were taken earlier for other purposes.

The Government's plans for the privatized and internal market sectors aimed at:

1 The insinuation of commercial thinking to the top managerial levels to replace the political thinking of ministers, councillors and senior civil/public servants.
   It was considered that the replacement of administrators by business leaders would be sufficient to ensure that commercial values would permeate strategic thinking and actual performance in the new units. There is no documentary evidence to suggest that the members of the new boards were selected against criteria other than those of commercial experience.
2 The empowerment of management (local directorates) to devise operating strategies and policies for their services or units with which to achieve the expenditure and value-for-money targets set by government and to comply with other operational rules emanating from the same source.
   Where the companies were exposed to commercial competition, no special arrangements were called for but where a degree of monopoly remained, 'Regulators' were appointed to prevent abuse of monopoly power. Outside the context of outright privatization, however, limits were placed on the managers' power by way of budgets, imposed targets, direct operational instructions and other constraints designed to

preserve and protect the State interest in the actions they take.

Nevertheless, the success of the Government's plans depends, not simply upon the personnel and structures put in place, but upon their capacity for and competence in effecting changes in the operational systems so that services are delivered at lower social costs and/or with greater efficiency than before. They must, in other words, produce a 'managerial' response to the challenges of delivering the services in question, and there is some reason to suppose that the two sectors differ on this score.

A managerial response

The managements of the privatized companies, trusts, schools, and executive agencies have responded to their new statuses in a broadly similar fashion, but following different time-tables. The companies privatized early in the programme have incorporated business leaders into their directorates, evolved new commercial strategies and cultures and progressively induced lower levels of personnel to develop a commitment to them. Although they find this no easier to achieve than in the generality of firms (de Meyer and Ferdows, 1991), they are helped in these endeavours by the existence of a relevant private enterprise model which can be drawn upon simply as a guide to 'best practice'.

The directing organs of 'privatized' management units within internal markets are usually less dominated by persons bringing business experience to bear on their decisions, and do not have a ready-made model of practice which they can emulate. This, coupled with their later creation and the different 'rules of engagement' which have been applied to them by Government, may account for their relatively slow and cautious responses to their new circumstances. Their intention appears to be to follow a similar route to that taken by the privatized companies, but the goal is pursued less single-minded and aggressively, possibly because they have to create new ad hoc strategies and cultures.

Thus, the mission statements of the privatized companies, in common with those of many other private companies, tend to elevate the importance of the customer as arbiter of corporate action and employee behaviours, because this is seen to be necessary to secure market shares. Superficially, those of the internal market organizations are similar in this respect, in that they predicate all activity on the needs of the client, patient or student; but in these cases, the reason for so doing may be as much the need to act in accordance with the Citizen's Charter as any need to satisfy the customers in order to maintain their goodwill and custom (Heller, 1993).

Another difference concerns the approach to and extent of disaffiliating senior and middle management from their unions (which has been common in all parts of the public sector). Many privatized companies achieved this by inducing them to accept 'personal contracts' (offering a better package of benefits) 'to bring them into line with their private enterprise colleagues'. De-recognition of the managers' union(s) was rarely made an issue but the extent of take-up of personal contracts usually meant that the union(s) involved simply withered on the vine.

In the internal market sector, personal contracts have been offered to general managers and those occupying what might be termed chief executive positions (such as that of head-teacher) but more sparingly to senior administrative managers. They have been offered even less frequently to senior professional personnel services, although bargaining over employment terms has been 'allowed to lapse' in some cases (such as senior nurses). The existence of strong professional, as distinct from union, affiliations amongst these personnel may impose a constraint less often encountered in the privatized company.

Actions of these kinds are designed to equip the organization with a commercially-orientated management 'team', which will be prepared to take and implement decisions which will either reduce costs or yield efficiency gains or both. These gains are achievable only if management can reduce the numbers employed without reducing outputs and/or effect changes in the practices which pervaded the preceding systems to give a net gain with the same workforce. The short-term response is one emphasizing labour shedding but the longer-term response demands changes in the ways in which the ends of activity are defined, the work is divided and allocated to workers, and the workers are mobilized and motivated to perform.

It is difficult to evaluate the extent to which the intention has been realized in the two sectors, although the impression given is that it is less in the internal market than in the privatized company sector. If this is indeed the case, it would, given the conclusions reached in evaluations of the achievements of privatized companies (Kay and Thompson, 1991; Haskel and Szymanshi, 1991), imply that the prospects for efficiency gains on the internal market sector will be more limited.

Progress - Privatization

It is not possible to evaluate the success of these strategies on constant criteria because the objectives are not constant for all affected parts of the former public sector.

(a) Outright privatization gave the Exchequer a windfall cash gain, but thereafter removed the new companies' transactions from the public accounts; henceforth, their performance could be measured in terms of profitability and efficiency in the same way as with existing private enterprise.
(b) The other two strategies involved no such initial windfall gains, and subsequent success is measured in terms of either the amount of reduction achieved in expenditure on acquiring the service or the number of successful responses to the new rules (as in CCT).

Measurement of achievement is also affected by the time which any affected organization has had in which to make adjustments to its new status or the new rules applicable to its operations.

The evidence from outright privatization (or threat of it) suggests that efficiency gains have been made although they have varied markedly in amount. They have been achieved mainly by shedding labour and varying the skill mix (by multi-skilling and enlargement of individual responsibility) rather than by depressing wage rates. Haskel and Szymanski's examination (1991) of the experience of fifteen companies, for example, found that

- employment had been reduced by more than a quarter in the past decade as companies changed their objectives to become more profit-orientated whether or not this occurred in the context of actual privatization, proposals to privatize or some form of internal re-organization.
- the wages of those remaining in employment had not fallen relative to the wages of those in comparable groups, except where competition had increased and led to a fall in market share.

Reductions in employment often precede the formal act of reorganization, either to make a transfer to private ownership a more attractive proposition or to prepare the way for market-testing. In its early life, a privatized company with a reasonable market share can usually achieve staff reductions by offering generous early-retirement and redundancy packages, where other forms of privatization are not so favourably placed. However, if the need to reduce the payroll persists over time for any reason, compulsion may have to be introduced.

Many privatized companies, in common with many existing private companies, took the opportunity to shed more labour during the recent recession in order to adjust to their reduced market shares as competition increased. British Telecom, for example, reduced its workforce from 210,500 to under 171,000, between April, 1992, and March, 1993, under its voluntary Release 92 scheme, but further promized downsizing is expected to call for compulsory redundancies. Consequently, further efficiency gains can be expected to accrue from this strategy which relies on numerical flexibility to effect adjustments.

This is usually accompanied in the privatized trading organizations by a strategy aimed at increasing functional flexibility by re-structuring and extending the boundaries of work roles and removing demarcations between jobs. Modern electronic devices (such as, for example, computer allocation of service calls in telecommunications or gas) may be developed both to assist in this process and to give closer control of operations.

Where the revenue flows permit this, re-training of those remaining in employment is provided by the employer, with the amount depending on the current and projected levels of profitability. Where downsizing is usually arranged by making deals with individual workers, training programmes may be agreed after discussion with the unions, in effect, treating the union as a cartel which can (at least help to) deliver members' motivation to accept the new working system.

The same condition, that cash is and is projected to be available, enables these companies to put together a contribution-and-reward package containing elements of functional and pay (usually PRP) flexibility. These offers have, in many but not all cases, proved acceptable to employees (even if less attractive to union representatives), but disillusion often occurs when experience of the operation of the elaborate appraisal systems which are used to link the two elements together has been gained (Richardson and Marsden, 1991; Rowland and Robinson, 1993).

Such contribution-and-reward packages are commonly initiated to apply to senior management grades and then progressively extended downwards to other categories of staff in turn, as changes in roles and responsibilities are introduced. At all levels, and independently of their specific merit as pay systems, they are often intended to serve as catalysts in changing the way in which people think about performing their redefined tasks, within the new 'consumer-orientated' corporate cultures.

In the privatized company sector, there has been little evidence of precipitate action to change industrial relations structures and processes. Where the former organization was fragmented (as, for example, with water or electricity distribution), localized bargaining arrangements were substituted for national ones, as in many other industries at the time and Welsh Water de-recognized the NUPE at this stage. Ogden (1990) records little change in either union membership (except as might be accounted for by reductions in employment) or the scope of bargaining (except in respect of the more senior managerial and professional staff grades offered personal contracts).

Although open confrontations have occurred, (as often in the run-up to privatization as after it), companies sought to avoid them whilst changes in work roles and performance standards were put in place, in the belief that if they occurred they would reduce the speed at which workers could be induced to accept new commercial cultural values in place of the existing political and bureaucratic ones (Kay and Thompson, 1991). The willingness of these companies to continue to negotiate issues with their local union representatives, is, however, one of the features which tends to distinguish them from the organizations affected by contracting out and internal market developments.

Market testing

Market testing differs from the other two strategies in that it relates to specific activities within organizations, rather than to the organization as an entity. This does not imply that the exercise had no impact on the organization or its 'culture' but that to a degree, certain (usually 'core') activities were insulated from its direct effects.

Contracting out effected savings in costs and increases in labour productivity which have been analyzed, although the resultant estimates of how much improvement has been made vary. Szymanski (1993) estimated that 217 local authorities in England and Wales showed on average saving of 27 per cent (within a range of 5 to 42 per cent) on their 1988 costs of refuse collection, although administration costs (a possible 4 per cent) have not been off-set against these.

The Institute of Local Government Studies, using a sample comprising building cleaning, street cleaning, catering, ground maintenance, refuse collection, vehicle fleet management and sport and leisure management (and taking account of administrative costs not included in Szymanski's analysis), estimated that competitive tendering had achieved on average reduction in costs of about 6.5 per cent, or about £500,000 per authority (*Financial Times*, 15 July, 1993). This is close to the estimate of 7 per cent made by the Audit Commission (1993, p. 9).

In the NHS, tendering was said to have saved £105,861,000, by April, 1988, an amount equivalent to about 0.4 per cent of the total NHS expenditure in 1988. Savings on in-house contracts accounted for three-quarters of this, most of which accrued to contracts for building cleaning.

The prevalence of complaints about reduced standards of performance by contractors raise doubts about whether this amounted to a real increase in productivity or to the substitution of an inferior service. The JNHSPRU records 103 'failures' by private contractors (24 per cent of the contracts awarded) during 1983-89, (where 'failure' is defined to include reduced standards, inadequate performance, withdrawal or dismissal). Since the rate of failure increased over the period, they cannot be attributed solely to teething troubles or the need to develop experience.

The gains achieved reflect two fundamental changes in the employment relationship which result from market testing:

(a) the modification of the existing division of labour (the way jobs are defined and related to one another) by limiting tasks to those for which the employer is commercially contracted and discontinuing any which relate to the service needs not specified in the contract; and
(b) the re-distribution of authority (who is permitted to influence decisions) to give the management increased autonomy and the workers and their unions less influence on decisions relating to workloads and remuneration.

The need to prepare task specifications carefully as a basis for tendering challenges existing definitions and results in new job descriptions which the in-house or private contractor workers must then follow. This in itself usually reduces the significance of the context within which the jobs are to be performed, but any such wider commitment is also discouraged by the fragmentation and re-scheduling of the work (to enable less skilled and/or part-time workers to perform it at lower costs than before). The traditional bases of a person's work identity are removed by these actions and unless new ones are substituted, commitment tends to fall.

Authority and power are re-distributed in management's favour on the pretext of meeting competition and retaining contacts and maintaining employment. This results from the progressive marginalization (in trusts, agencies or direct labour organizations) or the complete denial (in many private contracting firms) of the influence of workers individually or collectively on decisions about terms and conditions of employment.

The re-scheduling of work to enable it to be done by part-timers, many of them women, creates a situation in which unionization will be less prevalent. Even where workers remain unionized (as in direct labour organizations), the constant threat of contract switch tends to have the same consequence. Workers are forced to rely more on their low individual bargaining power to secure their terms and conditions and this is reflected in the savings and gains made by the employers and the losses of income and security sustained by the workers.

What occurs in the context of market testing, therefore, is a structural change which almost inherently creates conditions in which further deliberate actions to marginalize the influence of either individual workers or organized labour are unnecessary. The workers' increased insecurity and uncertainty are sufficient to secure both objectives. The impact is, however, limited to certain identified categories, and securing its spread to others depends upon market testing being allied with the other strategy of creating competition within internal markets.

Internal markets

No robust statistics are yet available on the achievements of units placed in internal markets in the health, education and civil service (executive agency) sectors. Achievements therefore tend to be expressed projectively and in terms of expected financial savings - regardless of any consequences they might have for the amounts or standards of service delivered. Typical was the announcement in June, 1993, that the Frenchay Hospital Trust in Bristol was to shed eighty-nine jobs over the following year, in order to reduce its spending by 2.3 million; other Trusts have made similar announcements. Some saving on expenditure might therefore be expected when these intentions have been carried into effect, but this may not amount to an efficiency gain unless overall performance is maintained.

The reports on actions taken by NHS trusts, maintained schools and executive agencies in the civil service suggest that they are reducing employment, but usually to reduce the level of spending rather than as a strategy. An IRS survey (June, 1993) of the 160 first and second wave NHS Self-governing Trusts found that more of their respondents had cut staff (12) than had increased employment (10) since becoming a Trust, and 40 per cent expected staff numbers to fall over the following 18 months.

Formal declarations of redundancy (whether voluntary or compulsory) are comparatively rate, as the rate of labour turnover often enables numbers to be reduced by the expedient of not replacing leavers and allowing 'establishments' to lapse. This can lead to public resentment because it seems to ignore what is often a rising client demand for the service in question.

Nor do they appear to be consistently depressing wage and salary rates (except in so far as the public sector was generally restricted by Government decree to a 1.5 per cent increase in pay during 1992-93). Only a few Trusts have been reported to be making attempts to reduce pay rates of mainline staff (even for new entrants and newly promoted staff, as the terms of transfer permitted them to do); most have so far maintained the Whitley Council or Pay Review Body recommended rates

The fact that these exist, as it were independently of any actions that might be taken locally, may actually inhibit action at that level. It is possible for public sector managements to opt out, and the White Paper, People, Jobs and Opportunities (1992) encouraged them to do so, but few have yet taken advantage of this. IDS Study No 510 (July, 1992) recorded that about 30 councils, mainly in the South-east of England, had opted out of national pay rates and the machinery for determining them as had a smaller number of health units at that date. Since it appears that the uncertainty about the outcome of the General Election in 1992 (and the consequences this might have for privatization) was a factor inhibiting action, progress in this direction may be expected to accelerate during the next few years (IRS, June, 1993).

In this sector, the restructuring of work roles is occurring only slowly. Progress is retarded by:

(a) the existence of professional demarcations reinforced by the length of training programmes (as, for example, in the NHS) or of strongly-defended agreements (as, for example, in the educational sector or the prison service);

(b) the absence of 'new money' either to provide the training or to buy out working practices, which leads to changes being introduced by stealth rather than openly or by agreement. For example, some authorities assimilated nurses to their new (1988) clinical grades in a way which effected cost savings by simultaneously changing the skill/grade mix;

(c) the continued existence of a national pay structure and the mechanisms for maintaining or changing it which does more than provide the benchmark against which units can compare themselves: it creates a presumption that it will be improved upon if any improvement in performance is sought and given.

These come together to form a significant restraint on change. Professional bodies are likely to be able to mobilize public (and therefore voter) opinion to support the maintenance of the services which they currently provide and thus thwart attempts to secure improvements in performance in the absence of significant amounts of new money being put on the table. Since it is unlikely to be forthcoming from national sources, unless and until a resource cushion can be built up within these services, the Mexican stand-off is likely to persist.

Future developments

The gains which have so far been achieved tend to follow from the achievement of flexibility by varying the numbers of people in employment, that is, from following a conventional hiring and firing strategy. The efficiency gains to be made in future are likely to accrue from an extension of the functional flexibility principle: the employer re-distributes tasks between workers commanding different market rates and assumes responsibility for determining which competencies each will develop. This development will be facilitated in one of two ways:

* first, the possibility of manipulating the mix of staff grades and skills, facilitated by the long pay spines which were put in place in some services during the 1980s and by the creation of new jobs which are kept out of the traditional collective bargaining framework; and
* secondly, the possibility of changing the mix of public and private provision of core activities in health care or education and of supply of support services in these and other service areas.

Skill mix

The evolution of the role of Health Care Assistant (HCA) within health and local authority social services illustrates the processes involved in the first of these. Earlier health sector studies (for example, Robinson *et al.*, 1990) had argued that a reorganization of ward support services involving transfer of tasks from qualified nurses to less qualified assistants could produce benefits. As a result, the concept of the Health Care Assistant emerged as a role which would bring together tasks previously performed by three distinct occupational groups, unqualified auxiliary nurses, ward housekeepers and ward clerks.

The new job possessed no 'obvious' occupational affiliation because it assembled tasks from three conventional job families. The opportunity was taken to remove it from the scope of all existing mechanisms for determining terms and conditions of employment while giving it a free-standing role. Fixing the range of tasks, the work schedules and the rewards to suit local requirements was left to management's discretion and not made subject to negotiation with any representative group.

Changes of a not very dissimilar kind were introduced at other boundaries between established occupational groups. The development of 'clinical directorates' (by which clinical staff were drawn into sharing some managerial responsibilities in return for which they received what were in effect honoraria rather than a rate for the job) reduced the demarcation between clinical and managerial work. The 'New Deal' for junior hospital doctors led to some duties (such as taking blood or setting up intravenous drips) being transferred from doctors to nurses and laboratory technicians (phlebotomists).

On the face of it, such changes in grade and staff mix match those made in existing and newly-privatized companies - under the headings of job enlargement, reduction of job demarcations, multi-skilling, or functional flexibility. But where private (and privatized) industry generally has been prepared to negotiate changes locally with recognized unions (Ingram, 1981: Kirosingh, 1989), a greater proportion of NHS Trusts appear to have introduced them without agreements being reached or even attempted.

The perpetuation of the national structure of negotiation and the absence of local bargaining structures may, in part, account for this difference in approach. But the existence of strongly-entrenched professional bodies, many of which are able to mobilize public opinion to support their objections to changing their practice when the necessity for it can be assigned to a desire to commercialize the process of delivering the service, may provide a more cogent reason. That being the case, it becomes more imperative to introduce other and greater structural changes in order to generate greater destabilization of existing institutions.

Mixed provision

This is currently being pursued in a strategy of mixing public and private provision. Where commercial practice provides little warrant for contracting out core activities (although it is not unknown), the development of 'networks' or 'operating partnerships' between otherwise separate commercial organizations provides a more pertinent model to follow for this purpose.

Certain services are already beginning to create a mixed (private and public) service, by combining the internal markets with contracting-out core activities. Networking, in one guise or another, is already under consideration or test in the health, education and prison services. NHS hospitals are being drawn into arrangements with private health care organizations to create 'mixed health care systems' (Cook, 1990; Harrison, 1993) in which each may perform fee-earning services for the other. The prison service has recently been opened up to accept a private contribution and eventually a similar partnership arrangement could develop. More use may also be made of the scope for partnerships between the public and private components in education.

Developments of this kind may appear to be a far cry from the rather simple expedients of contracting out cleaning, laundry and refuse collection activities. However, the principle remains the same. The main difference lies in the complexity of the institutions involved in that they depend upon a more complex combination of capital and (professional) labour resources than the activities initially contracted out. The level of efficiency gain which can be expected to accrue, is likely to be lower for the reason that gains cannot be made by simply shedding labour as a way of reducing labour costs in services for which demand continues to rise.

Such developments hold some promise of breaking the hold which professional bodies, with their widely accepted 'service ideals', retain over working practices within the core services of many of these internal market organizations. Arguably, these ideals and the appeal which they have to the clients or the public constitute the major threat to the development of the 'commercial orientation', which on the evidence of outright privatization (Bishop and Thompson, 1991; Parker and Hartley, 1991), yields the gains which can be shown to have accrued there.

It may therefore be expected that the strategies adopted in the internal market sector will become more complex as more destabilization is attempted. Simple expedients, such as contracting out, may transfer the actual costs and risks to the affected workers, but to bring such misery within the reach of everyone employed in a service may create nothing more than a self-defeating strategy. In order to solve the problem of adjusting what is delivered to what we think we can or should spend on these services, may call for a cleverer strategy which produces a more equitable distribution of costs and benefits between the various stakeholders.

Conclusion

Whether current strategies are producing effective convergence between public and private sector management may be doubted. Three main factors appear to reduce certainly the speed and probably the likelihood of the 'internal market' segment of the public sector ever developing the same approach and the same outcomes as the private or the privatized sectors:

(a) the nature of the employment relationship found originally (say in 1979) in the particular part of the public sector; this differed in significant respects (division of labour practized, patterns of interdependence fostered, methods used to determine rewards, human resource management strategies followed), from that found in trading organizations;

(b) the extent to which the strategy adopted can create conditions in which it will be difficult for management to succeed in its tasks without it absorbing and effectively disseminating commercial principles to all employees;

(c) the extent to which professional values sustained by strong professional organizations can delay or prevent the development of a managerial approach which fosters the adoption of commercial values as guides to action within the service.

Introducing a new realism into organizations whose core workers are strongly organized into professions may prove to be a significantly more difficult task than introducing it to unionized workforces - and even there it is not yet clear that success has been achieved.

References

Audit Commission Office (1993), *Realising the Benefits of Competition: The Client Role for Contracted Services,* (HMSO, London).

Authers, J. (1993a), 'Competitive Tender Myth Challenged', in *Financial Times*, 9 July and (1993b), 'Council Tendering "saves average of 6.5%" in England', in *Financial Times*, 15 July.

Bach, S. (1990), 'Competitive Tendering and Contracting Out: Prospects for the Future', in *Haydn Cook* (1990) q.v. pp. 13-31.

Bargaining Report, 'Personal Contracts - Protecting Yourself' in *Bargaining Report*, 110, October, 1991, pp. 13-15.

Beaumont, P.H. and Harris, R.I.D. (1991), 'Trade Union Recognition and Employment Contraction, Britain, 1980-84', in *British Journal of Industrial Relations*, 29 (1), March, 1991, pp. 49-58.

Bishop, G. and Lewin, R. (1993), 'Short-circuiting old Bargaining Machinery' in *Personnel Management*, March, pp. 28-32.

Bishop, M. and Kay, J. (1988), *Does Privatization Work? Lessons from the UK,* Centre for Business Strategy, London Business School, Sussex Place, London, NW1 4SA.

Central Office of Information (1990), *Britain's Privatization Policy,* COI, London.

Colling, T. (1991), 'Privatization and the Management of IR in Electricity Distribution', in *Industrial Relations Journal*, 22 (2), Summer, pp. 117-29.

Cook, H. (1990), *The NHS/Private Health Sector Interface,* (Longman,

London).

Corby, S. (1993), 'One More Step for the Civil Service', in *Personnel Management*, August, pp. 30-31.

Cross, M. (1988), 'Changes in Working Practices in Manufacturing, 1981-88', in *Industrial Relations Review and Report*, No 415; and (1990), *Changes in Working Practices in UK Manufacturing, 1981-1990* (Manchester Business School, June).

Daniel, W.W. (1987), *Workplace Industrial Relations and Technological Change*, Francis Pinter and Policy Studies Institute, 1987.

Davies, A. (1991), 'Restructuring Pay and Grading in a Civil Service Agency', in *Personnel Management*, October, pp. 52-53.

de Meyer, A. and Ferdows, K. (1990), *Removing the Barriers in Manufacturing; Report on the 1990 European Manufacturing Futures Survey* (INSEAD, Boulevard de Constance, 7730S, Fontainbleu Cedex. France).

Department of Education and Science (1986), *Education Reform: The Government's Proposals for Schools,* (DES, London).

Department of Education and Science (1987), *Maintained Further Education: Financing, Governance and Law,* (DES, London).

Department of Education and Science (1986), *Education Reform: The Government's Proposals for Schools*, (DES, London).

Dyson, R. (1991), *Changing Labour Utilization in the NHS Trusts* (Department of Health, London); (1992): *Hospital Doctors' Contracts,* (Mercia Publications, Keele).

Edwards, P.K. (1987), *Managing the Factory* (Blackwell, Oxford).

Efficiency Unit (1988), *Improving Management in Government: The Next Steps*, (A Report to the Prime Minister) (HMSO, 1988).

Enthoven, A.C. (1985), *Reflections on the Management of the NHS: An American Looks at Incentives to Efficiency in Health Services Management in the UK* (Nuffield Provincial Hospital Trust, London).

Fairbairns, J. (1991), 'Civil Service Decentralization: Reality or Rhetoric?', in *Personnel Management*, February, pp. 38-42.

Ferner, A. (1990), 'The Changing Influence of the Personnel Function: Privatization and Organizational Politics in Electricity Generation' in *Human Resource Management Journal*, 1, pp. 12-30.

Ferner, A. and Colling, T. (1991), 'Privatization, Regulation and Industrial Relations', in *British Journal of Industrial Relations*, 29 (3), September, 1991, pp. 391-409.

Freeman, R. and Pelletier, J. (1990), 'The Impact of Industrial Relations Legislation on British Union Density', in *British Journal of Industrial Relations*, 28 (2), June, 1990, pp. 141-64.

Gallie, D. and White, M. (1993), *Employee Commitment and the Skills Revolution: First Findings from the Employment Survey*, London: Policy Studies Institute Publishing.

Green, F. (1992), 'Recent Trends in British Trade Union Density: How much is a composition Effect?', in *British Journal of Industrial Relations*, 30 (3), September, 1992, pp. 445-58.

Harrison, A., (ed.) (1993), *Health Care UK, 1992/93,* (Kings' Fund Institute, London).

Haskel, J., and Szymanski, S. (1991), 'Privatization, Jobs and Wages' in *Employment Institute Economic Report*, 6 (7), December, (The Employment Institute, Southbank House, Black Prince Road, London, SE1 7SJ).

Heald, D. (1983), *Public Expenditure* (Basil Blackwell, Oxford).

Health, Department of (1989a), *Working for Patients,* (Cmnd 555, HMSO, London).

Health, Department of (1989b), *Caring for People; Community Care in the Next Decade and Beyond,* (Cmnd 859, HMSO, London).

Health, Department of (1989c): *Self-Governing Hospitals* (Working Paper No 1) (HMSO, London).

Heller, R., (1993), 'The Royal Mail finds a Culture', in *Management Today*, April, pp. 30-34.

Herd, S.B. (1986), *Industrial Relations in the National Health Service* (Health Services Management Unit, Dept of Social Administration, University of Manchester, Working Paper No. 24).

HM Treasury (1987), *Flexible Pay - A New Pay Regime for the Civil Service,* (COI, London).

Industrial Relations Review and Report (1989), 'Industrial Relations after Privatization' in *IRS Employment Trends,* No 439, May, 1989, pp. 12-14.

Industrial Relations Review and Report (1993), *Employment Trends*, No. 537, June, 1993, pp. 7-16. (IRS, 18-20, Highbury Place, London, N5 1 QP). By subscription.

Ingram, P.N. (1991), 'Changes in Working Practices in British Manufacturing Industry in the 1980s', in *British Journal of Industrial Relations*, 29 (1), March, 1991, pp. 1-17.

Institute of Public Finance (1993), *CCT and the Private Sector,* (Volume 2), IPF, PO Box 4, Croydon, CR9 1AT).

Joint NHS Privatization Research Unit (1990), *The NHS Privatization Experience,* (Joint NHS Privatization Research Unit, 20, Grand Depot Road, Woolwich, London, SE18 6SF).

Kay, J., Mayer, C. and Thompson, D.J. (eds.) (1986), *Privatization and Regulation: The UK Experience,* (Clarendon Press, Oxford).

Kay, J. and Thompson, D.J. (1986), 'Privatization: A Policy in Search of a Rationale' in *Economic Journal*, 96, pp. 18-32.

Kirosingh, M. (1989), 'Changed Working Practices', in *Employment Gazette*, August, 1989, pp. 422-29.

Labour Research Department (1987), *Privatization: Paying the Price,* (LRD Publications Ltd., London).

Lord McCarthy (1988), 'Privatization and the Employee' in Ramanadham, W., (ed.), *Privatization in the UK,* (Routledge, London) pp. 73-84.

Marginson, P., Edwards., P.K., Purcell, J., and Sisson, K. (1986), *Beyond the Workplace: Managing industrial relation in the Multi-establishment Enterprise*, (Basil Blackwell, Oxford).

Millward, N. and Stevens, M. (1986), *British Workplace Industrial Relations, 1980-84*, Gower.

National Audit Office (1986-7), *Competitive Tendering for Support Services in the NHS,* (No. 318, NAO, London).

National Economic Development Office (1986), *Changing Working Patterns: How Companies Achieve Flexibility to meet new Needs,* (NEDO, London).

Ogden, S. (1990), 'The Impact of Privatization on Industrial Relations in the Water Industry' (Paper for the Employment Research Unit Conference: Employment Relations in the Enterprise Culture; Cardiff Business School, 18-19 September, 1990).

Parker, D. and Hartley, K. (1990), 'Organizational Status and Performance: the Effects on Employment' in *Applied Economics*, 23, pp. 403-16.

Pendleton, A. (1991), 'Integration and De-alignment in Public Enterprise Industrial Relations: A Study of British Rail' in *British Journal of Industrial Relations*, 29 (3), September, 1991, on 411-426.

Peters, T.J. and Waterman, R.H. (1982), *In Search of Excellence: Lessons from America's Best-run Companies,* (Harper and Row, New York) .

Price Waterhouse (1987), *Privatization: The Facts,* (Price Waterhouse. London).

Prime Minister's Office (1991), *The Citizen's Charter,* (HMSO, London).

Public Services Privatization Research Unit, (1992), *Privatization: Disaster for Quality,* (PSPR Unit, 20, Grand Depot Road, Woolwich, London, SE18 6SF, March).

Richardson, R. and Marsden, D. (1991), *Does Performance Pay Motivate?: A Study of Inland Revenue Staff,* (London School of Economics for the Inland Revenue Staff Federation, September).

Robinson, J. *et al.*(1990), *The Role of the Support Worker in the Ward Health Care Team* (Institute of Nursing Studies, University of Warwick, Coventry).

Roots, P. (1990), 'Industrial Relations: An Alternative View', in *Employment Bulletin and Industrial Relations Digest*, 6 (2), pp. 1-2.
Rowland, V. and Robinson, I. (1993), 'Personal Contracts: Union Responses', in *Employment Bulletin and IR Digest,* 9 (2), 1993, p. 4.
Szymanski, S. (1993), Quoted by Authers (1993a) q.v.
Thomason, G. (1990a), 'Realism for the Professionals' in *Employment Bulletin and IR Digest*, 6 (2), 1990, p. 7.
Towl, G. and Gilbert, A. (1993), 'The Great Escape from Whitehall' in *Personnel Management*, May, pp. 24-27. (prisons)
Trades Union Congress (1986), *Bargaining in Privatized Companies,* (TUC, London).
Veljanovski, C. (ed.), (1989), *Privatization and Competition: A Market Prospectus,* (Institute of Economic Affairs, London)
Veljanovski, C. (1987), *Selling the State: Privatization In Britain,* (Weidenfeld and Nicolson, London).
Walsh, K. (1993), 'Compulsory Competitive Tendering' (INLOGOY, Birmingham) quoted in *Financial Times*, 15 July, 1993.
Winterton, J. (1990), 'Private Power and Public Relations: the Effects of Privatization upon Industrial Relations in British Coal' in Jenkins, G. and Poole, M. (eds), (1990), *New Forms of Ownership,* (Routledge, London).

15 Consumers and privatization: The case of the water industry

Peter Saunders

Introduction

This chapter draws on my recent research concerned with the sociological significance of the privatization programme (see Saunders and Harris 1994). The research focused on the impact of water privatization on different sections of the population, including domestic consumers, employees and managers, voters, share buyers and organized interests and pressure groups. In this chapter I shall review the findings as regards consumers, while in Chapter 16, Colin Harris draws on the same project to discuss the impact of privatization upon employees.

The research principally took the form of a panel survey of 828 members of the public and 107 water industry employees, all of whom were interviewed in 1989, several months before the privatization of the water authorities in England and Wales, and were then re-interviewed in 1991, some eighteen months after the sale. Although the case study focused specifically on the privatization of water (still the most difficult and contentious of all the sales to have occurred since 1979), evidence from other industries was also considered.

Most members of the public were (and still are) opposed to the privatization of water, and public hostility to the sale has been fuelled since 1989 by an escalation of water charges which have risen much faster than the rate of inflation. Yet despite the fact that most consumers did not want water to be privatized, the evidence from this (as from other sales) indicates that most consumers have probably gained more than they have lost by the sale of the industry into the private sector. In this chapter I shall try to demonstrate this with reference to changes since privatization in price levels, quality of provision and corporate accountability to customers.

A note on Ernst's 'Whose Utility?'

Before reviewing the evidence, it is necessary to refer to a major new study of the privatized utilities which has been published since my own work was completed. John Ernst's *Whose Utility?* (1994) is one of the few studies to date to consider the significance of privatization for consumers, and its findings tend to be much more critical than those of my own study. The two accounts are not wholly incompatible - we agree, for example, that the public now has access to better and fuller information about these industries than it ever had when they were owned by government, that the privatized companies are no harsher in their treatment of customers in debt than they were before privatization, and that consumers in general do not seem noticeably more or less satisfied with the service they are getting than they were before. Ernst neverthless suggests that 'the outcomes for consumers in general...have been mixed' and that 'low income consumers have been affected more adversely than the generality of consumers' (p.174). This leads him to conclude that, while privatization of the utilities cannot be dismissed as 'an unmitigated disaster' (as critics have often claimed), nor is it the case that consumers have benefited (as the Government claimed they would) through 'lower prices and better services'.

Since it is my claim in this paper that consumers *have* generally benefited from lower prices and better services, it is necessary to consider how the divergence between Ernst's findings and my own has come about. Four factors are pertinent here.

First, although it is represented as an analysis of the privatized utilities as a whole, Ernst's book actually ignores one of the four key utility industries, namely telecommunications. Since the privatization of BT has arguably been the most successful of the four as regards lower prices and improved service quality, and given that BT has been in the private sector for longer than the other utilities and reveals the greatest development of effective competition for customers, this omission is likely to be critical in shaping Ernst's overall conclusions. In this chapter I shall include evidence on BT's performance along with that pertaining to the gas, water and electricity industries.

A second point is that Ernst's study has no direct evidence on how consumers fared when these industries were still in the public sector. He himself recognizes that this is a major problem: 'A "before-and-after" approach, involving a direct comparison of the service systems of the public utilities under nationalized and subsequently, privatized regimes, would be instructive, but is made difficult due to the absence of comparable data' (p.4). Lacking such data, he resorts to comparisons of the situation now with various normative ideals (such as 'equity' and 'social justice') which he deems important, an approach almost guaranteed to generate critical evaluation since social institutions rarely if ever live up to the perfect ideals we may demand of them. In contrast to his approach, my research did collect information before as well as after the privatization of the water industry, and my evaluations are based mainly on these empirical comparisons. Thus, while I accept that the record of the privatized industries in relation to domestic consumers may fall short of some perfect ideal standard, my 'before-and-after' analysis leads me to believe that their performance generally stands up rather well in comparison with the situation when these industries were owned and run by government.

Third, Ernst ignores the question of how privatization of the water and energy industries has affected the environment. Like the omission of BT, the neglect of the environmental question means that the book overlooks one of the major positive features of the privatization programme, at least as regards the water industry. In this chapter, I shall include an analysis of the environmental impact of privatization, for there seems no good reason to limit our analysis of consumers' concerns to the quality of the service delivered to them individually as opposed to the quality of the service they receive collectively as consumers of the shared environment.

Finally, Ernst's major concern is with low-income users and he writes as someone who has been personally involved in various campaigns claiming to represent the interests of low-income households in relation to the privatized utilities. Much of his analysis hinges upon this interest, and in particular on the distributive implications of privatization which he sees as broadly negative due to changes in tariff structures (such as the impending move to metering in the water industry) reflecting the shift from a 'public service' to a 'commodity' model of provision.

There is, of course, nothing 'wrong' with adopting such a perspective, but it is debatable whether a criterion of 'distributive justice' is an appropriate yardstick by which to gauge the performance of the privatized utilities. In Ernst's view, 'public utilities are the bedrock of social welfare' (p.195), and this therefore justifies much tighter regulation of the privatized utilities in order to reduce their profits, to control their investment decisions and to oblige them to offer discounts to low income customers. Such conclusions only follow, however, if we are already committed to a political perspective which is antithetical to the stated aims and objectives of privatization and which believes that consumer welfare is best served by extending state regulation and control. It is, of course, true by definition that privatized companies are less easily controlled by the state than are nationalized enterprises, so if we assume from the outset that consumers' interests are best safeguarded by state control and political lobbying by consumer organizations, Ernst's conclusion will necessarily follow. The approach adopted in this paper is rather different, for it is by no means self-evident that the water and energy companies should function as extensions of the state system of social security in the way that Ernst suggests. An evaluation of the impact of privatization on consumers needs to look at the empirical evidence on how prices, quality and accountability have actually changed in practice, and this evidence points, I believe, to a much more optimistic conclusion than that reached by Ernst.

Why might we expect consumers to benefit?

One of the principal justifications for the privatization programme has been the claim that the shift from public to private ownership forces companies to pay more attention to what consumers want. In an article published jointly with Michael Beesley in 1983, for example, Stephen Littlechild (who was later to become the chief regulator of the privatized electricity industry) argued that, 'Privatization will generate benefits for consumers because privately-owned companies have a greater incentive to produce goods and services in the quantity and variety which consumers prefer. Companies which succeed in discovering and meeting consumer needs make profits and grow; the less successful wither and die' (1986, p.38). Similarly, the minister responsible for the early privatization programme, John Moore, made it clear in a speech he gave in 1983 that 'the main prize' from the policy would accrue, not to employees, nor even to the company managements, but to the consumers (p.13). In this view, therefore, it is the 'hidden hand' of the market rather than the clumsy hand of government and lobbyists which will best serve the interests of consumers.

Consumers are said to gain from privatization in three specific ways. First, prices should fall as a result of efficiency and productivity gains. Where firms operate in a competitive market they will be obliged to keep prices down in order to maintain or expand their market share, but even when they operate with little or no competition, price regulation should ensure that prices remain low and that customers reap the benefit of improved efficiency and the introduction of new technologies. Secondly, the quality of the good or service should improve. Privatized companies can raise more money for new investment and will be more concerned to innovate in order to attract new customers, and these changes should result in a better product. Furthermore, government regulation of privatized enterprises is likely to be more effective than when government departments are called upon to regulate industries which they themselves are responsible for administering. Thirdly, privatized firms should be more responsive to consumers, for they will be more concerned about their pubic image than the old nationalized industries ever needed to be. Complaints will therefore be dealt with more quickly, back-up services will be better organized, consumers' views will be more assiduously sought out, and so on.

The Conservative MP, John Redwood, summed all this up when he claimed: 'That can be the deal for the customer: a much better deal on price, on service, on delivery, on the whole operation' (Redwood, 1990, p.2). But has it happened?

The consumer experience of prices

All the privatized utilities currently operate under a price-capping system in which a regulatory body sets an overall limit to price rises in an attempt to simulate the effects of competition in forcing efficiency gains. This limit is set with reference to the Retail Price Index (RPI) rather than with reference to the companies' profit margins and rates of return (as happens in the USA). This means that the privatized utilities are expected to keep price levels below a set ceiling but are then in principle left free to make such profits and rates of return on their capital as are possible within this limit. The system is designed to encourage companies to make efficiency savings in order to increase their profit margins.

When BT was privatized in 1984, the price cap was set for ten years (with provision for a review after five) at RPI minus 3 per cent. In other words, BT was expected to keep its aggregate annual price rises at 3 per cent below the prevailing rate of inflation. Most of the other utilities have similarly been set targets below the inflation rate.

As things turned out, BT was able to meet this initial price cap fairly comfortably, for new technology enabled it to reduce costs by shedding labour. Higher than expected profits then led the regulator, OFTEL, to tighten the 'RPI-x' formula at the first opportunity in 1988 by raising 'x' from 3 to 4.5. In 1991, three years before the next review was due, OFTEL asked for the formula to be changed again and raized the value of 'x' from 4.5 to 6.25. Then, just one year after that, OFTEL intervened yet again. This time it not only changed the value of 'x' (raising it to a remarkably stringent 7.5), but it also enforced a cut in installation charges and laid down certain stipulations regarding the company's capital programme, setting targets for the installation of fibre optic cable and the extension of the digital telephone service. The company issued a statement complaining at what it termed this new form of 'interventionist regulation' (*The Guardian*, 10.6.92), but in the end it complied with OFTEL's ruling rather than appeal to the Monopolies and Mergers Commission (MMC) and risk an even more adverse judgement.

By 1992, it was clear that OFTEL had effectively moved away from the original spirit and intention of the 'RPI-x' system of regulation. Whereas it was originally intended that 'x' should be set for ten years, with the possibility of review after five, and that BT should be able to retain the fruits of any efficiency gains achieved over and above this figure, OFTEL in fact revized 'x' upwards three times in four years in response to evidence that the company was making high profits. The 1991 review was prompted by the political controversy provoked by the company's £3 billion profits that year, and it suggests that the regulator was in effect capping profits rather than prices. BT's customers have clearly benefited from this successive tightening of the price regime, at least in the short term, for it is highly unlikely that such dramatic cuts in price would have occurred under government ownership.

Much the same pattern has been repeated in the other utilities privatized since BT. At British Gas, for example, the value of 'x' was originally set at two, but at the first opportunity for review in 1991, the regulator (OFGAS) raized this to five following a 46 per cent profits rise in 1990. As in telecommunications, there is no doubt that domestic customers have benefited from lower prices as a result of privatization, for when they were in the public sector, neither British Telecom nor British Gas ever came anywhere near to holding price rises year on year to 7.5 per cent and 5 per cent respectively below the rate of inflation.

The water industry, however, has been different. Here there is little prospect of effective competition emerging, although the existence of ten different regional companies does in principle enable the regulator, OFWAT, to gauge relative performance and to penalize the less efficient companies. The really distinctive feature of the water industry, however, is that prices have been rising rather than falling in real terms. The price cap formula for the water plcs is 'RPI + k' where 'k' represents a company's projected future capital expenditure requirements less an 'x' factor for increased efficiency. Because it was recognized in 1989 that all ten plcs would need to expand investment in real terms in order to meet EC standards on drinking water quality and on disposal of sewage, the initial value of 'k' was positive for all ten companies, varying from a low of 3.0 for Yorkshire Water to a high of 7.0 for Northumbrian (see Price Waterhouse 1990). In every case except Southern (whose 'k' falls to zero after 1995), substantial price rises were therefore anticipated when the industry was privatized, with average prices set nearly to double in real terms over the ensuing ten years (Carney 1992). Indeed, provision was also made at the time of privatization for a so-called 'cost pass-through' or 'interim adjustment' mechanism which would allow price caps to be varied if company investment costs suddenly changed as a result of, say, increased prices in the construction industry or new regulations from Brussels imposing higher quality standards. Alone among the regulators, OFWAT is charged with the responsibility of ensuring that the companies can make profits at a level high enough to attract sufficient funds to enable them to carry out their future investment plans.

As in the telecommunications and gas industries, the regulator has, however, put pressure on the companies to keep price rises below the full value of 'k' as a result of their higher-than-expected profits in the first two years. By insisting on reducing prices after just one or two years of good results, rather than waiting for the full five years before a formal review was due, OFWAT has followed OFTEL and OFGAS in effectively introducing a system of profit-capping rather than price-capping (see Wright, 1992).

It seems from all this that it is proving difficult for regulators of monopoly industries to permit privatized companies to make high profits and to pay high dividends, irrespective of whether or not this is the result of efficiency gains, for politicians and the public become restive when they see these companies making high profits, and people are generally ignorant about how the price-capping system works. Few members of the public seem to understand the complexities of the 'RPI+k' formula in the water industry, few are aware of the investment programmes which the companies have embarked upon, and many apparently therefore believe that increased prices are a direct result of the privatization of water and the subsequent exploitation by the companies of their monopoly position. According to an OFWAT survey, over a quarter of the population attributes increased water bills to privatization (OFWAT, 1992, p.26). Public cynicism has been fuelled by the higher than average profits recorded by the companies and the substantial salary increases paid to senior managers, and this has undoubtedly put pressure on OFWAT to keep prices and profits down.

Despite OFWAT's success in keeping price rises in 1992 below the level of 'k', average (non-metered) water bills still rose from £119 to £169 between 1989 and 1992. In my two case study regions, average annual water bills had risen by 1992 to £174 in Southern and £156 in North West. In international terms, these are not high figures - Germany, Belgium, France and the Netherlands all pay higher water charges than in Britain (*The Independent,* 23.9.92) - and relative to the cost of other commodities, it may still be argued that water supply and sewage treatment represents good value at around three pounds per week. The fact remains, however, that the rate of increase in water prices is much faster than that of most other commodities, for price rises have been steep and have far outstripped the general rate of inflation. On average, water bills increased 20 per cent in real terms in the first three years after privatization (see CRI, 1992).

These increases are, as we have seen, due mainly to the massive new investment programmes forced upon the companies by EC directives and by the dilapidated state of much of the sewerage system, and there are some signs from my survey that customers are beginning to understand this and are perhaps becoming rather less inclined to blame price rises on privatization per se. While a substantial majority (91 per cent) believed in 1989 that privatization would increase prices, only 68 per cent believed that it actually had done when they were reinterviewed in 1991. People know full well that prices have risen, but they are now less certain than they were that privatization is the culprit.

Customers also apparently remain reasonably satisfied that they are getting value for money. In 1989, two-thirds of my sample described the charge they were paying for water as 'very' or 'fairly' reasonable with around a quarter thinking it was unreasonable. Eighteen months later there had certainly been a shift in attitudes following the price rises, but half of the sample still felt that charges were reasonable while 38 per cent thought they were not.

Drawing together all the evidence, it seems that, even where privatized companies have enjoyed effective monopoly or near-monopoly markets, consumers have objectively gained as regards the prices they have to pay. The fear has often been expressed that prices will rise when an enterprise is privatized since it will need to pay dividends to shareholders. Yet the experience in Britain over the last ten years or so suggests that any additional costs incurred by having to pay dividends are more than cancelled out by the gains from efficiency savings[1]. In the case of BT and British Gas, price rises are now pegged in both cases substantially below inflation. In the water industry, the picture is more complicated given the rising real charges and the concern of OFWAT that the companies are enjoying too high a rate of return on their capital, but it is important to remember that here too, there is an 'x' efficiency factor being imposed.

Price regulation by OFWAT has succeeded in creating a quasi-competitive environment in the industry, and the use of yardstick competition to fix the values of 'k' after 1994 will reinforce this. If anything, OFWAT, like the other regulators, is erring more on the side of the consumer than on the side of the companies it is regulating, and there is no evidence to support the views expressed by critics of water privatization that the regulator would prove too weak or would be 'captured' by the companies. On price, therefore, it is hard to avoid the conclusion that consumers do seem objectively to have benefited from privatization, although it also has to be recognized that many consumers subjectively still believe that the companies are making large profits at their expense.

The consumer experience of quality

Opponents of privatization often maintain that the quality of service deteriorates as newly privatized enterprises foresake their old commitment to a 'public service' ethos and seek ways of cutting corners in order to maximize returns. In this view, even if the regulators succeed in keeping price rises below inflation, the companies only meet these targets by reducing service quality.

In the years immediately following the BT privatization, such claims had some plausibility. When BT was sold in 1984, there was considerable anxiety about how diligent the company would be in maintaining essential but unprofitable services such as the network of public call boxes and the emergency 999 service, and the company's performance soon became subject to widespread criticism. Just two years after privatization, for example, 21 per cent of public call boxes were out of order and the volume of complaints to the Telecom Users' Association doubled between 1986 and 1987 (Thompson, 1988). In 1987, OFTEL reported that faults on exchange lines were taking longer to rectify, delays were increasing in providing new lines, and operator and directory enquiry services were unsatisfactory, and in 1988, OFTEL found that only 74 per cent of faults were being repaired within one day as compared with 85 per cent or 90 per cent a few years earlier. In 1989 OFTEL received thirty-two thousand complaints about BT, an increase of more than a third over the previous year (Chapman, 1990).

The suspicion was that BT was cutting the quality of its service in order to maximize its profits, and critics claimed that the rapid reduction in staffing levels after privatization resulted in increased delays and a poorer quality of service. More recently, however, perhaps because competition from Mercury, Cellnet and cable operators has intensified, BT has made stringent efforts to improve on all the quality of service indicators. The poor publicity has been countered and connections and repairs have speeded up. The Director General of OFTEL, writing in 1989, professed himself reasonably well pleased: 'The range of services now available and the range of apparatus are much wider and much better than in the days before privatization and liberalization. Some improvements would no doubt have come about anyway, as a result of improved technology, but I do not believe they would have matched the scale of what has actually happened' (Carsberg, 1989, p.94).

The early BT experience has nevertheless left its mark on a sceptical public, and by the time water came to be privatized there was widespread concern that the private sector could not be trusted to maintain quality standards in so vital a service. In the run-up to privatization, consumer bodies like the National Consumer Council began to warn that provisions for consumer protection were inadequate (Gordon 1989), and leading Labour Party politicians such as the late John Smith claimed that pursuit of profit by privatized water companies would prove incompatible with concern for quality standards (*The Independent*, 4.2.89). In May 1989, *Which?* magazine reported that nearly 60 per cent of people disagreed with the government's claim that privatization would lead to improvements in water quality, and in my survey in September of that year, less than a quarter believed that privatization would improve water quality while half believed it would not.

Many people, however, believed that improvements were required. In the *Which*? survey, more than 20 per cent of consumers said they were not satisfied with water quality, most of the complaints being about discolouration or taste, and in a Harris survey for the *Observer* (2.7.89), nearly one-third of respondents were dissatisfied with drinking water quality. My 1989 survey generated very similar findings to the *Which*? report, 21 per cent of respondents being either 'dissatisfied' or 'very dissatisfied' with the drinking water delivered to their taps.

Since the industry was privatized in 1989, quality standards have been policed by a number of different government agencies. Three new agencies established in 1989 are the key ones. First, the Drinking Water Inspectorate (DWI) monitors the water coming through the tap to ensure that it meets public health standards. Second, the Office of Water Services (OFWAT), whose main job is to regulate prices in the industry, also keeps a check on the quality of the service being offered by the water companies and seeks to ensure that they carry out all the requirements of their licences. Third, the National Rivers Authority (NRA) is responsible for managing and controlling the water environment. In addition, the water services plcs are also subject to regulation by Her Majesty's Inspectorate of Pollution (HMIP), the Office of Fair Trading and the Monopolies and Mergers Commission, government departments such as the DoE and the Ministry of Agriculture, Fisheries and Food (MAFF), and the EC. As Michael Carney observes, 'The most obvious point about...the regulators is that there are an awful lot of them' (1992, p.43).

One consequence of all this regulation and monitoring is that there is generally good information on various quality standards since privatization. Indeed, in the water industry, as in a number of other privatizations, it seems that the switch out of the public sector has increased the amount of information available and the amount of publicity about it (something which Ernst 1994 also recognizes). This is true for drinking water quality, monitored by DWI, environmental quality, monitored by NRA, and quality of service, monitored by OFWAT, for in all three areas data are gathered and published today which were never available before 1989.

(i) Drinking water quality

Objective indicators suggest that the quality of tap water is high. According to the DWI's first report, drinking water quality in England and Wales was 'generally of a high standard and much was of an exceptionally high standard' (*The Times,* 15.8.91). In over three million tests carried out through 1990, the DWI found that all of the quality criteria established at the time of privatization were met in 99 per cent of water samples. Objectively, therefore, water quality is good, but subjectively, many consumers do not believe it.

There are various reasons for this. One is the well-publicized failure of the British water industry to achieve the high drinking water standards laid down in the EC directive of 1980 which sought to reduce the level of nitrates and other contaminants in the water supply. In January 1992, the European Court found the British government guilty of failing to comply with this directive, although Britain is not alone in this transgression, for none of the twelve EC states currently achieves the extremely low levels of contamination which it lays down. Britain was prosecuted, not so much because it is any worse than the others, but because British pressure groups like Friends of the Earth have been particularly active in campaigning in Brussels.

The problem of contamination arises mainly because fertilizers and pesticides used by farmers end up in the water system. It is an issue which has received enormous publicity, but there are many in the industry in Britain who argue that the £2 billion now being spent by the water companies to reduce contamination, and the billions more likely to be spent in the future, represents a misuse of resources. EC standards on pesticides, for example, have been set at or even below the lowest concentrations which can be detected (0.1 micrograms per litre, or one part in ten billion, equivalent to just two litres of any pesticides in the entire daily water supply of England and Wales). Effectively this is a zero target, and it is some twenty times more stringent than the levels deemed safe to drink in the USA or, for that matter, in Britain before the directive came into force (*The Independent*, 22.7.91).

Regulators, of course, do not have to concern themselves with the costs of compliance, and it will always be in the interests of a regulatory agency to err on the side of caution, for the public is unlikely to complain that standards are too high, and extremely high standards also help pacify vociferous pressure groups. For the industry, however, the costs of bringing about marginal improvements are huge. Even pressure groups like Friends of the Earth accept that British drinking water is perfectly safe and that there is no need for anyone to buy mineral water or water purifiers on health grounds (*The Times,* 15.8.91). It also seems unlikely that domestic consumers will notice any difference in taste, colour or quality of their drinking water once the improvements have been made, although they will almost certainly notice a difference in their bills (Carney, 1992, p.35).

Whether or not some of the EC standards are unrealistic or unnecessary, many domestic consumers are clearly worried by constant reminders that their water supplies fail to comply with EC standards. This has undoubtedly contributed to an increased awareness and concern about tap water quality, even though there is no evidence that water quality is any worse than it has ever been. Certainly there are no grounds for believing that privatization is reducing water quality, but consumer expectations are rising, and privatization has contributed to this by drawing people's attention to an industry which they previously took very much for granted. Over the next few years, the quality of drinking water in Britain will rise, but it may not rise fast enough to match the growing expectations of those who consume it.

(ii) Quality of the water environment

One of the most significant changes brought about by the privatization of the water industry has been the marked improvement in the water environment. This is a reflection of the unsurprising fact that government agencies seem much better at regulating private sector organizations than they are at regulating themselves.

In 1989, when the water industry was privatized, years of relative neglect of the water environment had resulted in a major build-up of problems which required huge sums of new investment to rectify. Real capital spending by water authorities virtually halved between 1974 and 1985, and this was reflected in growing environmental problems such as nitrate and lead pollution of drinking water, fouling of bathing waters and beaches and widespread pollution of the river system. By the time they were privatized, most authorities were in breach of EC environmental standards.

In 1988, there were over 23,000 recorded incidents of water pollution (Gordon, 1989). More than one-third of these were caused by industry, and one-fifth were caused by agriculture, but a further 20 per cent of them were caused by water authorities themselves. The UK was, for example, the only country in the EC which was still disposing of raw sewage at sea, and this resulted in the failure of 23 per cent of the designated bathing beaches in England and Wales to comply with the EC Bathing Water Directive (NRA 1991, p.13). There was a 22 per cent failure rate at sewage treatment works, often resulting in pollution of rivers, and increasing numbers of sewage treatment plants were failing to meet their consent conditions (Rees and Synott 1988). Although the 1974 Control of Pollution Act gave members of the public the right to sue water authorities for such failures, only one successful prosecution was ever brought (*The Independent,* 22.7.88).

River quality, which improved through the 1960s and 1970s due mainly to the replacement of dirty industries by cleaner ones (*The Economist,* 25.2.89), deteriorated during the 1980s. Despite well-publicized triumphs such as the reintroduction of salmon into the Thames, a report on freshwater quality by the standing Royal Commission on Environmental Pollution shows that river quality deteriorated between 1980 and 1990 and that there is now extensive pollution of acquifiers, the underground sources of water (*The Times,* 11.6.92). The NRA's map of river quality published in 1991 also showed a deterioration between 1985 and 1990, although it did indicate that 65 per cent of river length in England and Wales is still of 'good' quality (class I), and this compared favourably with the EC as a whole where only 39 per cent of rivers were class I (*Financial Times,* 18.3.89). Nevertheless, during the 1980s more lengths of rivers were downgraded than were upgraded with a net deterioration of 1200km of rivers or more than 3 per cent of the total (*The Economist,* 25.2.89).

In the run-up to privatization, government ministers claimed that it would improve the water environment, partly because the privatized companies would have access to new sources of capital which they could use to fund long overdue investment, and partly because regulation would be made more effective by removing the regulatory powers previously exercized by the water authorities themselves and vesting them in a new independent agency, the National Rivers Authority. Critics, including the Labour Party and pressure groups such as Friends of the Earth, rejected these claims and argued instead that privatization would result in less concern generally for the environment than had been shown by water authorities when they were in the public sector. According to this view, public authorities are more trustworthy than private ones, partly because they are likely to be motivated at least in part by a public service ethos, and partly because they are indirectly accountable to the public through the medium of elected government. Most members of the public seemed to agree with the critics, for in my survey, 55 per cent of those questioned in 1989 agreed that the environment was likely to suffer as a result of water privatization while only 26 per cent disagreed.

As things have turned out, however, fears that privatization would result in a further decline in environmental standards have been misplaced, and it was noticeable in the 1991 survey repeat interviews that this particular worry had diminished significantly among the general public in the eighteen months following the sale. The 1991 responses from the survey revealed that, while 55 per cent of people had expected things to get worse as a result of privatization, only 28 per cent now believed that this had happened.

All the plcs are now engaged on a massive spending programme to improve water quality in rivers, at bathing beaches and through the tap. This investment programme has, of course, been forced upon the companies by the EU. What has changed as a direct result of privatization, however, is the stringency with which such standards are being enforced, and the professed concern of the companies themselves to be seen to be doing something to improve environmental quality. Both of these factors have been important in the move to improve environmental standards.

Before 1989, the Regional Water Authorities both provided water and sewerage services and regulated them. The result was that regulation was generally lax. As we have seen, the water authorities themselves were responsible for 20 per cent of all incidents of water pollution (mainly as a result of leakage from sewage treatment plants - Gordon, 1989). Not only did they often condone their own polluting activities, but they were also on very weak ground when it came to prosecuting farmers or industrialists for doing the same thing. The result was that environmental standards were often not enforced and the quality of the water environment continued to decline. By removing the utility functions into the private sector while retaining the regulatory functions in a new public sector agency (the NRA), privatization broke this pattern by separating the water utility poachers from the water regulation gamekeeper, and the environment has benefited as a result.

Part of the evidence for this can be seen in the rate of prosecutions brought by the NRA since it was set up in 1989; in its first full year of operation, the NRA brought 309 successful prosecutions for pollution, and this figure rose to 484 the year after that including 17 cases brought against water plcs. Data on the period before privatization are difficult to compile, but the NRA itself claimed in its first annual report that 'enforcement activity has increased significantly compared with previous years' (NRA, 1990, p.18). But the evidence goes beyond simply the rate of prosecutions.

One of the NRA's key responsibilities, in addition to issuing discharge consents and prosecuting those who break or disregard them, is to license abstraction from rivers. Licensing was previously in the hands of the RWAs which were of course themselves by far the largest volume abstractors. The NRA has attempted to improve river flows by reducing the amounts taken by water companies from rivers which are in danger of drying up, and in 1993 it introduced a national charging scheme for abstraction of water which is likely to reduce the overall volume of water abstracted in the future.

The NRA's functions also cover land drainage and flood protection and my interviewee at English Nature reported in 1991 that the threats to wildlife posed by drainage of wetlands were now, as a result of the establishment of the NRA, much less worrying than before. In addition, the NRA also has a responsibility for fisheries, navigation, conservation and recreation. Here it works by a code of practice agreed by the DoE at the time of privatization and designed to safeguard existing recreational uses while balancing them against the conservation of wildlife and its habitats and the need of the water plcs to make a return on their assets. According to my interviewee at the National Anglers Council, this code is working well as regards the safeguarding of existing recreational uses. There has been no deterioration in fish stocks since privatization, nor have the water plcs dramatically raized their charges (as was feared before 1989) to those using rivers or reservoirs for fishing or other leisure pursuits.

Privatization, in short, has resulted in environmental issues being accorded a higher priority than before. My interviewee at English Nature, who had been critical of the privatization plans in 1989, explained two years later: 'I don't like to say it, but I think it's been a great improvement over the previous system. One reason is that the water companies have got someone to control them now which they didn't have before... [Another is that] the NRA is more sympathetic to us than the RWAs were. We didn't have anyone nationally to talk to before.'

Not only does the NRA appear more receptive to the environmental lobby than the RWAs tended to be, but the new water plcs also seem more concerned to respond to environmental concerns than was the case with their predecessors. As private sector companies, they are now more sensitive to criticisms than they were when they were in the public sector. Precisely because privatization was so unpopular, and public distrust of the new plcs is so widespread, the companies have been concerned to do all they can to improve their public image. Privatization has raized the public profile of their activities and has therefore pushed environmental questions higher up their scale of priorities.

There is also a very real sense in which the water companies themselves have a vested interest in improving the water environment. As Michael Carney of the Water Services Association points out, cleaner rivers mean that the industry has to spend less time and money on purifying the water which it supplies to its customers (Carney, 1992). Furthermore, environmental improvements mean an expansion of business for the companies with increased turnover and increased investment, and the pricing regulations under which they operate mean that the companies can cover these costs through increased charges without losing customers. Seen in this way, there is little reason for believing that a private water industry will be any less asiduous in raising environmental quality than a public one.

Summarizing all of this, we can conclude that nature conservation is now accorded a higher priority than it was before 1989, that the activities of the water industry in over-abstracting or polluting rivers are now much more closely monitored and tightly controlled, that pollution by other users is also now more stringently regulated, that recreational users are no worse off than before, and that the environmental lobby has strengthened its position relative to that of producer groups like the farmers and landowners who enjoyed an inside track under the old arrangements. The result of all this is a clear improvement in water quality - the NRA reported in 1994 that river quality had improved by 10 per cent over the previous two years and that the long-term decline since the early 1970s had been reversed (*The Guardian*, 1.6.94).

It is possible, of course, that all of this could have been achieved by reforming the water industry rather than privatizing it, but this would have been much more difficult to achieve. The establishment of the NRA has been crucial, but such a radical reform might have been politically impossible in the absence of privatization, for most water professionals were strongly committed to retaining the 1974 principle of integrated river basin management, and the strength of opposition by the RWA chairmen to splitting their regulatory powers from their utility functions would have been even more difficult to counter without the move into private ownership. Even if the NRA could have been established while leaving the rest of the industry in public ownership, there is also the lingering doubt whether a public sector regulator would have pursued its objectives quite as keenly against other public sector agencies as it has done against the private sector water plcs which enjoy little public sympathy and which remain so acutely concerned about their corporate imagery. It is difficult to believe that the Treasury would happily have sanctioned expenditure of millions of pounds of public money to meet conditions imposed by a public sector NRA on a public sector water industry.

These considerations lead me to conclude that privatization has enabled government regulation to become effective, perhaps for the first time. The history of the water industry clearly demonstrates not only that private companies (even big and powerful companies which enjoy effective monopolies) can be regulated effectively by state agencies, but also that state agencies seem particularly bad at regulating themselves. Whatever else one thinks about the benefits and costs of water privatization, the division which it forced between those who provide the water and those who regulate its use must count as an unambiguous bonus.

(iii) Quality of service indicators

The performance of the privatized water companies can also be evaluated on a range of other criteria which are now closely monitored by OFWAT. These include, for example, imposition of hosepipe bans, incidence of interrupted supplies, reductions in mains water pressure, and incidence of flooding due to inadequate sewer provision (see CRI, 1992).

Statistics are collected on each of these indicators for each water plc, and this enables OFWAT to draw comparisons between the different companies and to judge whether standards of service are rising or falling over time. The figures show that there are problems, notably in London and the south-east where a series of unusually dry summers has reduced river flows and depleted water tables to a point where hosepipe bans have become common and some households have been forced to rely for supplies on standpipes. These, however, are problems of long standing and can hardly be blamed upon privatization. On the key question of whether things have been getting better or worse since 1989, OFWAT reports 'a mixed picture with some improvements but in some cases a deterioration of service' (OFWAT 1992, p.11). It is, of course, early days, and all that can really be said with any confidence at this stage is that quality of service is now being rigorously monitored for the first time. With more and better quality of service indicators being added (e.g. in 1993 OFWAT began to measure levels of water leakage and to penalize those companies with the worst records), it is clearly going to be difficult for the companies to increase profits by allowing the service to deteriorate, even if they wished to do so.

Much the same conclusion can probably be drawn for the other privatized utilities as well. In 1992 Parliament passed the Competition and Service (Utilities) Act. This gave all the regulators of privatized companies the same powers to obtain information on service quality and imposed on them the responsibility to ensure that companies did not sacrifice service quality in an attempt to expand profits. It also introduced automatic payment of penalties to customers in the event on non-performance (an idea which has also been extended recently to public sector services through the introduction of 'citizens' charters' and which has been in operation in the water industry since 1990/91). In 1993, a government survey found that 89 per cent of consumers believed that the quality of service offered by BT and by British Gas had improved over the previous twelve months - a higher figure than for virtually any other company or public service included in the survey (*The Independent,* 22.8.93).

While there are undoubtedly problems in measuring service quality, in collating all the data which are needed in order to judge it, and in devising effective compensation where quality is found to be sub-standard, it is fair to conclude that privatization has created for the first time a framework of regulation from which consumers should begin to benefit. The least that can be said is that they are unlikely to lose.

Accountability to customers

There are four measures which may be taken to judge this aspect of the companies' performance: the knowledge which customers have about the company; the viability of watchdog bodies operating on behalf of consumers; the volume of complaints received from customers; and the way the companies handle customers with problems.

(i) Company visibility

In most industries, privatization seems to have had the paradoxical effect of removing enterprises from the public domain of politics while at the same time making their affairs much more publicized and much more politicized. This process was particularly marked in the case of water, an industry which attracted very little public attention before privatization, yet which has had a high profile ever since (Chapman, 1990).

Increased visibility should be of benefit to consumers, for the glare of publicity not only enhances their knowledge and understanding about a service for which they are paying, but also acts as a safeguard against bad practice by the companies themselves. However, there are grounds for believing that the post-privatization water industry is not well understood by many people despite the publicity and despite the attempts by the companies themselves to project a corporate identity through expensive advertising campaigns. Very few people have any direct contact with those who provide them with water and take away their sewage - in my survey, only 11 per cent (before privatization) and 12 per cent (after privatization) of the population claimed to have had any direct contact with their water or sewerage company over the previous twelve months. Nor is there any direct link between the amount of water which people consume and the amount they pay, and this arguably further distances the companies from their customers since consumers are never encouraged or obliged to think about how much of the product they are using or where it comes from. For most people, before and after privatization, the water and sewerage undertaking is a remote institution with which they will never have personal contact.

The companies have tried to raise their visibility to their customers, partly by advertising and partly by innovations such as public open days or the publication of 'customer charters'. Despite this, however, many people seem to have only the haziest idea about the company which provides them with this most basic of services, and for this reason, effective accountability is likely to depend more upon the regulators than on direct contacts between the companies and the public they serve.

(ii) Consumer watchdogs

Since privatization, responsibility for the defence of consumer interests has fallen to OFWAT and its ten new regional Customer Services Committees (CSCs). These are committes of twelve people each, all of whom are appointed by OFWAT from among consumer organizations, welfare groups, women's organizations, trade and professional associations and groups representing the disabled. These committees hold various consultation exercises and are responsible in the first instance for handling customer complaints. OFWAT believes they 'play a vital role in customer protection' (*OFWAT*, 1992, p.15), and since 1993 this role has been strengthened through the establishment of a National Customer Council consisting of the Director General and the various CSC chairmen.

Unfortunately, however, few customers seem to know about the CSCs. A survey commissioned by OFWAT in 1991 found that few people even knew of its existence and activities, let alone the role of the CSCs. While 37 per cent of the population was apparently aware that an organization had been established to regulate prices and look after the interests of customers, only 6 per cent of them (or just 2 per cent of the population as a whole) could actually name it (*OFWAT*, 1992, p.68). This low level of public awareness seems no better than the situation before privatization - Customer Services Committees have replaced Consumer Consultative Committees, but there are few people outside the industry who know about either!

This is confirmed by my survey in which consumers were asked to whom they would complain if a grievance was not resolved by their water supplier. In 1989, before the industry was privatized, just 3 per cent of consumers thought of approaching the CCCs which had by then been in existence for six years. Most people put their faith in the political process - 28 per cent said they would contact their MP and 5 per cent mentioned their local councillor - or in government bureaucracies such as the Environmental Health Officer (10 per cent) or, fifteen years after water was removed from local government, the Town Hall (15 per cent). Twenty-two per cent admitted that they did not have a clue. Eighteen months later, notwithstanding OFWAT's efforts to publicize complaints procedures through a leaflet sent to every household, just 4 per cent of customers mentioned the CSCs with another 1 per cent each mentioning OFWAT or its Director General. People do seem to have become aware that water has been removed from the public arena, for resort to explicitly political channels such as MPs and councillors had decreased significantly (to 20 per cent and 3 per cent respectively), but so too had the proportion of respondents having any idea at all where they might complain (the percentage who could not answer the question rose from 22 per cent to 27 per cent). OFWAT and its CSCs may or may not be doing an effective job in safeguarding the interests of consumers, but it is clear that many consumers themselves are blissfully unaware of what is being done on their behalf and are by and large as ignorant of complaints procedures as they were before privatization[2].

(iii) Number of complaints

An important measure of how well companies are meeting the expectations of their customers is the number of complaints received against them. Because an independent complaints procedure with computerized records was only established after privatization, it is difficult to gauge how far complaint rates have changed as compared with when the industry was in the public sector, but it is obvious from the rate of increase in complaints since 1989 that many more people are formally expressing grievances today than ever occurred before water was privatized.

This *may* partly be explained by the very existence of a new complaints procedure. Give people a means to complain, and that is exactly what they will do. Three factors suggest that this cannot be the full explanation, however. First, as we saw earlier, customers are actually less satisfied than they were with the quality of service they are receiving. Secondly, we have also seen that most members of the public are still completely ignorant about OFWAT's existence, and it is therefore difficult to explain away the rising tide of complaints simply as the product of the increased visibility of the complaints procedure. And thirdly, customers do not themselves believe that it is any easier for them to make their views heard than it ever was.

One factor which undoubtedly does help to explain the growing number of complaints is the increased publicity and controversy surrounding the water industry. All the press and media attention which has been paid to water quality and environmental issues, together with the sharp rise in charges, has almost certainly prompted many more people to express their anger and frustration. Things may not have got any worse since 1989, but privatization has made people much more alert to them. In this sense, it can be argued that privatization has enabled the expression of grievances, not so much because it has led to the establishment of formal complaints procedures, but because the very act of privatizing the industry itself focused public attention on it and therefore prompted people to complain when things went wrong.

OFWAT records that, in their first year of operation (1990/91), the ten Customer Services Committees received 4613 complaints - a rate of 1.7 for every ten thousand connections. Just one year later, this had increased to 10635, or 4.0 per ten thousand connections (OFWAT 1992). These are not huge figures, although it should be remembered that they refer not to the total number of complaints made, but rather to the numbers of people who complained to the CSCs. Given that the complaints procedure requires that customers first take up their grievances with their local company, and only approach their CSC if the company fails to satisfy them, the total number of initial complaints in the industry as a whole is therefore likely to be much higher than the level recorded by OFWAT.

In my survey, 1.5 per cent of customers interviewed in 1991 claimed to have contacted their water services company to complain about some aspect of the service over the previous twelve months - a much larger proportion than that officially recorded as having contacted a CSC. It is also interesting to note, however, that this figure for the total number of initial complaints is virtually unchanged since before privatization, for the 1989 survey found that 1.4 per cent of customers had complained to their RWA during the previous year. This would seem to give some support to OFWAT's claim that the rising number of complaints brought to its attention should not be taken as an indicator of declining service quality, but is rather a reflection of more people learning how to use the official channels. Indeed, of the complaints dealt with by CSCs in 1991/92, most concerned either charges (38 per cent) or billing (25 per cent). Clearly, then, a large proportion of the increase in complaints is explained, not by any deterioration in service, but by the rise in water charges (and, indeed, in water company profits) which many customers resent or do not understand.

(iv) Dealing with problems

With the substantial increases in water charges since privatization, the problem of arrears and non-payment has been increasing. In June 1992, the Citizens Advice Bureau reported that more people were now seeking help with 'water debt' than were approaching it with problems of tax, telephone debt or social fund payments (*The Times*, 5.6.92). In order to protect customers from arbitrary abuse of monopoly power, water services companies are obliged to seek a court order before proceeding to disconnect households who fail to pay their bills. In 1991, a staggering nine hundred thousand court summonses were issued (OFWAT 1992, p.39).

The number of households disconnected from the water supply fell substantially at the time of privatization - from 5902 in the six months to September 1989 to just 2524 in the six months to March 1990. Since then, however, the figure has been rising again, to 7662 in September 1991 and to 21,286 twelve months after that - considerably higher than the pre-privatization levels and reflecting the increases in real charges since 1989. The rate of disconnection varies widely between different companies and seems to reflect differences in company policies. In 1991, OFWAT published a set of agreed guidelines designed to reduce the number of disconnections, but some companies seem to be observing the letter of the Code of Practice while continuing to offer their customers little help or advice in paying off debts (see Southern CSC, 1992, p.5), and in June 1992 the Director General publicly condemned the dramatic rise in the number of customers cut off (*The Guardian* 10.6.92).

The companies, of course, have a right to payment for the services they provide, and there is a view held by some that much of the arrears is the product of a refusal to pay rather than an inability to do so. Nevertheless, the issue of nearly one million court summonses is a major indictment of the companies' failure to make contact with their customers, explain why prices have risen, and investigate genuine cases of hardship. Also, the substantial increase in the rate of disconnections is a disturbing sign that some companies at least are less concerned with their customers' welfare than they claim to be in their propoganda[3].

Conclusion

In most of the industries which have been privatized, consumers have benefited on prices. As nationalized industries, these firms were constantly subject to political intervention on prices, sometimes holding them down (when the government was concerned about inflation), but sometimes pushing them up (when the government wanted to pay off debt). Privatized industries operating in a competitive environment have escaped such regulation altogether, and the competition itself has helped increase efficiency and keep prices down (Kay, 1987). The quasi-monopolistic privatized industries have been subject to tight controls by government regulators, and this too has tended to reduce prices. At British Gas and BT, for example, real prices now fall each year by 5 per cent and 7.5 per cent respectively, and such achievements were never matched when these industries were under direct state control. As regards water, where real prices are rising, efficiency gains are still being imposed by the regulator and the increased charges are being used to finance a massive new investment programme whose costs would in any case have fallen on water users, taxpayers, or both. On prices, therefore, the consumer has gained from privatization.

On quality and accountability, however, we should remain more circumspect. The obvious temptation of price-capped companies operating in a non-competitive environment will always be to short-cut quality standards in order to raise profit margins. The government has now moved to plug that gap with the 1992 Competition and Service (Utilities) Act, and regulators like OFWAT have made important progress in identifying measurable criteria of quality against which different suppliers can be evaluated. It is also the case, as we saw in the example of the NRA, that government regulation of externality effects is almost certainly more effective when the operators are in the private sector than when they are shielded under another wing of Whitehall. As a tentative conclusion, therefore, we may suggest that quality seems not to have fallen in any of the privatized utilities, that it has improved markedly in some cases, and that it is now being monitored much more carefully than it ever was before.

On accountability, the case of the water industry at least suggests that customers have gained little if anything from privatization, and that some may have lost. The companies are still experienced by most customers as remote agencies about which they know little or nothing. Despite considerable publicity by the companies and by OFWAT, most people still have no idea about the regulatory regime, nor about how to pursue complaints. The number of complaints has risen, though two-thirds of them have to do with charges rather than service quality, and the companies are generally seen by their customers as unaccountable - an impression likely to be reinforced by heavy-handed actions against those in arrears.

The privatization of the utilities, and especially water, was hugely unpopular. Now they are privatized, the public still seems sceptical about their performance. It is this scepticism which may help keep prices down and quality up in the future, for these companies are aware of their poor corporate image and of the need to improve it by developing a strong customer service ethic. This at least marks a positive change from the era of nationalization.

References

Beesley, M. and Littlechild, S. (1986), 'Privatization: Principles, problems and priorities' in Kay, J., Mayer, C. and Thompson, D. (eds) *Privatization and Regulation,* Oxford, Clarendon Press.

Carney, M. (1992), 'The cost of compliance with ever higher quality standards' in Gilland, T. (ed.) *The Changing Water Business,* London, Centre for the Study of Regulated Industries.

Carsberg, B. (1989), 'Injecting competition into telecommunications' in Veljanovski, C. (ed.) *Privatization and Competition,* London, Institute of Economic Affairs.

CBI (1990), *A Nation of Shareholders* London, Confederation of British Industry.

Chapman, C. (1990), *Selling the Family Silver,* London, Hutchinson.

CRI 1992, *The UK Water Industry: Water Services and Costs 1990/91,* London, Public Finance Foundation Centre for the Study of Regulated Industries.

Ernst, J. (1994), *Whose Utility?,* Buckingham, Open University Press.

Gordon, S. 1989, *Down the Drain: Water, Pollution and Privatization,* London, Macdonald & Co.

Kay, J. (1987), *The State and the Market: The UK Experience of Privatization,* New York and London, Group of Thirty Occasional Paper, no.23.

Moore, J. (1983), *Why Privatise?,* London, Conservative Political Centre.

National Rivers Authority (various years), *Annual Report and Accounts,* Bristol, NRA.

OFWAT (1992), *1991 Report of the Director General of Water Services,* London, HMSO.

Pirie, M. (1988), *Privatization,* Aldershot: Wildwood House.

Price Waterhouse (1989), *Privatization: The Facts,* London, Price Waterhouse.

Redwood, J. (1990), 'Spreading popular capitalism' in Butler, E. (ed.), *Privatization Now!,* London, Adam Smith Institute.

Rees, J. and Synott, M. (1988): 'Privatization and social objectives' in C. Whitehead (ed.) *Reshaping the nationalized industries* Oxford, RTransaction books.

Saunders, P. and Harris, C. (1994), *Privatization and Popular Capitalism,* Buckingham, Open University Press.

Wright, J. (1992), 'Economic regulation in the water industry' in Gilland, T. (ed.) *The Changing Water Business,* London, Centre for the Study of Regulated Industries.

Footnotes

1 These, of course, have generally entailed staff cuts. Consumers have gained, but as Colin Harris shows in Chapter 13, producers (workers) have often lost out as regards job security. It is interesting that Ernst accepts that labour-shedding has led to efficiency gains (p.104), yet he is reluctant to conclude from this that consumers have correspondingly gained from price reductions. Where he does recognize that prices have fallen, he complains that companies have still been making large profits and deduces from this that prices could therefore have been pushed even lower. This argument is based, however, on a comparison of the existing situation with some idealized norm rather than with the actual pattern before privatization when these industries were highly unionized, wage rises were kept above average levels in the private sector, and prices rose each year rather than falling.

2 This lack of public knowledge and concern about consumer representative bodies represents a major problem for those, like Ernst, who believe that political representation can function as an effective safeguard for consumers of public services.

3 The heavy rise in disconnections reflects the real price rises and the uncoupling of water charges from rents by local authorities. Even Ernst recognizes that the disconnection practices and policies of the privatized water companies are probably no more stringent, and may even be 'better', than when they were in the public sector (p.151).

16 Empowering the consumer: The case of social housing

Robert Smith, Richard Walker and Peter Williams

Introduction

In the last fifteen years successive Conservative Governments have followed a programme of replacing welfare state systems of collective provision and public funding with more individual and privatized systems. Whole areas of welfare state programmes have been cut back in real terms, partly in response to the Government perceived need to limit public expenditure (and a desire to cut direct taxation) but also because of an ideological opposition to the direct public provision of services. The commitment of central Government to private market solutions has been based upon a view of both what are seen as the inherent inefficiencies of different forms of state intervention and a commitment to privatization and the extension of market mechanisms. The latter are seen as the most effective way of promoting economic efficiency and of meeting individual preferences for services, enabling more people to exercise their own choices and at the same time reducing their dependence on what is seen as 'the nanny state'. However, as Saunders (1986) has noted:

> Customers can exert power (albeit limited) within a market through their purses, pockets and pouches, but this is denied to a client within a system of state provision. Clients can complain, can vote, can demand, but in the end they have no where else to go, and no choice but to accept

what they are offered. They are, in short, dependent in a way that is never true of customers in a competitive market.

The dilemma then is to deliver efficient, high quality publicly subsidized services which meet the requirements of users, without disadvantaging those unable to meet their market costs.

The chapter explores some of the housing dimensions of these processes. It begins by examining the different approaches to housing provision and allocation, setting social housing in the context of the different political attitudes towards the public and private provision of housing. It briefly examines the way in which free market approaches to housing have been strongly advocated in the last fifteen years and the impact which the Government policies have had in shifting housing further into the private domain. The analysis then examines the changing position of the consumer in the social housing sector, focusing on the ways in which policies have been designed and implemented with the interest of the consumer in mind. It concludes that, despite advances in the attitudes of housing professionals towards consumers, and measures to increase their relative power and control through increased rights (to be consulted, to change landlord, to buy one's own home etc.) and higher standards of housing management performance, the shift in emphasis towards increasing privatization, whilst benefiting some, has also led to a significant decline in the general quality and opportunities offered by social housing. It has created real problems for those less well-equipped to compete in the housing market, making access to a decent, affordable home for those in need often difficult to attain.

Historical approaches to housing provision and allocation

It can be argued historically that the shape and structure of state involvement in housing has meant that it has never been at the fulcrum of the welfare state. Although the quality of housing across all tenures has been regulated in terms of its design, structural soundness, sanitation and fitness, its finance, production and allocation have traditionally been dominated by the private, as opposed to the public sector. Unlike education or health service provision there has never been a commitment on the part of any Government, of whatever political persuasion, to support a near universal housing service designed to meet the needs of all households. Although history has pointed to the need for substantial state intervention in the housing market, and governments have interceded both directly and indirectly since the mid-nineteenth century, direct public provision has always catered for a minority of the population. At its peak, about a third of UK housing stock was owned and managed by the public sector though there were important regional and local variations. In Scotland 43.7 per cent of the housing stock was in council ownership in 1990 whilst specific authorities in England housed well over half their local population. Council landlords dominated the rented sector, a position dissimilar to that in other Western European countries, where rented housing has traditionally been provided by a more diverse range of private and non-profit making organizations (Kroes, Ymkers and Mulder, 1988). However, the traditional role of social housing (and in particular council housing) has been to provide a redistribution of housing resources in favour of those in housing need, irrespective of ability to pay for its consumption. Only in the last fifteen years has this role been reversed, with social housing playing a more limited and targeted role.

Whilst housing has not been recognized as a part of a comprehensive social service and the attitude of individual governments towards the public and private provision of housing has differed according to their political colour, until 1979 it can be argued that post-war British housing policy represented an example of consensus politics. For the last fifty years, the private rented sector has continued its long-term decline despite modest attempts to revive it (most notably in 1957), both Labour and Conservative governments sought to woo the owner-occupier and council housing continued to expand, although from the mid 1970s housing associations were encouraged as a 'third arm' of housing, between council renting and owner-occupation.

Although the emphases varied somewhat this consensus ran from 1945 to the late 1970s. Despite this, there have been substantial and continuous criticisms of housing policies over the years. Those on the political left have argued for an increased role for the state in housing (Merrett, 1979); on the right have been those who have argued for greater freedom for the market (Stafford, 1978). The last fifteen years has represented a triumph for those who have argued in favour of housing being increasingly provided, funded and allocated by the private market. However, whilst it has traditionally been part of Conservative philosophy to place considerable reliance on the market and defend the interests of the private sector, what has been most evident in this recent period has been the direct attack on the very existence of public housing. Although this began in 1979 with the promotion of home ownership via the 'Right to Buy' by the end of the 1980s this assault had taken a very different form.

Privatization has not only meant the easing of rent controls in the private rented sector and a reduction in state subsidies in the social sector; it has also involved a significant reduction in direct state provision, the selling off of public housing into private ownership (most notably under the right-to-buy) and increased competition for the ownership and management of state housing between public and private service providers. The rationale for such policies has been not only a commitment to market mechanisms but a belief that Government's direct interventions in the housing market have failed to solve housing problems and in some instances have exacerbated them. The counter arguments have suggested that the attributes of housing are such that its private production and allocation is likely to be more efficient than public and that satisfying individual consumer preference will meet social objectives. As Pennance and Gray (1968) argued;

> If there are no restrictions on price, consumer choice or the entry of new producers or sellers, a strongly competitive market will ensure that the size, quantity and quality of houses that are built and the distribution of existing stock will be dictated by the tastes, incomes and preferences of consumers.

On the face of it the consumer would seem to have much to gain from the encouragement of market mechanisms and increased privatization. So how extensive has been the pursuit of policies designed to provide this degree of consumer sovereignty within the social housing sector?

It would be entirely misleading to argue that the 'public choice' based critique of UK housing policy is entirely without foundation. Intervention by the state in housing markets has created as well as solved problems. Rent controls in the private sector have certainly contributed to its long-term decline, the provision of large scale non-traditional public housing in the 1960s is widely regarded as an expensive and unpopular failure, which has had detrimental effects on the lives of council tenants (albeit that this form of housing was promoted by central Government and given very favourable subsidy treatment); and the management of public housing has often left a great deal to be desired, certainly from a tenant's perspective. These are powerful arguments - but whether for non-intervention and increased privatization or for trying to improve the ways in which policies are implemented is a subject for legitimate debate.

It is arguable whether public housing in Britain was ever fully conceived as part of the welfare state (Kirwan, 1984). Merrett (1979) has argued that the origins of direct council provision served the state's legitimatory and reproductive objectives as well as underpinning the political philosophy of social democracy. However, he and others have argued that since the early 1950s it has been perceived by both main political parties as the provision of housing for the minority of the population unable or unwilling to buy. In that sense it has never been seen as a direct substitute for home ownership, albeit that on occasions state provision has been on a larger scale than private speculative development.

The growth of council housing between 1919 and 1980 and its shifts from just providing 'housing for the working classes' has meant that the state has directly provided for the housing needs of a significant minority of the population. However, the development of state housing was underpinned by concepts of central bureaucratic hierarchies and a uniformity of service delivery, irrespective of locality. It can also be argued that the growth of social housing has been accompanied by the emergence of a professionalized class of housing managers acting as intermediaries between the state and the individual, controlling access and limiting the voice of the consumer. Although in its 1959 Report 'Councils and their Houses' (MHLG, 1959) the Central Housing Advisory Committee argued that housing management should seek to encourage a sense of independence among tenants, whilst fostering a sense of personal relationship between tenants and their landlord, it was recognized that this might become harder to maintain as the scale of the landlord's undertaking grew. In many cases it was not until the 1980s that we began to see real moves in this direction, following a growth in criticism of the ways in which public housing services were provided. Council landlords came to be seen as unresponsive, inefficient and ineffective providers of often poor quality services (Housing Research Group, 1981), and it is partly in response to such criticisms that the voice of the consumer has become more significant.

Responses to criticism of publicly provided services have taken two distinct forms. On the one hand arguments have been developed in favour of bringing services closer to the consumer either through decentralization (Cole, Arnold and Windle, 1991), a priority estates approach to housing management (Power, 1991) or increasing the role of residents, via increased tenant participation and self-management, for example through tenant managed co-operatives (Clapham and Kintrea, 1992). Some of these issues are considered more fully in the next section.

The alternative view, from the political right, has been that the problems inherent in the management of council housing in Britain can only be resolved by the use of the market and private sector competition. In the last decade successive Conservative governments have developed policies towards the public sector in general, and council housing in particular, based upon financial controls, internal markets, more tightly defined trading accounts (e.g. the Housing Revenue Account), competitive tendering, contracting out, clearer divisions between purchasers and providers and an increasing emphasis upon performance management. During the 1990s this has been taken a stage further with the introduction of performance indicator Reports to Tenants, following the Local Government and Housing Act 1989 (Marsh et. al., 1993, Walker, 1992) and the introduction of the Citizen's Charter (Cabinet Office, 1991). The debates have moved on from initial concerns with efficiency, effectiveness and quality (though these remain important) to giving greater attention to tenants rights and looking at the housing service from the perspective of those who use and pay for them. The next section examines in detail ways in which change has been introduced in the social housing sector with a view to empowering tenants and improving service standards and the accountability of providers. It then examines the shift towards consumerism in the social housing sector in the context in which social landlords have been operating during the last fifteen years, with the emphasis on privatizing public housing and providing alternatives to council housing, before concluding with an evaluation of the achievements and failings of the changes which have been introduced.

Privatization and tenant power in the 1980s and 1990s

It was not until the 1980 Housing Act that social housing tenants were given explicit rights. The Tenants Charter contained in this Act provided security of tenure, the Right to Buy, the right to exchange and a range of other measures. This Act can be seen as a first stage in a series of attempts to diversify and privatize the provision and management of social housing during the 1980s and 1990s. These attempts to diversify and privatize the public sector follow three broad themes. The first theme has been that of individual privatization seen through the Right to Buy (RTB) and more recently through the Rents to Mortgages (RTM) scheme. The second theme has seen a shift in provision way from local housing authorities to housing associations, whom the Government views as private sector organizations. The role of local authorities is being increasingly transformed from that of provider to enabler of provision. The pace with which this is happening varies reflecting partly the very varied size of the local authority stock in each area and political commitment. However, it is gaining pace and authorities are now in the process of being forced to compete for the provision of their housing management services. Aligned to these changes have been significant alterations in the funding and financial basis of local housing authorities. We return to these last two issues in section 4 of this chapter.

The third theme is that of consumerist and collectivist approaches to tenant involvement. The consumerist approach has been typified by attempting to increase the responsiveness of local Government whilst collective approaches have attempted to give tenants (consumers) the power to make democratic decisions about levels of service provision or opting out of local Government control. This has been achieved through a number of mechanisms. First, mechanisms have been put in place to increase the accountability of the total authority housing service to its tenants. At the same time tenants have been brought into the decision-making processes of housing management. Increasingly their views have been canvassed and acted upon. Tenants have been given information to aid this process which will allow them to make 'informed' decisions, primarily by the introduction of performance indicators for housing management. Second, tenants have been given powers to manage their own homes but still within the local Government arena through, for example, tenant management co-ops (TMCs) or Estate Management Boards (EMBs). Third, tenants have been given the opportunities to transfer to another landlord, either voluntarily or through compulsion via a number of routes; Tenants' Choice, large scale voluntary transfers (LSVT) and Housing Action Trusts (HATs). These first two options identified are forms of diversification of local authority housing, whilst the latter is a more direct way in which the Government has attempted to privatize the service. These issues are now explored in more detail.

Tenant involvement

During the 1980s the Government has become increasingly concerned about tenant involvement in housing management. It has promoted tenant participation for a number of reasons; first, as a means of increasing the accountability of housing management services; second, to improve standards as tenants question and challenge service provision; and finally, the Government has promoted participation, and in particular co-ops, because it is seen to discourage dependence and encourage self-reliance. To meet these aims a plethora of initiatives has been developed ranging from broad-based community associations, which extend their role beyond housing and deal with social, community or employment issues to specific housing management organizations such as TMCs and EMBs. The Government has also been active in sponsoring and encouraging a range of organizations to promote participation, notably the Tenant Participation Advisory Service, whilst providing direct funding to tenants' organizations through the Department of the Environment (DoE)/Welsh Office for local Government and Housing Corporation/Tai Cymru for associations. This promotion has also produced a small industry centred on tenant participation with numerous consultancies offering their advice to tenants and landlords and series of publications promoting the best ways to achieve successful participation (e.g. IoH/TPAS, 1990; NFHA, 1991).

The origins of the participation initiatives can be dated back to the 1970s. Government promoted TMCs under the 1975 Housing Rents and Subsidies Act and through the Priority Estates Project established in 1979. These two initiatives aimed to involve tenants in improving difficult to let/manage estates. However, the reasons for this promotion, as identified in the 1977 Housing Policy Review (DoE, 1977), were as much concerned with participation as mechanisms to reduce problems on housing estates, (for example vandalism) rather than promote consumer involvement per se.

On balance one has to argue that the Government has been successful in promoting tenant involvement, at least from a consumerist perspective, when we note the now extensive use of tenant satisfaction surveys and the growth of tenants' associations. However, the more formal, or collectivist, forms of participation, TMCs, EMBs, Estate Sub-committees etc. have been less successful. The levels of responsibility that tenants have to take on board to run these organizations is quite considerable and they typically take two or more years to develop. The imminent introduction of compulsory competitive tendering (CCT) of housing management has also laid down a challenge to tenants. The legislation allows tenants to by-pass the tendering procedures by setting up tenant managed organizations (TMOs). The extent to which tenants will take over the decision making of their estates, rather than see them go out to contract, where they have no veto over who wins the contract, is unknown. However, the demonstrable success of some forms of tenant participation, of which there are a growing though limited number, may lead to many tenants groups opting to set up TMOs.

One can challenge the perceived wisdom of tenant participation. Real questions have to be asked about the extent to which tenants want to become involved in the management of their homes. Research has shown that successful tenant participation schemes are based on the desire of tenants to alter or change the way in which things are done and often centre on a particular issue (Clapham and Kintrea, 1993). However, the DoE have drawn tenant participation into the resource allocation procedures. The Estate Action initiative established in 1985 in England competitively allocates funds to authorities to deal with problematic estates. This funding comes through the Housing Investment Programme (HIP) and is top-sliced from the total credit approvals available. Successful bids have to combine an innovative approach to solutions and to involve tenants. More recently councils have been penalized, in their HIP allocation, when they have not had a tenant participation strategy and active tenants groups. This raises issues about why groups exist and how they feed into decision-making processes. Yet despite all these measures and developments the 1989 Local Government and Housing Act restricts the role of tenant representatives on council committees and sub-committees (where they are not allowed to vote on decisions, the only exception to this being Estate Sub-committees) and reinforces the consumerist approach to tenant involvement, rather than a collectivist one.

The performance measurement regime to tenants

Performance measurement regimes have operated in the public sector throughout the mid to late 1980s following the launch of the Financial Management Initiative in 1982. However, a formalized regime was not introduced in local Government housing until the enactment of the 1989 Housing and Local Government Act. Section 167(1) of this Act introduced the Report to Tenants Determination Etc. Order (hereon in referred to as the Report to Tenants) which requires local housing authorities in England and Wales to provide every tenant with a report on housing management performance. The information contained in the report is determined by the relevant Secretary of State. The Report to Tenants together with the new financial regime introduced in 1990, the Citizen's Charter, the Government's White Paper 'Competing for Quality' (H.M. Treasury, 1991), and the consultation paper on competing for quality in housing management (DoE/WO, 1992) have all increased the pressure on local authorities to focus their attention on performance measurement and the setting of performance targets and improving service delivery. Although in the past local authorities have not been in the forefront of developing performance measures or of understanding the requirements of their customers, the challenge of legislation and the importance now attached to tenant participation, has forced them to develop a co-ordinated approach to performance measurement, target setting and outcome monitoring.

The stated legislative aims of the Report to Tenants is to allow local authority tenants to judge whether they are getting value for money from their local housing authority. In addition, one can identify attempts to further establish a dialogue between landlords and tenants about the housing service and to increase the accountability of the service. However, to date the success of the Report to Tenants in developing tenant awareness of services and establishing a dialogue between tenants and landlords has been limited. Research undertaken for the Department of the Environment (Marsh *et al.*, 1993) and the Welsh Office (Walker, 1992) suggested that housing officers were sceptical about how interesting or useful tenants would find the reports. Overall these assumptions were unfounded; tenants found the report interesting and useful, at the same time identifying a range of problems with it. Tenants in England found some of the detailed statistical information presented in the Report 'dry' and of little interest. In Wales specific indicators were felt to be inappropriate and tenants were more concerned with qualitative output data and information on policies and procedures, rather than performance data. Tenants in England and Wales found district-wide data unhelpful, preferring to see estate/decentralized information. Presentation of the reports was also often poor. Although the majority of tenants interviewed in the research projects felt that their authority should produce a report and found the reports useful there was little evidence of tenants using the report to press for improvements in services (Marsh *et al.*, 1993).

The lack of use of the Reports by tenants can also be traced back to the performance indicators adopted by the Government. Although the content of the reports varies between England and Wales the indicators are reliant on input measures (which relate to the economy of the service, providing data for example on costs of service provision) and not output/outcome measures (which measure effectiveness and what has been achieved) (Smith and Walker, 1994). The reliance on input information also suggests that the indicators are more concerned with providing standardized data for all authorities which will aid in establishing service costs and feed into the process of CCT for housing management services rather than to help users press for service improvements, particularly when they have no basis of comparison. The future of the Report to Tenants is now under question following the introduction of the Citizen's Charter performance indicators (Audit Commission, 1993) which duplicates and covers many of the same issues.

Collective privatisation

The successes of the Right to Buy, the tightening financial regime placed on local authorities in the early 1980s, which has forced some landlords to dispose of stock to cross subsidize refurbishment, and a general belief by the Government that tenants were trapped recipients of welfare services, led to the enactment of the 1988 Housing Act. This Act aimed to fundamentally restructure the provision of socially rented housing. It introduced private financing for housing associations (see below) and attempted to extend the process of privatization of local authority housing by giving tenants the collective right to opt for a different landlord, via Tenants' Choice, or be compulsorily transferred to a new landlord, Housing Action Trusts (HAT).

These last two initiatives have failed spectacularly, in terms of their initial aims and structure.

In terms of providing collectivist exit routes from social housing it can be argued that the Government has misjudged the feelings and views of council tenants. The introduction of this Act followed the third electoral success of Mrs Thatcher's Government and the transfer of over one million individual public sector homes into over-occupation under the Right to Buy. In comparison to this success Tenants' Choice has produced only three transfers, of which two have been highly controversial. Glyntaff Farm in Taff-Ely BC and Walterton and Elgin in Westminster have seen local authority stock transferred to a local housing association and community based association, respectively. However, in reality these transfers have not represented a rejection of council housing but have been a means to secure the necessary funding to repair and rehabilitate the stock.

Glyntaff Farm illustrates this point. The estate was built between 1967-70 and is of non-traditional construction. Not long after its completion design faults emerged which have manifested themselves in severe structural problems. The tenants' group on the estate had been fighting for many years to get the necessary resources from the local authority to repair the estate. To this end the estate received Priority Estate Project (PEP) status in 1987. However, the PEP brought only intensive management practices and not a capital repair programme. In 1989 a technical survey revealed the need for over £15 million of remedial work. The local authority was not in a position to fund this work and the tenants' group began to explore options. Tenants' Choice was chosen as a mechanism to improve the estate as the repair problems would lead to a negative valuation of the estate which would have to be funded. After four years of protracted negotiations the tenants have opted to transfer to Newydd Housing Association with a dowry from the authority of £25 million. In the case of Glyntaff Farm and Walterton and Elgin Tenants' Choice represented 'Hobsons choice' rather than true choice for the tenants groups, as this proved to be the only mechanisms available to access resources (and these resources are top-sliced from the resources available to all local authorities). In other words, it's a reallocation of existing resources rather than any additional funding.

Housing Action Trusts represented a very different form of transfer. The Government took an approach which developed upon that of the Urban Development Corporations. They believed that the solution to some of the worst local authority estates lay in private sector intervention. The initial conception of HATs was to identify estates and compulsorily transfer them into trusts which would undertake renovation work and then sell on the estates to other landlords (excluding local authorities). Even whilst the Act was progressing through Parliament the viability of HATs was challenged and their nature fundamentally altered. During the Parliamentary stage 18 estates in six authorities were identified as potential HATs. Objection to the designations were vehement, particularly in relation to the lack of tenant consultation over establishing a HAT and the fact that there was no option to return to the local authority. This opposition came from tenants and the House of Lords. The statutory framework laid down in the Act finally allowed tenants' views to be canvassed and for them to return to the local authority but was left deliberately vague (as was the Tenants' Choice legislation). The outcome from the identified estates was outright rejection of the concept. Even though it could result in substantially increased levels of funding to tenants it smacked of privatization and conjured up images of private landlordism. HATs were 'saved' by local authorities persuading the Government that a more liberal and voluntary regime could be introduced. HATs which declared (for example North Hull) have typically been on estates where the physical fabric is not fundamentally problematic and where social problems are not as severe as those orginally identified.

The future of both HATs and Tenants' Choice has to be seen as limited. Both involve top slicing monies from capital allocations. If they were to take off on many estates the Government would be left with no funding to put into council housing. For example, the transfer at Glyntaff Farm involved top slicing £5 million a year for five years which represents approximately 2 per cent of total public housing investment per annum in Wales. If a significant number of transfers or HATs were to proceed little cash would be left for other schemes. As Karn (1993) has noted those HATs which have been developed have been taken forward to save face.

Privatization and the Welfare State

As we have already indicated the pressures on local authority housing and the local authority housing service have been exerted in a number of ways. These have included pressures from tenants and councillors demanding better services (in part due to the Government supported programmes of participation and through new legal rights, but also because of 'the new consumerism' and a new generation of tenants whose expectations were much higher than previously), from regulatory and supervisory bodies such as the Audit Commission identifying weaknesses in performance and seeking improvements, from increasing demand from the homeless and from the combined impacts of new financial regimes and the range of mechanisms designed to ensure properties move outside the ownership and/or control of the local authority.

The emphasis in this section is on the changes in the financial regimes under which local authority housing has increasly operated. Overall these changes have both stimulated and directly resulted in privatization. As Whitehead (1993) notes with respect to UK housing;

> At its simplest privatisation can be seen as simply the transfer of ownership from the public to the private sector. In fact over the years the idea of privatisation has become far more complex, so that it is necessary to distinguish at least four different elements; the transfer of residual rights; the transfer of management of assets...; the transfer of finance...; and the transfer of risk.

Changing regimes

Whitehead's remarks are an important reminder. Privatization takes many forms and in housing changes in the financial regimes have been an important part of the process. The regime has changed in a number of ways. These include;

* shifts in the rent regime from one based upon historic costs (albeit modified by a cost pooling arrangement) to one based upon a return based on current values (albeit modified to ensure rents cannot fall) and with annual guideline increases imposed by Central Government.
* creation of a negative subsidy arrangement whereby entitlement to subsidy rests upon a Central Government calculation of entitlement. Moreover rents and rent increases now produce revenue which offsets subsidy entitlement in relation to housing benefit. As notional income grows so overall subsidy falls. Many authorities are now out of subsidy and local authority housing is forecast to contribute well over £820 million in 1993/94 to reducing the benefit bill.
* requiring local authorities to meet the cost of backdated housing benefit claims and to contribute financially to the cost of private sector renovation grants.
* ring fencing the housing revenue account (the trading account for the local authority housing service) to prevent cross subsidy from other council activities and introducing a tight specification as to what can be charged against the account.

* requiring local authorities to use the capital receipts from the sale of housing to offset debt (thus speeding up the process by which local authorities pass out of subsidy).
* reducing that portion of the receipt which authorities can spend on housing (from 50 per cent to 25 per cent) and taking away the entitlement to spend 100 per cent via 'the cascade system'. Combined with reductions in basic credit approvals (permission to borrow money for capital works) this has meant authorities have had less money to spend on improving and repairing their own housing stock.
* providing a 'capital receipts holiday' in 1993 by which local authorities could spend 100 per cent of their receipts as an added incentive to dispose of land and property.
* a very strong signal to all authorities that they are not to engage in new building and that requests for funds for new building will damage their overall position.

The consequences of these changes is that in general terms expenditure has fallen year on year in terms of local authority housing. For example, capital expenditure on local authority new house building in England fell from £2704 million in 1979/80 to £197 million in 1992/93. Central Government subsidy to the housing revenue account of all local authorities in Great Britain has fallen from £1719 million in 1980/81 to £554 million in 1992/93. Alongside this £28 billion has been raised from the sale of council owned dwellings in Great Britain, outstripping any other privatization receipts by a great margin. Moreover, that portion of capital receipts which could be used for housing has become ever more important as a source of income in the light of the reduction in overall expenditure (as have revenue contributions to capital outlays, an estimated £497 million in 1992/93).

The downward pressure on subsidy and loan approval has been matched by an upward pressure on rents. In England average rents have risen from £7.71 a week in 1980 to £30.65 a week in 1992, nearly doubling as a proportion of average male earnings. More recently the Government has begun to restrict the increase in management and maintenance allowances built into subsidy calculations as a means of forcing local authorities to seek economies. Detailed research on management costs has however revealed that there is no systematic set of factors associated with management cost variations making it difficult for the Department of the Environment to put in place the revised formula which can achieve this without producing perverse outcomes (DoE, 1992). However, it is clear there is a view that both local authority and housing association management and maintenance costs are too high and that they must be reduced. Most recently the same view has been expressed about staffing levels although here too the fact that associations have a much higher staff to property ratio means that the Government can less easily claim local government is being inefficient.

Housing has been subject to severe reductions in public expenditure since the late 1970s, and increasingly the financial mechanisms employed have been used to both encourage privatization and cut welfare spending. At the same time public spending has been increasingly directed ('targeted') towards those in greatest need who are unable to provide for themselves. The costs of social housing have been increasingly shifted away from society as a whole and towards the individual.

Competition

The planned introduction of CCT for the housing management function in part resolves the problems of housing management costs. The test of market forces and disciplines can be seen as one way of getting round the difficulties of trying to devise administrative formulae. The evidence from current competitive tendering is that it has produced savings and introduced new rigour into the process. However, a broader view of CCT would also point to the costs of preparing for tendering and the negative impacts on the service provided. It is too early to state categorically what the outcome of CCT for housing management will be. It is now evident that a number of private companies are preparing to tender (e.g., Business Expansion scheme landlords, managed services companies and probably some housing associations, as well as in-house teams from most, if not all, of the local authorities) and this will reveal how competitive current management costs are (albeit that in-house bids, despite all the longer term risks, will probably be pitched below current costs to try to ensure they win the contract).

The Government has thus moved the local authority sector a long way in terms of its costs, prices and competition. It is now much more nearly a market sector than ever before even though more and more of its users, the tenants, have to be subsidized to gain access to it. These solutions to privatizing the public sector may satisfy the Government despite its earlier wish to see the local authorities divest themselves entirely of the landlord role. As this section goes on to show, the success of programmes to dispose of local authority housing via sales have been considerable even though a very large stock remains which may never be sold.

From Right to Buy to Rent to Mortgage

The right of secure tenants to buy their council property has been proclaimed as one of the great successes of the Conservative governments since 1979. Via discretionary sales, earlier sales schemes and the legally imposed Right to Buy, around 2 million council dwellings have been sold in the UK (with 1.4 million being sold via RTB over the period 1980 to 1992). Between a third and a half of the recorded 4 million household growth in home ownership in the period 1979 to 1990 came from the sale of council dwellings (Whitehead, 1993). Over the period the level of discount on the valuation of the dwellings was increased several times to make purchase more attractive and further rights to part purchase (the right to shared ownership) and to obtain a mortgage to assist the purchase (the right to a mortgage) have been included.

The Right to Buy has attracted some 1.4 million purchasers. Inevitably the volume of purchases has been influenced by the state of the housing market and the economy in general. As the decade progressed and the housing market boom built up so purchases increased (to a peak of 181,367 in 1989, although note an earlier peak of 196,591 in 1982). As the boom collapsed and recession bit so sales declined (to 63,402 in 1992). Currently they are severely depressed, ironically having a negative effect on authorities which had banked on receiving a specific level of capital receipts. The capital receipts holiday announced by the Chancellor in the 1992 Autumn statement was meant to give authorities an incentive to sell by any means but in reality it has triggered instead land sales, sales of other property and the sale of mortgage portfolios.

It was recognized in the late 1980s that the Right to Buy had limitations and was not likely to lead to the complete erosion of the local authority sector. Discussions about an automatic right to ownership after thirty years returned to the agenda, having last been mooted in the 1970s. From this upsurge in more radical thinking about privatization came the experiments via a new 'rents to mortgages' scheme. Piloted in Wales, Scotland and the remaining English new towns this scheme allowed tenants to convert their rental payment into a mortgage payment and to receive a discount on the value of the property. The residual value of the property, i.e., that not given away via the discount or being purchased via a mortgage payment, was to be held as a public sector debt repayable on the sale of the property concerned. RTM occupied a small niche below the market for RTB and was particularly attractive in periods of rising prices and high interest rates. As both of these factors changed so the potential attraction of RTM has declined. Despite this the Government launched a new national scheme in October 1993. Although it is directed at the 1.25 million council tenants not in receipt of housing benefit, the expectation is that it will not attract a large number of buyers and that the RTB will remain the more attractive scheme.

Where next?

One impact of these accumulated rights is to make the task of running a housing service ever more difficult. The size and composition of the stock is subject to continuous change (decline) and it is apparent that sales typically involve the most desirable types of property (Forrest and Murie, 1991). The result is a diminution of the local authority's ability to respond to the diversity of need and demand and thus a growing friction with remaining and potential tenants. As suggested already this may stimulate tenants to push forward with EMBs, Tenants' Choice applications and other arrangements such as HATs.

Contracting out

Quite naturally given the situation, the options of contracting out of the current system become attractive to many local authorities and their tenants. CCT will potentially usher in new managers even though the property will remain within the ownership of the local authority and it will be the local authority which sets up and controls the contract under which new managers may operate. Thus, although tenants will be consulted in this process the local authority's skill in setting up and managing the contract will be critical. As an initial alternative to CCT the authority can enter into a management agreement with a housing association to take over the running of its property possibly with the view that at the end of the contract the tenants will be balloted to see if they would like a change of ownership to the association.

The option of transferring the stock (or part of the stock) arises under two different routes. One is triggered by the tenants (at least notionally) under the so-called 'Tenants Choice' discussed above; the other is via what is termed 'Large Scale Voluntary Transfer' under the 1986 Housing and Planning Act. Here the local authority can opt to transfer its stock to the ownership of a housing association or other landlord. It can do this via transferring its entire stock, specific estates or via trickle transfer (individual properties as and when they become vacant). So far only three estates in Great Britain have been transferred under Tenants' Choice while some twenty-six councils have transferred their stock under LSVT.

Depending on the condition of the stock LSVT offers the transferring authority the prospect of a capital receipt. The new rules on receipts means that any outstanding debt has to be paid off first but in high value areas substantial receipts are still possible. It has soon become apparent to the Government that this process, which was largely local authority initiated and unanticipated, needed regulating and now the number of authorities which can transfer in any year is restricted. Part of the reason for this is that by shifting the stock into the private sector, typically a housing association, the full cost of housing benefit falls back upon the Exchequer. It has also been seen as a potentially very large call on the capital market with consequent upward pressure on interest rates.

Housing associations; the Trojan horse?

It might appear that within this process of privatizing social housing in general and local authority housing in particular, housing associations have escaped untouched. This is certainly not the case, although they do remain privileged within the overall scheme of things and they have been used by the Government as a mechanism to challenge the role and performance of local authorities. However it can be argued that it is ever more apparent that they were the means to an end rather than an end in themselves and their privileged position is being rapidly eroded.

The 1988 Housing Act introduced a new private finance regime for housing associations. Basically they now have to raise over one-third of the funding required for building from the market and this has brought with it an upward pressure on rents. Rents have been moved outside of the earlier fair rent regime (where they were set by a Government run rent officer service) to one where rents are set in the market place. This has raised concerns about the affordability of associations' rents to tenants, where in the period 1989 - 1991 rents rose by an average of 48.8 per cent in England, increasingly trapping tenants on welfare benefits. Whitehead (1993) notes that this aspect of privatization has not only resulted in the introduction of private finance at market rates but also a shift in risk to the private sector. It is evident that the private sector is still having some difficulties with this and considerable pressure remains for the Government to offer explicit guarantees. It is also worth noting this has resulted in a shift of risk onto the voluntary committee members who run housing associations and this voluntarism is increasingly at odds with the considerable scale of the businesses they are running.

Housing associations have thus also been exposed to the rigours of the market. Increasingly the competition is between housing associations rather than between housing associations and local Government. At the same time there is a growing critique of associations from within the Conservative

Party which points to their privileged status vis a vis the private sector in general. It has been suggested that the housing association grant which meets the other two-thirds of the cost of developing a dwelling should be available to other landlords and to private developers. Some have suggested that housing associations are increasingly local authorities in disguise (Coleman, 1991) and as such are no real alternative.

In Scotland the funding agency for housing associations, Scottish Homes, can offer 'grow grants' to the private sector and this is being explored as an option south of the border. Local authorities already have powers to give financial assistance to private landlords but few, if any, have chosen to do so (except in terms of grants to improve properties). Both of these mechanisms could be further developed as the Government seeks to extend the privatization of housing provision with the consequence that associations along with local Government will be placed in intensively competitive markets for both resources and roles.

Achievements?

Looking back over the last fifteen years we can note the very considerable efforts which have been made to empower consumers, most notably the 1.5 million tenants who have exercised the Right to Buy. The list of rights and options available for council tenants has grown significantly, albeit that take up has often been quite low. The Right to Repair is a case in point. It has been suggested that total take up of this right since its introduction has only been in the hundreds even though local authorities spent millions of pounds preparing for its introduction. The take up via Tenants Choice and Housing Action Trusts has also been very limited. Does this mean the policies have failed? In the simple sense of take up the answer must be yes. However it is clear that all these rights and options have forced local Government to take a much closer interest in its tenants. Certainly this could have been achieved in different ways but the change in stance has been considerable.

Having recognized this success it must be recognized that consumers have in some senses been used by Central Government in its 'campaign' against local Government. Although there has been a genuine desire to empower council tenants as council tenants it is evident that many of the powers granted to them were designed to ensure they left the sector. In other words their power was the power to exit. The Government has acted to enhance the appeal of this option by reducing the resources available to local Government and placing pressure on rents. Perhaps fortunately for local Government, as the pressures have heightened so the condition of the private housing market deteriorated. House price booms were followed by a deep depression creating conditions which deterred many would-be purchasers.

What has become ever more evident is that many council tenants want to remain council tenants and that many of the tenants who have bought their home could have entered owner occupation in the private market but chose to buy on council estates (Forrest, 1993). Certainly tenants have been critical of the performance of authorities and want to have a say in the way the housing service is run. However, many tenants wish to remain with their local authorities. The most obvious evidence of this is in the twenty-seven authorities which proposed voluntary transfer, eleven balloted the tenants and were rejected. While this is always a more complex issue than suggested, here it does give basic evidence of their wish to remain tenants of the local authority. Many other surveys have pointed in the same way although it is worth noting that the level of support for authorities tends to diminish as the age of the tenants fall. It is the youngest tenants who have the highest expectations and are most likely to be dissatisfied.

The Government's commitment to empower tenants has been somewhat tarnished recently by the powers they have been granted under compulsory competitive tendering mechanisms to veto proposed new landlords. At the end of the day the concern to introduce CCT and to pressure local authorities to move out of management has been more important than the views and feelings of the tenants themselves. However, some authorities and their tenants have recognized this weakness and decided to exploit the right to manage proposals which are also within the Act. As we noted earlier tenants can exercise their right to manage and hire back the former local authority staff to undertake the management task and this has been proposed for the entire stock of Kensington and Chelsea. This way they retain the management they have always had and the authority not only retains ownership but effectively ensures its staff continue to run the service. The Government achieves its goal of getting the service outside the local authority and without doubt over time the tenants will recognize that the power relationship will have changed. They now control their managers rather than vice versa.

Was there any other way of achieving this? Possibly not, for despite the best intentions it would take many years for local authorities to move down this path voluntarily, particularly as central Government has eroded the role of local authority members for whom council housing remains one of the few areas where they can directly exercise control and patronage.

Conclusions

What we have seen in Britain in the last decade has been the intention on the part of Central Government to bring about the gradual replacement of large scale often bureaucratic local government housing organizations by decentralized councils working in partnership with housing associations, the private sector and tenants' groups. The emphasis has been placed upon financial controls, increasing competition, market mechanisms, privatization, a contract culture, service quality and performance management, with the citizen viewed as the consumer. The implicit power of those who pay for publicly provided services has been used as a lever to promote change and, coupled with the continued attack on local government, has led to the diminution of the powers of local authorities, whilst paradoxically increasing tenants' power. Questions remain as to what CCT may bring to tenants, in terms of a better understood and costed service, but the concern must surely be that quality will be sacrificed on the altar of market forces which may put ecconomic costs ahead of consumerist benefits. In an increasingly residualized social housing sector the advantages of consumerism, in terms of power and choice, may only be available to some (e.g those who exit the council sector). At the end of the day the central problem remains of how to stimulate individual rights for the consumer without weakening the position of those in society who are reliant upon social housing. It is unclear that present housing policies have successfully addressed this dilemma whilst the position of others (including future generations) will be weakened.

References

Audit Commission (1993), *Citizen's Charter Indicators. Charting a Course,* London: HMSO.

Cabinet Office (1991), *Citizen's Charter: Raising the Standard*, London, HMSO.

Clapham D. and Kintrea, K. (1993), *Housing Co-operatives in Britain: achievements and future prospects,* Harlow: Longman.

Cole, I. Arnold, P., and Windle, K. (1991), 'Decentralised housing services - back to the future' in Dannison and Moderran D. (eds), *The Housing Service of the Future*, Coventry Institute of Housing/Longman.

Coleman, D. (1991), 'Government and the housing associations : A doomed romance?', *Housing Review*, 40:4, pp. 79-80.

Department of the Environment (1977), *Housing Policy: A Consultative Document*, London: HMSO.

Department of the Environment (1992), *Empirical Study into the Costs of Local Authority Housing Management*, London: HMSO.

Department of the Environment/Welsh Office (1992), *Competing for Quality in Housing. Competition in the provision of Housing Management: A Consultation Paper,* London: DoE/WO.

Forrest, R. (1993), 'Contracting housing provision: Competition and privatisation in the housing sector', in Taylor-Gooby P. and Lawson R. (eds), *Markets and Managers*, Buckingham: Open University Press.

Forrest, R. and Murie, A. (1991), *Selling the Welfare State. The Privatisation of Public Housing*, London: Routledge.

H.M. Treasury (1991), *Competing for Quality*, London: HMSO.

Housing Research Group City University (1981), *Could Local Authorities be Better Landlords?* London, City University.

Karn, V. (1993), 'Remodelling a HAT: the implementation of the Housing Action Trust legislation 1987-1992', in Malpass P. and Means R. (eds) *Implementing Housing Policy*, Buckingham: Open University Press.

Kirwan, R. M. (1984), 'The Demise of Public Housing?' in Le Grand, J. and Robinson, R. (eds), *Privatisation and the Welfare State*, London: George Allen and Unwin.

Kroes, H., Ymkers, F. and Mulder, A. (1988), *Between Owner-Occupation and Rented Sector, De Bilt*, The Netherlands Christian Institute for Social Housing.

Marsh, A., Niner, P. and Symon, P. (1993), *An Evaluation of the First Year Experience of the Local Authority Report to Tenants Regime,* London: HMSO.

Merrett, S. (1979), *State Housing in Britain*, London: RKP.

Ministry of Local Government and Housing (1958), *Councils and their Houses. The management of estates*, London: HMSO.

National Federation of Housing Associations (1991), *It's a Better Way of Working: Tenant Participation in Housing Associations*, London: NHFA.

Pennance, F. G. and Gray, H. (1968), *Choice in Housing*, London: Institute of Economic Affairs.

Power, A. (1991), *Housing Management: A guide to quality and creativity*, London, Longman.

Saunders, P. (1986), *Social Theory and the Urban Question*, London, Hutchinson.

Smith, R. S. G. and Walker, R. M. (1994), 'The role of performance indicators in housing management: a critique', *Environment and Planning A,* 26, pp. 609-621.

Stafford, D. (1978), *The Economics of Housing Policy*, London: Croom Helm.

Walker, R. M. (1992), 'Reporting to Tenants' *Welsh Housing Quarterly*, Issue 7 Summer pp.15-17.

Whitehead, C. (1993), 'Privatizing Housing: An assessment of U.K. experience', *Housing Policy and Debate*, Vol. 4 No 1 pp.101-139.

Author index